Critical Social Policy
A Reader

Critical Social Policy
A Reader

Social Policy and Social Relations

edited by
David Taylor

SAGE Publications
London • Thousand Oaks • New Delhi

First published 1996

SAGE Publications Ltd
6 Bonhill Street
London EC2A 4PU

SAGE Publications Inc
2455 Teller Road
Thousand Oaks, California 91320

SAGE Publications India Pvt Ltd
32, M-Block Market
Greater Kailash – I
New Delhi 110 048

British Library Cataloguing in Publication data

A catalogue record for this book is
available from the British Library

ISBN 0 7619 5033 8
ISBN 0 7619 5034 6 (pbk)

Library of Congress catalog record available

Typeset by Mayhew Typesetting, Rhayader, Powys
Printed in Great Britain by Redwood Books,
Trowbridge, Wiltshire

Contents

Notes on Contributors

Colin Barnes is a disabled activist, writer and researcher. He teaches disability studies in the School of Sociology and Social Policy at the University of Leeds. He is currently honorary research director for the British Council of Disabled People (formerly The British Council of Organizations of Disabled People), and an executive editor of the international journal *Disability and Society*.

Peter Beresford works with Open Services Project, teaches at Brunel University College and is a member of Survivors Speak Out. He has a long-standing involvement in issues of participation as a worker, service user and researcher. He has written widely on the subject, and with Suzy Croft is currently writing a book on the politics of participation.

Jean Carabine lectures in social policy in the Department of Social Sciences, Loughborough University. She has researched and published on issues concerned with sexuality in relation to social policy, feminist campaigning, politics and policy making, empowerment and on questions of difference. She is currently working on a book *Women, Sexuality and Social Policy*, to be published by Macmillan. She has been a member of the *Critical Social Policy* Editorial Collective since 1994.

Steve Cohen has been practising as an immigration lawyer for many years. He is presently co-ordinator of the Greater Manchester Immigration Aid Unit which is a unique venture funded by local authorities and offering free immigration advice and legal representation. He has published extensively on the politics, law and history of immigration control. His main area of academic interest is in the relationship between immigration controls and welfarism. He is currently writing a book for social workers and social policy teachers on children, the family and immigration control. He is actively involved politically in campaigns against immigration control.

Suzy Croft works with Open Services Project and as a social worker at St John's Hospice, London. She was previously co-organiser of Battersea Community Action. She has a long-standing involvement in issues of participation as a worker, service user and researcher and has written widely on the subject. She is a member of the Editorial Collective of *Critical Social Policy*.

Jay Ginn is employed at the National Institute of Social Work researching the careers of social services staff. She previously worked in the Sociology

Department of Surrey University researching gender differences in economic and health resources of elderly people and more recently the employment of women in mid-life. Publications focus on gender, employment and pensions. She co-authored *Gender and Later Life* (1991) and co-edited *Connecting Gender and Ageing* (1995), both with Sara Arber.

Martin Hewitt teaches at Hertfordshire University. He is author of *Ideology, Welfare and Needs* (1992) and several papers on welfare theory and ideology. He is currently writing a book on human nature and social policy which explores the exhaustion of social democratic and new right ideologies and the quest for new notions of human nature in politics.

Ruth Lister is Professor of Social Policy at Loughborough University and a former director of the Child Poverty Action Group and member of the Commission on Social Justice. She has published widely in the areas of poverty, income maintenance and citizenship and is currently writing a book on feminist perspectives on citizenship for Macmillan.

Mary McIntosh teaches sociology at the University of Essex. She has written on a variety of topics: 'The Homosexual Role' (1968), *The Organization of Crime* (1975), 'The State and the Oppression of Women' (1978), *The Anti-social Family* (with Michèle Barrett, 1982), *Sex Exposed: Sexuality and the Pornography Debate* (edited with Lynne Segal, 1992). Her current work is on prostitution and public policy.

Jenny Morris is a freelance researcher, consultant and trainer. Her most recent publications include *Gone Missing: A Research and Policy Review of Disabled Children Living Away from their Families* and *Encounters with Strangers: Feminism and Disability*. She is currently working on a research project concerning disabled children in care.

Paul Spicker is senior lecturer in Social Policy at the University of Dundee. He has taught and researched on a wide range of social policy topics, including social security, housing and community care. Much of his writing is concerned with the application of political and social theory to issues in social policy. His published work includes *Stigma and Social Welfare* (1984), *Principles of Social Welfare* (1988), *Poverty and Social Security: Concepts and Principles* (1993) and *Social Policy: Themes and Approaches* (1995).

David Taylor is Director of the MA Programme in Environmental and Social Studies at the University of North London. He was Visiting Associate Professor of Social Policy in the Department of Social Work and Social Policy, University of Sydney in 1995 and Visiting Associate Professor of Sociology at City College, City University of New York in 1985–6. He has been a member of the *Critical Social Policy* Editorial Collective since 1983 and was Production Editor from 1983–93.

Fiona Williams is Professor of Social Policy in the School of Sociology and Social Policy at Leeds University. She is author of *Social Policy: A Critical Introduction: Issues in Race, Class and Gender* (1989) and has researched and written widely on social divisions, social theory and social change in relation to social policy. She has been a member of the *Critical Social Policy* Editorial Collective since 1984.

Preface

The publication of this volume has been timed to coincide with the move of the journal *Critical Social Policy* to Sage Publications. It is an exciting time for *CSP* in many respects: the journal moves from three to four issues per year and a new international editorial board has been installed with the intention of reinforcing our commitment to fostering international debate. It also marks 15 years of uninterrupted publication of the journal. Since its inception *CSP* has been committed to radical analyses of social policy and to encouraging reports and reflections on current struggles and campaigns within welfare. From the outset *CSP* was committed to a socialist and feminist analysis, but in subsequent years has gone on to develop an awareness of the central role of other social relations such as race, sexuality, disability and age as they have emerged as forms of contestation, in shaping both the analysis and form of welfare provision. That these issues are increasingly seen as central to the discipline of social policy is testament to the perseverance of the Collective.

The articles in this volume represent one aspect of *CSP*'s history – the development of anti-discriminatory analyses of welfare. They also represent the effort of all those associated with the journal. *CSP* was, and remains, committed to working collectively. It was established by the enthusiasm of a group of people who believed in the need for new analyses of welfare which would challenge the then orthodoxy of Fabianism and the emerging critique from the New Right. From the beginning, the journal sought political as well as academic relevance and has always struggled to incorporate its political values and commitments into the working practices of the Collective.

Despite enormous changes in the welfare state and developments in the discipline, we believe a critical analysis of welfare remains as important and relevant as ever. Over the last 15 years *CSP* has been sustained by the efforts of its contributors, supporters and a changing collective, drawn both from academics and welfare practitioners. Below is a list of all those who have ever been members of the *CSP* Collective, with the current membership (January 1996) in bold: Peter Alcock, **Mary John Baptiste**, Reena Bhavnani, Avtar Brah, Graham Burgess, **Jean Carabine**, Marion Charlton, **Suzy Croft**, Jen Dale, Miriam David, **Lesley Day**, Bob Deacon, Judith De Witt, Lena Dominelli, Lesley Doyal, Eva Eberhardt, **Norman Ginsburg**, Ian Gough, Sue Harris, **Michael Hutchinson-Reis**, **Syd Jeffers**, Elly Karnavou, Hugh Kerr, **Phil Lee**, **Ruth Madigan**, Marg Mayo, **Karim Murji**, Gordon

Peters, Chris Phillipson, Geoff Rayner, **Naseem Shah, Tom Shakespeare, Sharon Smith, David Taylor**, Peter Taylor-Gooby, Sophie Watson, **Fiona Williams**, Elizabeth Wilson.

Critical Social Policy Editorial Collective

Acknowledgements

The existence of this book is testimony to the work of all the members of the *CSP* Collective since 1981. In addition to the support and friendship of my colleagues on *CSP* I must acknowledge the hospitality of the Department of Social Work and Social Policy at the University of Sydney from September to December 1995, and in particular the welcome extended by Stuart Rees, Lindsey Napier and Marie Wilkinson. My visit there and the work on this book was made possible by the award of a sabbatical from the University of North London.

Most of all, I would like to thank my partner Jackie Fosbury for her tolerance of my stresses and anxieties and for sharing morning cappuccinos in the 'Bondi Tratt' as I tweaked the copy.

David Taylor

Editor's Note

All the contributions to this volume, with the exception of the Postscript to Chapter 1, were previously published in the journal, *Critical Social Policy*. Original publication information is given at the start of each chapter. There are numerous references throughout the collection to campaigns, policies, agencies and political figures of the time. Some of the campaigns and agencies no longer exist, some policies have be superseded, and many politicians no longer hold office. The references have been left in their original form, however, to retain their historical integrity. Where contributors have referred to other articles included in this volume this has been indicated in the text and the appropriate page reference given.

PART I
SOCIAL POLICY AND SOCIAL RELATIONS

Introduction

David Taylor

Themes in Part I

The decade-and-a-half since the launch of the journal *Critical Social Policy* has been a turbulent one for the welfare state and the discipline of social policy. Alongside the restructuring of welfare undertaken by successive Conservative Governments (see Ginsburg, 1994, for a useful discussion of welfare restructuring) there has been an increasing recognition that the discipline of social policy must incorporate an understanding of social relations. As Fiona Williams (1994: 50) has written, 'social relations, not only of class but of gender and "race" – not to mention age, disability and sexuality . . . underpin welfare policies, their outcomes, the organisation of labour within the welfare state, the delivery of services, political pressures and ideologies, and patterns of consumption'. The acknowledgement of social relations has not simply been the product of an evolutionary self-awareness on the part of the discipline. Social relations are also relations of power and the struggles of groups who inhabit those social relations was, and remains, the painful component of change. As those who give voice to these struggles in the academic arena point out in this volume, political battles for acknowledgement have to be fought within the discipline as well as without.

A recognition of the need to develop new analyses of welfare was the initial impetus behind *CSP*. Our editorial statement in Issue 1 stated a belief in the 'inadequacies of Fabian and orthodox models' to meet the challenges facing the welfare state and the discipline, and our aim was 'to encourage and develop an understanding of welfare from socialist, feminist and radical perspectives'. In 1986 this statement was amended to include a specific acknowledgement of the experiences and writings of 'anti-racist writers and activists'. The articles in Part I all illustrate discriminatory practices in the welfare state and analytical absences in the discipline associated with gender, 'race', sexuality, age and disability. They do not, however, represent a unified approach to social relations, and in some cases appear to occupy contradictory positions. Yet despite the diversity of perspectives employed there are a number of issues raised in common by all contributors.

A shared starting point is the *exclusion* of different groups from both the *social rights within the welfare state* and the *frameworks employed in the discipline*. This may take the form of institutionalised dependency for women; the refusal to accept racialised groups as legitimate claimants; extreme social isolation and institutional discrimination against disabled people; discrimination against lesbian and gay people through the normative assumption of heterosexuality; or the marginalisation of older people. In each of these cases contributors use an *historical perspective* to show how social exclusion has been *integral* to the institutional structure and legitimating ideologies of the welfare state. Equally important, they show how academic analysis has frequently failed to incorporate an understanding of the associated relations of power and discrimination into its theoretical models. In this sense, each contribution is an argument for an extension or reorientation of the discipline. At the same time, however, it would be wrong to see each article contributing to the accumulative evolution of an *explicit* perspective. The various social relations discussed cannot simply be added together or aggregated into an expanded whole. Instead, the contributions raise questions of how far *the social relations of welfare* may be analytically separated or seen as mutually constituted; as reinforcing or contradictory. At another level, the concept of *social exclusion* raises the equally difficult issues of what exactly is meant by social *inclusion*, on the one hand, and the exact nature of *the social* from which individuals are included or excluded on the other (see Squires, 1990, for an interesting discussion of the 'the social').

If social policy is seen as operating on an axis of inclusion/exclusion, there may be a danger of reducing a complex interactive process to a single dimension consisting of discrete opposing poles. Levitas (1996) points out that contemporary discourses around social exclusion often counterpose two homogeneous groups – the excluded, who are frequently seen as an 'underclass' sharing a marginalised and pathological culture, and the included who are similarly assumed to be an homogeneous cohesive group integrated into the social sphere. The degree of inclusion/exclusion in such discourses is usually measured along the single dimension of participation in waged work. Levitas argues that such a debate masks, 'the degree of inequality among the 80 per cent (who are "included")' (p. 6), but additionally, it may mask other social relations of inclusion/exclusion associated with gender, 'race', age, sexual orientation and disability. For our purposes, we should note that alongside the idea of inclusion through the labour process, the parallel idea of *integration* via the welfare state may mask the role played by a variety of social relations in structuring individual and group participation in the social. At the same time, as Williams (1992: 214) points out, individuals experience a range of social relations which impact upon them differently in different situations: 'social divisions impact upon people, singly or in groups, in different ways at different times, in different situations. At one or many moments, in one or many places, issues of disability may be highlighted; at another moment the inequalities of class may predominate for the same person or group'. Taken together these points entail a rejection of the simple *binary opposition* of inclusion/ exclusion and perhaps direct us to look at the way various social relations interact to create particular circumstances and specific conditions for membership of the social. All the contributions here address the issue, in different ways, of the role of social policy in enabling or disabling social participation.

A second issue touched upon in these contributions, and important for a social relations of welfare perspective, is the construction of the individual inhabiting social relations. There has been a tendency to assume a *unitary category of the subject* – perhaps most obviously in the male breadwinner model of Beveridge's social insurance schemes – and each contribution here points to a reconceptualisation of the individual as gendered, 'racialised', with a particular sexuality, at different stages in the life course and socially disabled or enabled. On this point there is no necessary agreement amongst contributors and in some cases, one contribution may aim to 'deconstruct' the categories used by another, but taken together they make a powerful critique of the white, male, heterosexist, ablist and ageist assumptions of much social policy.

A social relations perspective, then, will ask questions about the way in which different forms of discrimination, oppression or exploitation under-pin *institutional forms* and *welfare outcomes*. It will also pose questions about the categories of the subject inherent in welfare discourses. These questions inform not only the larger macro-theoretical analyses but also investigations of the user/provider relationship and how this impacts on particular individuals as recipients of benefits and services. As many of the contributors point out, *inclusion* into the social rights of welfare, is not a simple positive to counterpose to the negative of *exclusion*. While many benefit from access to services, this access may also be at the cost of *internal control* or regulation by the state.

Articles in Part I

'Feminism and Social Policy' by Mary McIntosh (first published in 1981) was originally presented as a paper at the founding *CSP* conference in 1980. It is an early socialist feminist argument that the 'question of women [is] integral to an analysis of the welfare state' (p. 24). This was by no means the first contemporary feminist analysis of welfare, as the author herself points out, but this only gives more force to her argument that gender relations and women's position were ignored or excluded from the discipline. Acknowledging earlier work by Ruth Lister, Hilary Land,

Elizabeth Wilson and others she comments, 'what is disappointing is how little this critique has really affected thinking among other radicals about social policy' (p. 14). In her postscript written for this volume she accepts that feminism has now become a common sense for many women and some men, and that there has been a 'decisive shift towards an acceptance of some kind of feminist analysis' (p. 25), though this is 'too often . . . concerned with the immediate effects of social policy and policy changes on the lives of individual women as claimants or carers rather than with the more institutional or sociological effects that have consequences for all women' (ibid.).

Her starting point is the role of the welfare state in reinforcing women's dependence upon men: 'not merely . . . mothers and non-mothers, wives and non-wives, earners and non-earners – but . . . women as a whole category' (p. 14). All women, she argues, 'suffer from the stereotype of the woman as properly dependent upon a man' (ibid.). This dependency is constructed, in particular, through the aggregation of income for calculating benefit. 'The aggregation of the married couple into a tax unit and a means-testable unit – however it may be dressed up in unisex clothing – represents women's dependence on their husbands' (p. 21). The origins of this dependency and its concomitant sexual division are firmly located in the family. One challenge to this dependency was the campaign for 'disaggregation' (for equal entitlement to benefit for women irrespective of any relationship to a man) described by the author. This campaign highlighted the exclusion of women from equal treatment within the social security and other benefit structures of the welfare state. At the same time, however, there was 'a growing awareness of women as state employees' (p. 14) in the 'lower ranks' of welfare bureaucracies and institutions, and of the close articulation between women's enforced dependency in the family and exclusion from equal participation in the *labour market*.

McIntosh considers possible strategies for socialist feminists at that time in the light of critiques of the welfare state as reinforcing dependency within the family. Should feminists 'opt out' of state provision in favour of separatist self-help organisations? Her answer is clear – 'voluntary' efforts are not likely to sustain long-term independence for women, and, 'faced with the choice between a chancy dependence upon a man on the one hand, and dependence upon the state or exploitation in waged work on the other, feminists opt for the state and the wage' (p. 15). This is because, 'with all their problems . . . the state and the employer can be fought collectively and unlike modern marriage are not intrinsically patriarchal' (p. 15). She is equally clear on strategies for income maintenance. Demands for a 'guaranteed minimum income' (in some ways a forerunner of the contemporary Basic Income debate) are rejected as 'socialism by the back door' in favour of 'furthering the process of proletarianisation of women and rescuing women from pre-proletarian dependence' (p. 23). Such a strategy would be part of a wider socialist feminist struggle to end capitalist waged labour.

In the postscript to *Feminism and Social Policy*, the author argues that, while in 1980 'the central political issue was the "cohabitation rule" . . . now the central issue is "child support" and the role of the Child Support Agency' (p 25) and suggests that 'the article is of historical interest rather than immediate practical relevance'. Nevertheless, it represents an important *socialist feminist* component of early contemporary feminist accounts of the welfare state.

Since the original publication of 'Feminism and Social Policy' Black and anti-racist writers, and those concerned with discrimination based on sexuality, age and disability, have challenged notions of women as an homogeneous group with a unitary set of interests, and have looked at the way the welfare state relates differently to different women. In this volume, Fiona Williams, Jean Carabine and Jenny Morris all point out the way in which Black and ethnic minority women, lesbians and disabled women's interests have often been subsumed or marginalised under the general category 'women'.

In 'Anti-semitism, Immigration Controls and the Welfare State' (originally published in 1985), Steve Cohen argues that racism and immigration controls are central to the welfare state. Taking an historical perspective, Cohen points out the continuity between the anti-semitism of the first half of the twentieth century and post-war racism, both underpinned by immigration controls. It is a powerful argument that *social exclusion* is integral to the welfare state, and, equally importantly, that exclusion has been supported by policies of *internal control* against Jews and Black people. Cohen shows how, from as early as the turn of the century, 'entitlement to a whole series of welfare benefits have themselves become linked to immigration status'(p. 27) and looks at the role that welfare agencies have played in policing immigration.

The author attempts to retrieve 'the hidden history of the relationship between nationalism and welfare' (p. 27) and shows how eugenics, efficiency and empire were used to bolster a racist and exclusionary *nationalism* at the time. The key legislation which ensured exclusion was the Aliens Act of 1905, implemented by the reforming Lloyd George government. As the author points out 'the major welfare legislation passed by the 1906 government made eligibility for benefit dependent upon immigration status' (p. 28) and drew heavily on the residency and citizenship requirements outlined in the Act. The racially constructed Alien was seen as a threat to national efficiency, 'British culture' and to the interests of the labour movement itself. In respect of the latter, Cohen provides damning evidence of support for immigration controls amongst some sections of the labour movement at the time, and highlights how a eugenicist standpoint was embraced by many of the Fabian reformers.

In terms of welfare legislation the author shows how the Old Age Pensions Act of 1908 and the National Insurance Act of 1911 excluded whole categories of potential claimants and marginalised others through limited entitlement and reduced benefits. In relation to the contributory health insurance scheme, 'male non-British deposit contributors were only eligible for seven-ninths of the normal rate of benefit, and women were only eligible for three-quarters. It was at this point', he goes on, 'that racism met sexism' (p. 38). This racism remained at the heart of the welfare state and Cohen goes on to show the articulation of notions of 'Britishness' and the 'British race' in Beveridge and its relation to the assumed dependency of '*British*' women in the family. 'Alien' women, therefore, suffered a double social exclusion. Cohen draws a number of contemporary parallels including the exclusion and control of Asian women revealed by the case of Nasira Begum in 1979 (p. 48). In addition to demonstrating exclusion and internal control, then, Cohen reveals the role played by an *essentialist* notion of 'Britishness' in constructing another dimension of legitimacy for would-be claimants.

These arguments are taken further by Fiona Williams in 'Racism and the Discipline of Social Policy' (first published in 1987). Like Cohen, she draws out the central role of nationalism and racism both in welfare theory and policy, and launches a critique of the discipline for its failure to incorporate an understanding of 'race' and racism.

> My contention is [she states] that the discipline of social administration has been disinclined, or unable, to take account of the welfare experiences of Black people. Put differently, those who fought Beveridge's five giants – Want, Squalor, Idleness, Ignorance and Disease, hid the giants of racism and sexism (and the fights against them) behind statues to the Nation and the White Family. (p. 48)

Reviewing a range of general texts published up to that time she argues that 'race' has not been *integrated* into the analysis of the welfare state, but treated, at best, 'like gender, as a discrete issue, a dimension of inequality, an "ethnic" or minority group, a group with "special needs"' (p. 49). Instead she presents a

> framework for understanding the relationship between racism and social policy, in terms of the historical development of the welfare state in the context of capitalism and imperialism, a context which places racist ideology and practice as an unsurprising outcome of some of the dominant characteristics of the welfare state, and in terms which imply changes to welfare theory and strategy if racism and the struggles against Black oppression are to be taken seriously. (p. 48)

She proceeds by an analysis of the major approaches to welfare theory which she categorises into four groups: anti-collectivism – essentially the neo-liberalism and the neo-conservatism of the New Right; Social Reformism, which is divided into three streams – 'mainstream', 'radical' and 'non-socialist'; the Political Economy of Welfare; and the Feminist Critique of Welfare. While Political Economy and the Feminist Critique hold out the best prospects for developing an integrated approach to 'race', she concludes by pointing out the limitations of all four approaches:

> the individualism of anti-collectivism fails to register structural racism; the methods of the mainstream social administration approach . . . have inhibited any more than a very marginal acknowledgement of racism. Further, the influences on Fabianism of familism and nationalism . . . have reinforced this marginalisation. The political economy approach, whilst its framework offers the

possibility for the analysis of some aspects of racism, has also neglected it . . . taking the unitariness of 'class struggle' for granted. It has also prevented a full appreciation of some of the more controlling features of the state. In addition, it has lacked an international perspective of global divisions which are necessary to the analysis of racism. Finally, the critical method of feminism has much in common with an anti-racist analysis, but in its assumption of a 'false universalism' of the family as the site of oppression, and patriarchy as the root of oppression, it has ignored the impact of racism on Black women. (p. 61)

She next explores three different theoretical analyses of 'race' and racism 'which have emerged from the recent debate around the relationship of *race* to *class* and which have particular significance for a study of the welfare state' (p. 62): John Rex's underclass model of social exclusion; Ben-Tovim and Gabriel's view of racism as an 'autonomous ideology'; and the 'modality' approach of Gilroy, Hall and others. Rex's 'ungendered' account of the exclusion of Black people from the social rights of the welfare state, 'tends to an uncritical view of those rights themselves' (p. 63) and shares with the 'autonomous ideology' view of racism a lack of historical understanding of the material basis for exclusion in the historical structures of the welfare state. The 'modality' approach offers the best hope of showing 'how the various historical, political and economic features of the welfare state [have] been affected by "race" and in their turn contributed to elements of "race" and racism' (p. 63).

Combining aspects of the political economy and feminist approaches to welfare with the modality approach to racism, the author goes on to outline a framework for the analysis of 'race', racism and social policy. Such a framework would have to consider the following: (a) the historical cast of welfare reforms – in particular the roles played by imperialism, nationalism and immigration controls (p. 64); (b) the role of Black workers in maintaining lower social expenditure (p. 65); (c) the social reproduction of a racially stratified workforce and the maintenance of the white population but the limitation of the Black (p. 66); (d) the social control of Black welfare users (p. 68); and (e) struggles against Black oppression (p. 70).

This powerful critique shows how Black people's *social exclusion* is paralleled by the *exclusion of Black experiences from a theoretical analysis of the welfare state*. At the same time, it forces us to 'deconstruct' some of the *universalist categories* and assumed *unitary interests* of groups engaged in welfare struggles such as 'women' and 'the working class'.

Deconstructing the category 'women' is at the heart of Jenny Morris' contribution, '"Us" and "Them"? Feminist Research, Community Care and Disability' (first published in 1991). 'Both disability and "community care" are issues of fundamental interest to women', she writes, 'yet the feminist concern with community care has been partisan in that it is almost entirely from the point of view of non-disabled and younger women' (p. 77). She shows how, 'for feminists writing and researching on carers, the category "women" does not generally include those who need physical assistance' (p. 83). Her contribution clearly highlights how the *social relation of disability* cannot be divorced from *social relations of gender* when considering the user/provider relationship in the delivery of 'care'. Those who take a *unitary* gender perspective in their research tend to focus, she argues, on women's role as *carers* to the exclusion of women as the *cared-for*. This focus sees care in the community and residential care as simple oppositions in which the latter is preferred due to the possibilities it raises for 'collectivised' provision outside the family. The former is criticised because of its implicit expectation that women will fulfil an unpaid 'domestic responsibility' for care in the 'community'. This view is sustained by a particular feminist critique of familism and its implied dependency for women. The effect, argues Morris, is to marginalise the needs of the *cared-for* and to exclude *disabled women* from investigations of the care relationship.

While acknowledging the importance of previous feminist research which drew attention to women's unpaid work in the home she nevertheless argues that the critique of 'familism' has been generalised in some research, into an implicit critique of the *household* or *home* as a location for care. She says,

> Feminist research which incorporated the experiences of disabled and older people might also raise the question of the meaning of the word 'home', separating this out, in a conceptual and political sense, from the feminist critique of the family. Disabled feminists should be able to assert their right to live in their own home without being accused of supporting the oppression of women within the family. Indeed, non-disabled feminists in other contexts have insisted on women's rights to a home (for example, Watson, 1986) yet in their opposition to community care policies and in their aim of undermining the family and women's dependence within it, they are in danger of denying one group of women the right to a home. (p. 91)

Morris goes on to appeal to feminist researchers and academics (a group in which disabled people are under-represented) to focus less on *carers* and more on *caring as a relationship*. She also points out that the caring relationship is often not composed of the two *binary oppositions* – carer and *cared-for* but that roles may be blurred. 'If we focused not just on the subjective experience of those identified as carers', she writes, 'but also on the other party to the caring relationship we may find that in some situations the roles are blurred or shifting' (p. 92). Her point here highlights, once again, the danger of using a *uni-dimensional category of the subject* in policy analysis and of *excluding* the needs of particular individuals and groups.

This point is taken further in Colin Barnes' article, 'Institutional Discrimination against Disabled People and the Campaign for Anti-discrimination Legislation' (published first in 1992). The author defines institutional discrimination in the following way,

> institutional discrimination is evident when policies and activities of all types of modern organisation result in inequality between disabled people and non-disabled people. It is embedded in the excessive paternalism of contemporary welfare systems and is apparent when they are *systematically ignoring or meeting inadequately the needs of disabled people*. It is also evident when these agencies

are regularly interfering in the lives of disabled people as a means of social control. (p. 97, emphasis added)

This definition echoes Cohen's earlier characterisation of the relationship of the welfare state to racialised groups as double-edged – *social exclusion* on the one hand and *internal control* on the other.

The author adopts a 'social model of disability' in which the barriers imposed upon disabled people, such as 'restrictions . . . due to inaccessible built environments, the inability of the general public to use sign language, the lack of reading material in braille, or hostile public attitudes' (p. 97), are situated in the context of other social relations. These constraints are, 'compounded for disabled members of the lesbian and gay communities, Black people and women with impairments' (p. 96) – an important reminder that whilst there may be *universal barriers* experienced by all disabled people, social disability may interact with other social relations to produce *particular needs* for Black, women, older, gay or lesbian disabled people.

Like Jenny Morris, Barnes is clear that support services for disabled people must be offered in the community, 'independent living', he writes, 'means disabled people have access to and control of a range of community-based services which empower them to identify and pursue their own lifestyle' (p. 100). Unfortunately, current provision does little to empower disabled people when their circumstances have to be professionally assessed and 'managed' by 'care managers' who may not have appropriate services available.

> Consequently, the majority are forced to rely on informal unpaid helpers; this usually means women family members or friends . . . Current services, therefore, not only fail to provide disabled people with opportunities to live independently in the community, but also deny them the dignity of independence within the context of personal relationships and the family home. (p. 100)

This situation is increasingly being challenged by disabled people and their organisations who demand the introduction of anti-discrimination legislation,

> which; first establishes a suitable framework for the enforcement of policies which would ensure the meaningful integration of disabled people into the mainstream economic and social life of the community, such as the employment quota scheme, for example; and second provide public confirmation that discrimination against disabled people for whatever reason and in whatever form is no longer acceptable. (p. 107)

Such policies, however, will need to be supported by a whole range of other reforms to stand any chance of success. Referring to the work of Mike Oliver, Barnes suggests the following: freedom of information backed up by a supportive network of disabled people; demystification of professionalism; and a system of basic human rights which guarantees the voice of disabled people. This is a call, then, for legislation and policy reform which 'emphasises social rights rather than individual needs' (p. 107).

'"Constructing Women": Women's Sexuality and Social Policy', by Jean Carabine (first published in 1992), is an argument that social policy, both as a framework for action and as a discipline, is socially constructed on the basis of normative rules of heterosexuality. Like previous contributors, the author notes a failure to develop an *integrated* analysis of sexuality in the discipline. Once again, reviewing the current literature she points out, 'although feminists had written about sexuality and social control and women and social policy – all had failed to make the crucial link between women, sexuality, social policy and social control' (p. 113):

> Every day as women we are confronted with the relationship between our sexuality and social policy – like when we are deemed unfit mothers because we are single women or lesbians and have our children taken from us; or are considered 'unfit' to have children because we are not in a relationship with a man or when we fail to get work or promotion because it is known that we are lesbians; or where we have to deny our sexuality because we work with young girls. (p. 113)

This norm of heterosexuality is particularly evident in ideologies surrounding *motherhood* and *the family*: 'the concept of motherhood enshrined in social policies is one which is based on, and reinforces, an "ideal" . . . which is white heterosexual and "respectable"' (p. 122); it is also one which assumes the dependency of heterosexual women within the family.

In addition to this substantive critique, Carabine points to the way in which *sexual* identity interacts with other aspects of identity to produce a range of experiences in relation to welfare: 'women, depending on their sexual identity, "race", class, age and being differently bodied will all experience social policies differently, but all will still be affected by ideas about what is appropriate and acceptable sexuality' (p. 114). Discussing the example of racist stereotypes about Black women being too sexually active she says that, 'racist ideas about Black women's sexuality are so powerful that other forms of sexuality, for instance lesbianism, are invisible' (p. 118). The *universal exclusion* of lesbian and gay sexualities, then, interacts with other social relations of exclusion to produce particular experiences and needs, in a similar manner to that outlined by Barnes in relation to disabled people. The *social exclusion* suffered by gay men and lesbians is also the *social control* of their sexuality – a point made in parallel with Cohen's earlier analysis of 'race'.

In 'Grey Power: Age-based Organisations' Response to Structured Inequalities' (first published in 1993), Jay Ginn challenges 'the myth that elderly people have increasing affluence and political influence in Britain' (p. 128). She does this by 'reviewing the income of elderly people and the way their income is structured by gender, class and race' (ibid.) to show the economic and social marginalisation of the majority of older people:

> Low income is the most concrete manifestation of the social devaluation of those who do not participate in production. An industrial ideology in which production

is given priority over reproduction, the formal economy over the domestic, hardware over humans, leads to ageist prejudice; this in spite of the fact that retirement is socially created. (p. 132)

The status of older women is lower than older men – this 'derives from a combination of ageism and sexism: industrialism devalues age, patriarchy devalues femaleness' (p. 133). This situation is compounded further for ethnic minority older people when ageism and sexism meet racism. Ethnic minority older people are on average poorer, and 'face greater difficulties than other elderly people in obtaining health care, housing and social services' (p. 133). Despite ample evidence 'the oppression of older women . . . especially . . . ethnic minority older women' (p. 134) has been less visible in academic research . One reason which Ginn gives for this may be the same focus in some feminist research criticised by Morris: 'the "burden of caring" borne by daughters looking after elderly parents has received rather more research attention than the feelings of indignity and loss of autonomy in those receiving care' (ibid.).

Despite the low socio-economic status of older people, there has been a growth in 'conflictual ageism', whose roots, 'are to be found not in concern for younger generations but in an ideological preference for privatisation of pensions and in the interests of financial institutions' (p. 144). Contrary to those who see older people as already possessing disproportionate influence, Ginn concludes by stressing the need for self-empowerment through older people's organisations: 'However, combating ageist attitudes and practices will not be easy, as it entails a shift in power relationships. Just as younger women and black people led the campaigns against sexism and racism, the self-organisation of older people is crucial' (p. 135).

All the contributions to Part I, then, address the *social relations of welfare* from a variety of perspectives focusing on a range of experiences. They also point to the ways in which these experiences have been marginalised or ignored in the academic discipline of social policy. They show, too, how benefits, services and attendant welfare ideologies can be strategies of social control. At the same time, they point to the way in which marginalised or excluded groups have fought for social rights and social inclusion. These issues raise practical and theoretical questions about *particular needs* and *universal rights*; about the nature of *empowerment* and *participation*; and about *the bases of social inclusion*. These issues are explored further by the contributors to Part II.

References

Ginsburg, N. (1994) 'Agendas and prognoses for social policy; a selective review', in N. Manning and R. Page (eds), *Social Policy Review 6*. Canterbury: Social Policy Association.

Levitas, R. (1996) 'The concept of social exclusion and the new Durkheimian hegemony', *Critical Social Policy*, 46: 6–20.

Squires, P. (1990) *Anti-social Policy*. London: Harvester Wheatsheaf.

Williams, F. (1992) 'Somewhere over the rainbow: universality and diversity in social policy', in N. Manning and R. Page (eds), *Social Policy Review 4*. Canterbury: Social Policy Association.

Williams, F. (1994) 'Social relations, welfare and the post-Fordism debate', in R. Burrows and B. Loader (eds), *Towards a Post-Fordist Welfare State?* London: Routledge.

1

Feminism and Social Policy

Mary McIntosh

During the 1970s, feminists developed a critique of the welfare system that was both sophisticated and damning. It began in a fragmentary way in the early 1970s with specific protests about issues like the 'cohabitation rule' and the 'tax-credit' proposals. There was a growing awareness that women figure prominently among the clients of social workers, the inmates of geriatric and psychiatric hospitals, the claimants of supplementary benefits – despite the fact that married and cohabiting women are not eligible for many benefits. There was a resentment about the degrading way that women are treated when they need state benefits and state services.

The first responses were articulated most clearly by libertarian feminists, who could express vividly what women know of the conditions under which welfare is granted. They know the queues and the forms, the deference, the anger, the degradation, the sense of invisibility and the loss of autonomy. They see the mean, withholding face of the state and can readily take up the negative cry of 'Smash the state!' But the cohabitation campaign also raised deeper issues. It was not just that the 'SS' were 'sex snoopers' who prevented women claimants from drawing their benefit if they were suspected of living with a man. They also tried to force women into prostitutional dependence on the men they slept with. This raised the whole question of women's dependence on men and the fact that women were second-class citizens. The Women's Family Allowance Campaign against the Tory government's 1972 tax-credit proposals focused on the same problems. The family allowance, paid directly to a mother was preferable to the same, or even a greater, amount paid in tax credits through a father's pay packet. The model of the couple as a financial unit bore little relation to reality as many women experienced it. In the end, after we had defeated this aspect of the tax-credit scheme, the trade unions' reluctance to accept the loss of the child tax allowance that accompanied the improved child benefit only verified what we already knew: that money in a husband's pay packet was not equivalent to a direct payment to his wife.

In the context of the women's liberation movement, the developing

This article is based on a paper given by the author at the *Critical Social Policy* Conference, 'Crisis in the Welfare State' in November 1980, and was first published in *Critical Social Policy* 1(1), 1981.

awareness of women's relation to the welfare state was crystallised at the national conference in 1974. Elizabeth Wilson's pamphlet *Women and the Welfare State* (1974) was launched there and a new demand, for 'legal and financial independence', was adopted. The new demand, the fifth to be adopted by the movement, recognised clearly the relevance of the state in solving the problem of women's dependence upon men. The other demands (concerned with equal opportunities in jobs and training, equal pay, nurseries, abortion and contraception) all had a bearing on women's independence in their different ways. But this one, as the paper calling for it to be adopted expressed it, 'highlights the links between the state and the family, and the way in which the state systematically bolsters the dependent-woman family' (Gieve et al., 1974). It saw the relevance of state policy not merely to those categories of women who receive or are denied state benefits of various kinds – not merely to mothers and non-mothers, wives and non-wives, earners and non-earners – but to women as a whole category. For it saw how state policies play a part in constructing that category and in constructing the idea of the family in which it exists. All women suffer from a stereotype of the woman as properly dependent upon a man. But all women also suffer in quite practical terms from the fact that there are few viable alternatives to such dependence. (For an argument against this view, see Bennett et al., 1980.)

Since then, this critique of state policy has been detailed and sustained. Academic articles have been published (especially by Hilary Land, 1976, 1977), and so have pamphlets (for instance, Streather and Weir, 1974; Lister and Wilson, 1976). Many a parliamentary select committee and inter-departmental working party has been told of our views by various women's groups. Wider campaigns, like the rousing but in the end rather abortive one on wives' treatment under income tax, have been mounted. What is disappointing is how little this critique has really affected thinking among other radicals about social policy. Goodwill towards feminism expresses itself in manning the creche, going on the abortion demo and avoiding sexist styles of behaviour. But how many critics of the DHSS review of supplementary benefit a year or so ago – apart from women – argued against the aggregation of the income and resources of husband and wife? Yet separate treatment has been our demand ever since the first feminist critiques of the Beveridge Report in the early 1940s (see, for instance, Abbott and Bompas, 1943; Pierce, 1979).

At the same time as this awareness of how the state constructs dependent women, there was a growing awareness of women as state employees. Both the state bureaucracies and the institutions of health, education and welfare employ enormous numbers of women in their lower ranks; often their clients are women; and often they are engaged in classically 'feminine' types of work both in terms of the contents of their tasks and in terms of the social functions they fulfil. In fact, insofar as previously domestic functions like health care, child care and personal services have become socialised, the social tasks are frequently performed by women just as the private ones were. In struggles to improve social services and nurseries, and in struggles to unionise women workers and advance their position, feminist issues and the question of what women in different situations have in common were fought out time and again. 'The patter of tiny contradictions' was how Val Charlton (1974) described a child care centre started by some women's liberation groups in London.

All of these critical approaches to social policy were the feminist version of the radical and Marxist critiques of the 1960s and 1970s. The burden of these was that the welfare state is nothing of the kind: that it is not redistributive as between the social classes, but makes the working class pay for its own social casualties, that it does not even eliminate poverty at the bottom end of the scale, that it is not the harbinger of socialist provision according to need – neither in its style nor in its effects – and that it is an instrument of bourgeois control, forcing people to work and imposing standards of morality, decency and household management. To this, feminists add that the welfare state is especially oppressive to women, in that it harnesses them into the team that pulls the whole welfare charabanc along.

What was new, though, was that there was a clear recognition at the same time that women need state provision. Faced with a choice between a chancy dependence on a man on the one hand and dependence on the state or exploitation in waged work on the other, feminists opt for the state and the wage.

Personal dependence carries with it a whole baggage of psychological dependence. Lack of autonomy, deference, the need to manipulate personal relations, all tend to stunt women's potential and make us insecure and unadventurous. Indeed the characteristics of femininity which Juliet Mitchell (1974) has explained in terms of the experience of infancy – passivity, masochism and narcissism – could equally be explained by the adult experience of dependence and the practical need to seek support. This explanation would in fact fit better the reality, which is one of public passivity, based on self-repression and often masking an underlying attitude of cynicism and rebellion, similar to that of Franz Fanon's colonised people.

With all their problems, then, the state and the employer can be fought collectively and unlike modern marriage they are not intrinsically patriarchal. And whenever feminists have formulated the demand for the socialisation of housework and of personal care, it has been state provision rather than private commercial provision that they have had in mind.

Feminists in this country have never been for very long attracted to purely anti-statist positions. Such utopian individualism (or even small-scale collectivism) is a possible dream for men who can envisage a world of self-supporting able-bodied people. But women are usually concerned with how the other three-quarters live. They have argued for new forms of interdependence based in the community and not in the family, and these necessarily involve the state at one level or another.

There have been some interesting debates in the women's movement about the development and provision of feminist services. The question has

been: should we provide these ourselves or should we demand state provision and then fight about the form that provision should take? Nurseries,
playgroups, health care, advice on contraception and abortion, refuges for
battered women, rape crisis centres, legal and welfare rights advice all
clearly fall within the ambit of things that we expect to be provided by state
agencies. Yet these are either not available or, when they are, are inadequate and unfeminist in their approach. Setting up services like this is a
way both of meeting women's needs and also of developing public awareness of the effects of women's oppression, and providing a base for feminist
analysis and agitation around the issue (Flaskas and Hounslow, 1980). In
Australia and in the United States there has been a great proliferation of
feminist health and welfare services and the results have sometimes been
disappointing in that the energies of the women involved have been used up
in providing a good service so that the more forward-looking political tasks
have been neglected. In this country, with the notable exception of the
network of Women's Aid refuges for battered women, the tendency has
been to set up very few feminist agencies but to concentrate on campaigning for state provision. The more developed social and health services
in this country have made this a more promising direction to work in. It
also seems to me to be the right approach, since it can lead to more long-
term and more universal provision than any voluntary efforts are likely to
do. The character of such campaigns is also different and in some ways
more outgoing politically. Instead of the independent and sometimes rather
inward-looking group work involved in establishing and running a feminist
service, there is the need to make alliances and work in the existing political
arena. The struggle to develop the present services in a feminist direction
involves work in the unions and professional bodies of the service workers
as well as organising among clients and users.

Making claims on the state thus involves fruitful political work and
agitation at many levels and is far from being confined to the politics of
Westminster. So in this respect, as in some others, women have been at the
forefront of the rethinking of the rather facile radical libertarianism of the
1960s and early 1970s. (The other things that feminists questioned were the
general assumption that decriminalisation, decarceration and de-institutio-
nalisation were unambiguously progressive. Sometimes they have gone too
far as in calling for exceptionally heavy punishments and the suspension of
the usual rights of the accused in the cases of rape and of violence against
women, and in calling for increased state control over pornography. In
some spheres we have not yet gone far enough: we should be mounting a
much stronger criticism of present ideas of 'community care' and fighting
for new forms of institutional care that avoid the problems earlier radicals
have pointed to.)

Now, at the beginning of the 1980s, we have reached the point, feminists
and socialists alike, where it is generally agreed that we cannot afford the
luxury and purity of a simply critical stance. This, I take it, is why our

journal is called *Critical Social Policy*, rather than *Critique of Social Policy*. We have to develop ideas and organisations that enable us to engage with social policy as it forms. And this will mean discussing what sort of welfare state we do want, not just sniping at the existing one and waiting for The Revolution to put everything right.

However, for Marxists this cannot mean a Fabian-style formulation of gradual ameliorative goals and means. It must mean taking a very clear class position and working within the labour movement and all organisations that can take up an anti-capitalist position. It means working out what gains can be made in any given situation and what threats most need defending against, not assuming that social policy makers are people of goodwill who will see reason when a clear and forceful case is put to them. I suggest that, at the most general level, there are two key points to remember.

The first is that although the dominant factor affecting state policies will always be the long-term interests of the ruling class, and although the central interests of the working class and the capitalist class are antagonistic, it is not necessarily the case that their interests will be opposed on every single issue of social policy. The most fundamental reason for this is that, despite the fact that the wage relation is an antagonistic one, workers' and capitalists' interests coincide in requiring the satisfaction of the workers' basic needs, whether through the wage or by other means. The capitalist requires the reproduction of labour power; the worker requires food and clothing. Of course, they will differ widely over what sort of needs should be met and under what conditions: over what constitutes 'adequate' reproduction of labour power; and this is where struggles over social policy come in. The history of the growth of the welfare state and the growth of collective consumption (Grevet, 1976; Castells, 1978) in general in capitalist societies is thus neither a history of cherries snatched from the greedy hands of capitalists by a militant working class, nor is it a history of a crafty capitalist plot to control and enfeeble the workers in the interests of guaranteeing the reproduction of labour power and of the relations of production. It is both. The gains and losses have to be figured partly in terms of some felicific calculus and partly in political terms: are we better placed for the next battle? Has morale improved?

The second key point is that we need to keep in mind the limits that are set on social policy by the capital–labour contradiction. In particular, we need to recognise that the wage system is fundamental to capitalist production and that the primary means of the reproduction of labour power will be the wage. Social security provisions and collective consumptions will be designed in such a way as to minimise their interference with the labour market and with the existence of a proletariat obliged to sell its labour power in order to survive.

This means that demands for a 'guaranteed minimum income' have no connection with social policy in capitalist society. The 'guaranteed minimum income' is a demand adopted by the Claimants' Union as a radical solution to their degrading experiences at the hands of the social security officials. They see the problems of the means test, the search for a 'liable relative', and the obligation to sign on for employment as ways in which the working class are harassed and controlled. So they demand their abolition, the right of everyone to a guaranteed income regardless of whether or not they are willing to look for waged work. As a Claimants' Union representative argued in one of the workshops at the 'Crisis in the Welfare State' conference: 'People who don't have jobs need an income as much as those who do; it is hard work just staying alive in capitalist society.' The demand is thus very different from a demand for a minimum wage coupled with improved social security benefits at the same level. It is a demand that the need to sell one's labour power in order to survive should be abolished. So it is nothing less than a demand that socialism be introduced: but a demand ostensibly made of the capitalist state and a demand that socialism should enter through the back door, via the relations of distribution; rather than the front door, via the relations of production. It is thus, as its proponents are well aware, an unrealisable demand under capitalism, since it negates the wage relation which lies at the heart of capitalism. Any of their supporters who join the ranks because they think they might actually gain the demand have been sadly deceived. But the existence of such demands can have the depressing effect of making all real current struggles over policy look paltry and reformist by comparison.

Feminists have been very aware of this problem in relation to the demand for 'wages for housework', rejected by the women's liberation movement in this country in 1972, but still having a small, vocal following. Effectively this is a demand that women should have a guaranteed minimum income, since the idea that there should be any check on whether they actually do any housework is rejected. It is thus a demand that all women should be lifted out of the proletariat and put on a pension. It, too, can be dispiriting if it has the effect of making current struggles over matters like invalid care allowances or the infamous 'Housewife's Non-Contributory Disability Allowance' seem trivial and reformist.

Though dependence on the wage will continue to be the primary means of support for the working class, we have seen during the twentieth century a notable narrowing of the range of people who are expected to depend upon a wage. A wage-earner is no longer expected to provide the main support for old and disabled relatives, only for his wife and children (or, more rarely, her husband and children). The welfare state has defined whole categories of people out of the labour market – the old, the young, the disabled – enabling the capitalist work process to be intensified and many welfare benefits to be offered unconditionally and apparently benevolently. But there cannot be an infinite extension of such benefits unless the working class is to be de-proletarianised altogether.

These two key points are proposed as basic considerations for the formulation of any socialist strategy for social policy in capitalist societies. But I shall illustrate their importance by looking at the problems of feminist strategy. Women have to consider whether they have gained or lost by the policies accepted by the working class in the past, and how they should relate to working-class political organisation for the future. And we have to consider what relation we want women to have to wage labour. Should we become more fully proletarianised or should we seek better conditions of dependence on husbands or on state benefits?

I shall turn now to these more specific questions of feminist strategy. In some ways, the central problem is the same one that has plagued feminism ever since the achievement of the vote left the movement without a central rallying cry. The problem is whether to press for equality with men, usually in terms of legal, political and citizenship rights, or to press for greater support and respect for women in their roles as housewives and mothers: a right to an independent income and a recognition of the importance of their contribution.

The second position was that of the 'new feminists' who emerged after the First World War. So Eleanor Rathbone argued in 1925 that the point had been reached where women could say:

> At least we have done with the boring business of measuring everything women want, or that is offered to them, by men's phraseology. We can demand what we want for women, not because it is what men have got, but because it is what women need to fulfil the potentialities of their own natures and to adjust themselves to the circumstances of their own lives. (Rathbone, 1929, quoted in Lewis 1973)

The argument against the older equalitarianism took the form of a rejection of male definitions of women's work as inferior and a plea for a new dignity and new measures of protection. In some respects it was more progressive than equalitarianism: it sought to change the world, not merely to give women access to the better places in it. But in the end it was less radical because the changes it sought were too shallow. They were designed to ease the suffering where the shoe pinches rather than build a new shoe on a better last. For modern feminists it is easy to see why Rathbone's mountainous ideal of Family Endowment brought forth the rather ridiculous mouse of Child Benefit and why women's dependence is still a key issue today. As Hilary Land (1980: 75–6) put it: 'Eleanor Rathbone laid much emphasis on the unequal economic relationship between husband and wife, but had far less to say about the division of responsibilities for child care and housework.' A deeper analysis would have led her to see the two as inseparable within any wage-based economy. The problem as it was posed then is that of the impossibility either of the equalitarian ideal – which asks for equal treatment for unequal people – or of the 'new feminist' ideal – which asks for women to be treated as different but equal.

It is interesting to ask whether the difference between these two strategies has been transcended by the more recent feminism of the women's liberation movement. Certainly it is not the basis for the main divisions within the movement at present. And the modern movement is characterised much more by methods that have nothing to do with legal changes or state policies and so may appear to sidestep the problems of equalitarianism: cultural politics, the politics of lifestyle and changing household relationships, self-help and self-defence, support for victims of rape and violence, forming international links and (perhaps most distinctively) developing theoretical analyses of women's oppression.

Yet in many fields of work, the choice between those two strategies remains and continues to pose thorny problems. These tend to be the modern versions of the very issues of law and social policy that exercised our feminist grandmothers. The issue of protective legislation, restricting the hours and conditions of women's work in factories, is a conspicuous example. Feminists have been divided over it ever since it was first introduced during the nineteenth century. At that time equalitarianism was the dominant approach and such feminists as took an interest in the question opposed the legislation on the grounds that it infringed women's liberty and put them at a disadvantage in the labour market – a view which I think is justified by the historical evidence (Barrett and McIntosh, 1980; but for the opposite view, see Hutchins and Harrison, 1911; Humphries, 1977, 1981). Later the 'new feminists' attacked this stance and argued that women's functions of home-making and child-rearing could not be carried out properly if they were forced to work long hours and at night outside the home. This is not, of course, a defence that appeals to women's liberationists today.

However, the situation today is not at all comparable to that in the past. For one thing, we have formulated the goal of transforming the processes of home-making and child-rearing, so that if these are to be done privately we want men's factory hours to be limited as well. For another, while the CBI wants protective legislation ended, the TUC wants it continued and extended to cover men and to cover workers everywhere, not just in factory production. So when the Equal Opportunities Commission (1979) recently recommended abolishing the legislation it was siding with the bosses as well as taking an unhistorical perspective and thinking in terms of immediate equality of treatment (for the unequal) rather than of working to eliminate the underlying inequality.

However, it should be noted that the position that women's liberationists usually adopt on this issue depends upon trusting the TUC. If they are not genuine in their commitment to extend protection to men – or if they have no hope of carrying it through – our position becomes one that simply accepts the present role of women and seeks to protect us from some of its worst penalties. I shall come back later to the questions of political practice that this raises. I want first to say something about strategy in relation to one particular feminist campaign, that for 'disaggregation'. I focus on this campaign because it raises important problems and also because I happen to have been involved in it, rather than because I believe it to be any more or less important than other campaigns. It is obviously just one part of a wider struggle.

Socialist feminists in the women's liberation movement have transcended the old divide in the sense that they have questioned not only masculinity and femininity, not only man's place and woman's place, but also the very existence of social division and difference based on sex. We have firmly located the origin and support for this division in the family. This does not mean that we locate it in individual kin-based households, but in the institution of the family, with its ideology, its imperatives and its constraints, which spread far beyond households themselves and both cause and enable the organisation of everything else to be marked by gender division. Women's liberation depends upon the radical transformation of that family. However, although there is much disagreement about the relation of that family system to capitalism, most socialist feminists agree on two things: that the specific character of women's oppression at present is related to the articulation between the family system and the wage system; and that we should start working now towards the transformation of the family system as it will not automatically arrive along with socialism. Indeed, I would add that the family system is changing and is under great strain at present (and not only because of the resurgence of feminism), so that it is incumbent on us to play a part in determining what form that change takes.

On the whole we choose to campaign for those things that we know will both help with the immediate problems of many women and also help to open up possibilities for further and more far-reaching change. The demand for 'disaggregation' in social security, income tax, student grants and so on, is a good example. The aggregation of the married couple into a tax unit and into a means-testable unit – however it may be dressed up in unisex clothing – represents women's dependence on their husbands. This is a dependence that is unreliable and degrading when it does exist and which in any case is a less common pattern than is often supposed, since most women are breadwinners (Hamill, 1978). In terms of Social Security, disaggregation would mean that a married woman who could not get a job could claim supplementary benefit regardless of her husband's income. But it would also mean that a married man would get a single person's benefit with no allowance for the wife; she would have to claim herself and fulfil the usual conditions: unless she was responsible for caring for small children or an invalid or something like that, she would have to sign on for employment.

This is a demand that comes out of our own experience. Several of the group which formulated it had suffered indignities and deprivation at the hands of the social security. Even so, the chief argument for it is not that thousands of women will be better off. It is that all women will have rights to full social security and that all men will lose the right to state back-up for keeping their wives in dependence. We realise that some women, especially older ones who have not had recent experience of going out to work, will be disadvantaged. We realise that forcing women onto the labour market as it exists for them now is painful. But we believe that married women's dependence is in part responsible for their dreadful position in the labour market, and the movement is simultaneously fighting for better pay and conditions at work, including the part-time and low-paid jobs that many women are forced to take.

We realise, too, that many who are concerned about poverty will tell us that there are other groups worse off than married women, whose needs should be met first. I think that argument reveals one of the weaknesses of the approach to social policy that focuses on questions of income equality in terms of the outcome of distributional and redistributional processes, and does not look at the structure of relations involved in producing those outcomes. Our concern is with moving towards a structural change; by unhitching marriage from the social security system we hope to contribute to loosening its ties to the welfare system in general and ultimately to the wage system itself. We do believe that many unemployed married women are in poverty; those who are may benefit from the change. So we think that disaggregation would meet important immediate needs for some women, but more importantly it would help undermine the existing unequal marriage system. (Incidentally, I am not much swayed by the argument that disaggregation would remove one of the few advantages of forming households not based on the heterosexual pair-bond, and so provide another bonus for traditional marriage. For one thing, the argument considers individual types of household rather than the institutions as a whole. But, more importantly, it assumes that marriage would be strengthened because more people would be motivated to enter it, or to stay in it, and I doubt whether this would be true for many people.)

In the present situation, the main point of arguing for disaggregation is to get an acceptance of the principle as widely as possible: to get to the point where the chief basis for resistance to its cost and all the objections on principle have been rejected, both within the labour movement and in official circles. Some of the strongest arguments for it will, of course, be equalitarian ones, not because we want to conceal our real aims, but because equality is indeed an important dimension of the demand and one that people most readily latch on to. (In the social security field, arguments for equality will be undermined by some meretricious wording in the forthcoming legislation, which will use some euphemism like 'main breadwinner' to mask its sex discrimination.)

The day-to-day battles, unfortunately, are much more defensive ones against the cuts. But it is important to give these a feminist dimension, which often means one informed by the perspective of disaggregation, so that we recognise and attack cuts that force women further into dependence as well as those that take away their jobs or give them extra unpaid work. Disaggregation and protective legislation are only two examples. Similar strategic decisions have to be made in relation to almost every field. Should we press for a share of the matrimonial home and adequate maintenance for wives on the breakup of marriage (Law Commission, 1980)? Should we press for cohabitant women to be given rights equivalent to those of married women (Bottomley et al., 1981)? These fields need to be linked and seen as part of the overall strategy for women's liberation, which of course goes far beyond the confines of social policy, even in its broadest sense.

The positions that I have argued for here are adopted in the light of the two key points of guidance for socialist social policy that I outlined earlier. They are based on the belief that there can be significant gains for women and for the working class (real gains for women are also gains for working-class unity) within capitalist society, since not every working-glass gain is an immediate capitalist loss. And they are based on the belief that the wage system is fundamental to capitalist society, so that, despite all the disadvantages of wage work, the way forward must be through furthering the process of proletarianism of women and rescuing women from pre-proletarian dependence. The struggle to end capitalist wage labour cannot be helped by women opting out and can only be undertaken by a working class that is less divided by male domination than the present one.

I want to end with some remarks about problems of organisation in pursuing feminist goals in social policy. I shall not discuss questions of organisation for women's liberation in general, though what I shall say clearly reflects certain views on that.

First, I think we have got to develop a feminist presence in all the places where changes in social policy are fought for. This means within the left political parties, within the labour movement, within all the campaigning and lobbying bodies, and as much as possible in the women's organisations. Building up such a presence is often an unattractive activity for contemporary women's liberationists. Once we have experienced the joys and terrors of swimming in structureless movements like the women's liberation movement (if we managed to keep our heads above water), whose favourite forums are the mass meeting in an overcrowded school hall with an inadequate PA system, and the small intimate and supportive workgroup, we find it hard even to tread water in the structured world of jockeying for office, juggling agendas and bowing to the constraints of representative democracy. But we cannot by-pass those organisations; they exist, and each of them has carved out its own space of power. If we are not to be in constant opposition to them we must work within them as well as working in our own ways outside them. Sometimes this means challenging and transforming their styles of work and approach. Often, though, it means forming alliances where we have only a few points of agreement; and often it means compromises: avoiding taking a line that will lose us the support that we need for other more important battles. The question of protective legislation and the TUC, which I discussed earlier, is a case in point. Above all, it means getting in there and arguing our case in the context of on-going work.

The second remark I want to make is about men's relation to feminist social policy and to the women's liberation movement. I think it may be true to say that there is never an entirely acceptable stance for outsiders towards a movement of liberation. I have experienced this as a white person in relation to the Black movement in the 1960s and as a Briton in relation to anti-imperialist movements. It is easy to be caught in the double bind of being told simultaneously that we should not interfere, not impose our ideas, not assume we can escape being oppressors by an act of will, and leave the oppressed group to constitute its own autonomous movement. But it is easier still to use that double bind as an excuse for doing nothing to support the cause of liberation, for carrying on with our own struggles quite unaffected by those of our neighbours. Many men have used that double bind as a way of getting off the hook in relation to women's liberation. They respect the autonomy of the women's movement, wish it well, and there the matter can rest.

But such an easy benevolence is not appropriate to the case. We aim to overthrow men's dominance and remove their privileges as a gender. Our cause cannot just be added on to the list of radical causes. We are not a newly discovered minority group like dyslexics or people whose homes are threatened by road-widening, because our oppression is built in to the very structure of production and reproduction. So anyone concerned with social policy must decide what stand to take on the issues we raise and must see the question of women as integral to any analysis of social policy. We have been talking and writing for many years now about the inadequacy of existing analyses. Yet those of us who are teachers still find that our well-meaning male colleagues invite us to give a lecture or two on 'Women and welfare', 'Women and crime', or whatever. This is done with a modest, 'I am only a man; I can't speak for women.' But I sometimes wonder what they think the other 18 lectures in their course are about: men? neuters? a gender-free society? The welfare system as it stands (or totters) is utterly dependent upon a specific construction of gender. The Department of Health and Social Security is well aware of that and it is time that critics of social policy were as well.

Postscript

The 15 years since 'Feminism and Social Policy' was written have seen many changes in the politics of the welfare state. To some extent, then, the article is of historical interest rather than immediate practical relevance. Yet I think that the underlying analysis is still correct and many of the ideas still worth reading.

In the countries where the women's movement exploded in the 1970s, it has now disappeared as a recognisable entity, a set of groups and campaigns co-ordinated through mass conferences and newsletters. Feminism has become the common sense of progressive women – and some men – and is now the effective practice of many women active in local government, education, medical and social services, the voluntary sector, the arts and media and in political and trades union organisations. At the same time, feminist ideas have become much better established in universities and colleges. The enormous outpouring of women's studies books and journals is witness to the level of interest in these issues – and also means that there is no longer any excuse for teaching social policy in a way that does not recognise its deeply gendered nature. Too often, perhaps, the analysis is concerned with the immediate effects of social policy and policy changes on the lives of individual women as claimants or as carers, rather than with the more institutional and sociological effects that have consequences for all women. Nevertheless, there has been a decisive shift towards an acceptance of some kind of feminist analysis.

During this period of Conservative rule, the family has become more politicised than ever. The major parties compete for the title 'the party of the family'. One aspect of this is support for family values and opposition to divorce, lone parenthood, sexual non-conformity and non-family forms of household and solidarity. The other aspect is a reliance on the family to perform basic social functions of caring, financial support and social control. In the moral panic after the horrific murder of toddler Jamie Bulger by two 10-year-old boys, politicians vied for the limelight with their castigation of inadequate parents and their calls for a strengthening of the role of fathers in the moral education of their children. Community care has largely replaced care in large institutions and, although part of this is support for mentally ill and disabled people living independently and in small residential homes, a lot of it is care by families, and particularly by women within families. Mutual material support has always been an important function of the family, but the rise in divorce and the increasing number of unmarried heterosexual couples has destabilised this function and made it hard for the state to police. In 1980 the central political issue was the 'cohabitation rule', obliging a heterosexual couple to support each other even if they had chosen not to get married. Now the central issue is 'child support' and the role of the Child Support Agency in enforcing maintenance payments by absent parents is hotly disputed; but there are far fewer voices than there were 15 years ago calling for public support for children rather than private support based on biological paternity. Even the One Parent Families organisation now believes that mothers should get maintenance from the absent fathers of their children.

In this context, the call for 'disaggregating' married couples for the purposes of means testing may seem more utopian than ever. It is true that we have achieved disaggregation for the purposes of taxation, but this is not nearly as fundamental, or as costly to the Treasury, as income support. Child Benefit is the only remaining vestige of the ideal and it is an extraordinarily tenacious one which has survived repeated threats over the years. The ideal of disaggregation seems to me one that is worth retaining, however, if only as a reminder of how far we are from any true social justice for women and from any truly socialist concern for child welfare.

References

Abbot, Elizabeth and Bompas, Katherine (1943) *The Woman Citizen and Social Security: A Criticism of the Proposals Made in the Beveridge Report as they Affect Women*. London: Mrs Bompas.

Allen, S., Sanders, L. and Willis, J. (eds), *Conditions of Illusion*. Leeds: Feminist Books.

Barrett, Michele and McIntosh, Mary (1980) 'The family wage', *Capital and Class*, 11.

Bennett, Fran, Heys, Rosa and Coward, Rosalind (1980) 'The limitations of the demand for independence', *Politics and Power*, 1.

Bottomley, A., Gieve, K., Moon, G. and Weir, A. (1981) *The Cohabitation Handbook: A Woman's Guide to the Law*. London: Pluto Press.

Castells, Manuel (1978) 'Collective consumption and urban contradictions in advanced capitalism', in M. Castells, *City, Class and Power*. London: Macmillan.

Charlton, Valerie (1974) 'The patter of tiny contradictions', in Sandra Allen, et al. (eds), *Conditions of Illusion*. Leeds: Feminist Books.

Equal Opportunities Commission (1979) *Health and Safety Legislation: Should we Distinguish between Men and Women?* London: HMSO.

Flaskas, Carmel and Hounslow, Betty (1980) 'Government intervention and right-wing attacks on feminist services', *Scarlet Woman* (Australia), 11.

Gieve, K., Gilbert, L., McIntosh, M., Morton, L., Robinson, L., Wheatley, M. and Wilson, L. (1974) 'The independence demand' in Sandra Allen et al., eds.

Grevet, Patrice (1976) *Besoins populaires et financement public*. Paris: Editions Sociales.

Hamill, Lynn (1978) 'Wives as sole and joint breadwinners', paper presented to the Social Science Research Council, Social Security Research Workshop.

Humphries, Jane (1977) 'Class struggle and the persistence of the working-class family', *Cambridge Journal of Economics*, 1(3): 241–58.

Humphries, Jane (1981) 'Protective legislation, the capitalist state and working-class men: 1842 Mines Regulation Act', *Feminist Review*, 7.

Hutchins, B.L. and Harrison, A. (1911) *A History of Factory Legislation*, 2nd edn. London: P.S. King & Son.

Land, Hilary (1976) 'Women: supporters or supported?' in Diana Barker and Sheila Allen, *Sexual Divisions and Society: Process and Change*. London: Tavistock.

Land, Hilary (1977) 'Social security and the division of unpaid work in the home and paid employment in the labour market', in Department of Health and Social Security, *Social Security Research Seminar*. London: HMSO.

Land, Hilary (1980) 'The family wage', *Feminist Review*, 6.

Law Commission (1980) *Family Law: The Financial Consequences of Divorce: The Basic Policy: A Discussion Paper* (Law Com. No. 103). London: HMSO, Cmnd. 8041.

Lewis, Jane (1973) 'Eleanor Rathbone and the new feminism during the 1920s', unpublished mimeograph.

Lister, Ruth and Wilson, Leo (1976) *The Unequal Breadwinner*. London: National Council for Civil Liberties.

Mitchell, Juliet (1974) *Psychoanalysis and Feminism*. London: Allen Lane.

Pierce, Silvie (1979) 'Ideologies of female independence in the welfare state: women's response to the Beveridge Report', paper given at British Sociological Association Annual Conference.

Rathbone, Eleanor F. (1929) *Milestones: Presidential Addresses at the Annual Council Meetings of NUSEC*, London.

Streather, Jane and Weir, Stuart (1974) *Social Insecurity: Single Mothers on Social Security*, Child Poverty Action Group, Poverty Pamphlet No. 16.

Wilson, Elizabeth (1974) *Women and the Welfare State*, Red Rag Pamphlet No. 2, London.

2

Anti-semitism, Immigration Controls and the Welfare State

Steve Cohen

The history of the British welfare state has been marked by the existence of two related forms of institutionalised racism. First, there has been, since the Commonwealth Immigrants Act of 1962, ever-increasing immigration controls against Black people. Second, entitlement to a whole series of welfare benefits have themselves become linked to immigration status. This is now the case, to take just a few examples, in respect of supplementary benefit, housing benefit, student awards and NHS hospital treatment. The consequence of all this is internal controls against Black people. There is a daily working relationship between the welfare, supposedly caring, agencies of the state and its repressive apparatus as represented by the Home Office (Cohen, 1980; 1981).

This appears paradoxical and poses a fundamental question. Is institutional racism of this nature merely coincidental to the welfare state or is it in some sense intrinsic to it? The present chapter attempts to answer the question historically through retrieving the hidden history of the relationship between nationalism and welfare. It does this by pursuing the two main themes of *welfarism* and *labourism*. On the one hand it looks at how the ideological concepts of efficiency, eugenics, nation and empire have been a constant in the debates about welfare throughout this century. On the other hand it emphasises how the labour movement played a central role from an early date in popularising these concepts in relation to welfare. The hidden history that highlights these themes is also the hidden history of anti-semitism. It centres around the struggle against Jewish immigration which was successfully concluded with the Aliens Act of 1905. Although this is now forgotten it is crucial – not least because it was enforced by the Liberal government of 1906. This was the government which legitimised state provision of welfare through the introduction of its pension and national insurance schemes and as such it laid the basis of the future welfare state. It was not thought inconsistent with these welfare innovations that Jews be excluded from the country. Indeed, there was a link between welfare and exclusion. The major welfare legislation passed by the 1906

First published in *Critical Social Policy*, 13, 1985.

government made eligibility for benefit dependent on immigration status. The parallels with the modern welfare state are, of course, remarkable. However the combination of immigration control and internal control has been developed in every decade in this century – though for the people unaffected by this development it has often remained hidden.

The chapter concludes that the welfare state is intrinsically racist since the provision of welfare is premised on the ideological acceptance, historically long-held, of immigration controls.

Opposition to Jewish Immigration

Major Jewish immigration to the UK began in the last quarter of the 19th century. It was a response to organised anti-semitism throughout Eastern Europe – particularly after 1882 and the enactment of the May Laws in Russia which confined the Jewish masses to the Pale of Settlement. Probably 700,000 Jews fled persecution by coming here. They entered a country which was itself profoundly anti-semitic. England had a history of Jew-hatred going back to the time of the Crusades. The massacre of the Jews of York by the assembled Crusaders in 1190 is one example. This was followed in the next century by pogroms in Lincoln and Norwich. The entire Jewish population was finally expelled from England in 1290. The imagery of anti-Jewish mythology flourished through religion and art. The figures of Shylock and Fagin were typical of popular myth.

Immediately on arriving in this country Jews were faced with the demand for immigration control. This demand was supported by the Tories and though the Liberals were in nominal opposition it was they who enforced the 1905 Act. The situation was similar to the paper objection of the Labour Party to the 1962 Commonwealth Immigrants Act but their enforcement of it when they came to power in 1964. The rhetoric of immigration control against Jews was also remarkably similar to that used against Black people decades later. Here is a quote from William Evans Gordon, Tory MP and a major advocate of control:

> Not a day passes but English families are ruthlessly turned out to make room for foreign invaders . . . Out they go to make room for Rumanians, Russians and Poles . . . It is only a matter of time before the population becomes entirely foreign . . . The rates are burdened with the education of thousands of children of foreign parents . . . The working classes know that new buildings are erected not for them but for strangers from abroad. (*Hansard*, 29.1.1902)

This appeal to the 'working classes' and their material interests is significant because the battle against Jewish immigration was won as a result of the active support of the British working and unemployed classes. It is doubtful whether, without the incessant demands for exclusion from this direction, the immigration control legislation would have been passed. For over 20 years the British masses campaigned for control. This campaign was so successful that by the time of the 1962 Immigration Act, the labour movement was to regard immigration controls as 'natural'. However the ideology of control had only been legitimised 60 years previously. The struggle of the masses took place on two levels. On the one hand there was agitation by the organised trade union and socialist movement. On the other hand there was agitation by a truly proto-fascist organisation, the British Brothers League. That these could exist in parallel says a lot about the ideology of British labourism. It also says a lot about the ideology of British welfarism. Popular support for immigration controls was not solely based on a generalised anti-semitism. There was also specific agreement both that Jews were detrimental to the welfare of the British and should be denied entry to the country and also that Jews already in the country had to be excluded from any proposed welfare reform. In this way the demand for immigration control became inextricably linked within the labour movement with the struggle for welfare and social legislation.

The Trade Union and Socialist Movement

The hostile attitude of major sections of the labour movement to Jewish immigration is crucial to an understanding of labour history. The struggle for immigration controls was actually being waged simultaneously with the creation of both industrial unionism and socialist organisation in this country. The consequence was that chauvinism became virtually inbuilt into the modern labour movement at its commencement.

From 1892 onwards the TUC was committed to a resolution excluding Jews. In the same year W.H. Wilkins, a fanatical advocate of control, published his book *The Alien Invasion*. This listed 43 other labour organisations in favour of restricting Jews. These included the National Boiler Makers, the Durham Miners and Liverpool Trades Council. Many other trades councils supported control in this period. These included London (*London Evening News*, 27.5.1891 and 19.6.1891), Manchester (Trades Council Report, 1892) and Leeds (evidence of its Secretary to the 1903 Royal Commission on Alien Immigration). J.H. Wilson, MP and Secretary to the Seaman's Union was one of the first to propose legislation in Parliament (*Hansard*, 11.2.1893).

The position of the TUC is particularly relevant as it shows the intimate connection drawn within the labour movement between immigration control and welfare reform. In 1895 there was a special conference of the TUC called to compile a list of questions to be asked of all MPs in the coming general election (*Manchester Evening News*, 11.7.1895). These questions were described as 'a labour programme'. They included demands for the nationalisation of land, minerals and the means of production, for old age pensions, for adequate health and safety facilities, for abolition of the House of Lords, for workers' industrial injury compensation, for the 8-hour day and for the reform of the poor law system. Radical as these were they also included one other demand – the restriction of Jewish immigration.

One of the platform speakers at this TUC conference was Ben Tillett who actively supported this form of questioning of MPs and spoke in its favour. Tillett has a place on the pantheon of labour heroes because of his militancy as a rank and file docker's leader. In fact he also spoke at the London Trades Council in support of immigration control along with another docker's leader Tom Mann (*London Evening News*). Tillett was renowned as a socialist. As a member of the Independent Labour Party he often used its journal to attack Jews. For instance he wrote,

> If getting on is the most desirable thing in this earth then the Jew, as the most consistent and determined money grubber we know is worthy of the greatest respect. That his money grubbing is not universally respected only proves that the bulk of civilised nations, even now, do not believe in the commercialistic idea of clean hands and blood-stained money. (*Labour Leader*, 19.12.1894)

Tillett was not the only socialist to attack Jews and call for immigration controls. *Clarion*, the journal of Robert Blatchford, carried an article as early as 1895 which claimed that immigration control against Jews was a matter of 'legitimate self-preservation' and that 'there is scarcely any town of any dimensions in the country in which the foreign element has not injured and menaced the position of the local workmen' (12.10.1895). This was written by Leonard Hall who was ILP candidate for Salford South in 1892. By 1904 the *Clarion* was proclaiming 'it was high time that legislation dealing with the alien should be considered' (8.10.1904). The Social Democratic Federation, led by H.D. Hyndman with its paper *Justice*, was almost as bad. Hyndman, at a meeting called by Jewish socialists against controls, came and said he was opposed to 'the free admittance of aliens' and went on to attack Jews for living in ghettos and refusing to intermarry (*Jewish Chronicle*, 1.4.1904).

There were some exceptions to this Jew-hatred. The Socialist League of William Morris adopted a consistently principled position, opposed control and worked actively with Jewish trade unionists. However, by 1902 the League had collapsed. Moreover, even when some socialists claimed to be in opposition to control it was an ambivalent opposition. For instance in 1904 the ILP actually issued a pamphlet against control, *The Problem of Alien Immigration*. On its first page it mounted an attack on 'The rich Jew who has done his best to besmearch [sic] the fair name of England and to corrupt the sweetness of our national life and character.' This playing off of the 'rich Jew' and 'poor Jew' was frequent.

Fundamental to this hostile socialist response was obviously a generalised chauvinism against all foreigners. So Bruce Glasier of the ILP argued that 'Neither the principle of the brotherhood of man nor the principle of social equality implies that brother nations or brother men may crowd upon us in such numbers as to abuse our hospitality, overturn our institutions or violate our customs' (*Labour Leader*, 3.4.1904). Similarly,

Leonard Hall in his article had written that support for unrestricted immigration was 'inspired by a somewhat too sanguine estimate of the quality of fraternity . . . sheerest Utopian impracticableness . . . a squint-eyed patriotism and a spurious humanitarianism'. In addition to all of this, socialist hostility was directed against Jews *as Jews*. Hyndman believed that the Boer War was a Jewish plot (*Justice*, 25.4.1896) and that the English press was under Jewish control 'in accord with their fellow capitalist Jews all over the world' (*Justice*, 5.7.1890). *Labour Leader* could write 'Wherever there is trouble in Europe, whenever rumours of war circulate and men's minds are distraught with fear of change and calamity you may be sure a hook-nosed Rothschild is at his games' (19.12.1891). All of this draws on the most basic assumption of anti-semitism – namely that there exists a Jewish world conspiracy.

It is an indictment of the anti-semitism of early English socialism and of its campaign for immigration controls that the National Front has published at least one lengthy article in support of its tradition(*Spearhead*, March 1980). The article commences by stating 'Modern socialists who support the so-called Anti-Nazi League and other anti-racialist organisations would be highly embarrassed to learn of the nationalist and racialist attitudes displayed by many early British socialists.' It ends by praising 'the obvious patriotism and candid racialism of these early socialists'.

The Jewish Response

The only consistent opposition to immigration controls came from the Jewish community. This community was itself split on class lines. The way the British state tried to co-opt members of the community to do its dirty work is similar to its response to the immigration of Black people years later. Major sections of the Jewish leadership supported control. Benjamin Cohen MP, the President of the Jewish Board of Guardians, said he was positively 'disposed to assist in the establishment of such regulations as would discourage the immigration of undesirable persons' (*The Times*, 21.3.1894). Other elements of the leadership offered to police the Jewish community themselves as an alternative to legislative control. Lionel Alexander, Secretary to the Board of Guardians, publicly stated that 'My Board does not favour unwarranted immigration but do their utmost to check it by warnings rather than prohibitions . . . it is one of our largest operations sending people back who, having wandered here, prove useless' (evidence to the 1888 House of Commons Select Committee on Immigration). This attitude was remarkable not least because the Guardians were supposedly themselves the leading Jewish welfare organisation.

On the other hand groups of Jewish workers took up the struggle against immigration controls. In 1894 there was a major conference of Jewish trade unionists, organised in Whitechapel, to protest at the TUC's attack on immigration (*Jewish Chronicle*, 11.9.1894). In 1895 Jewish trade unionists, led by Joseph Finn, produced a leaflet against the TUC's policy, 'The

Voice of the Alien' (*Jewish Chronicle*, 14.2.1902). Shortly after the formation of the British Brothers League there was convened in Whitechapel a
'conference of delegates of trade unions and other Jewish bodies to organise
against the new threat' (*Jewish Chronicle*, 7.6.1901). The following year
there was established an Aliens Defence League in Brick Lane (*Jewish
Chronicle*, 24.1.1902). This activity, though ultimately unsuccessful, had
some positive resonance. First, it pressurised some of the Jewish establishment into permanent opposition to controls. Just as significant was the
fact that Jewish trade unionists and socialists forced some of their English
counterparts into action. This set a pattern which is obvious today – only
when the oppressed take the initiative will English workers respond. For
instance in 1903 over 3,000 people attended a protest meeting organised by
the Federated Jewish Tailors Union of London where the speakers included
W.P. Reeves of the Women's Union League, Margaret Bondfield, secretary
to the National Union of Shop Assistants and Frank Brien of the Dockers
Union (*Eastern Post*, 20.9.1902). A consequence of this is that although the
British labour movement did not campaign against controls, important
sections became neutralised. For example, both Manchester and Leeds
Trades Councils ceased to campaign for controls (in 1903 and 1905
respectively), and in 1905 the President of the TUC actually denounced
controls.

The explanation for this change of attitude does not necessarily lie in any
principled re-evaluation of the traditional chauvinism of the labour movement. Rather, it was a response to the wave of industrial militancy conducted by Jewish workers since the 1890s. Between 1890 and 1903 there
were a series of major Jewish strikes and it is not surprising, therefore, to
find the secretary of Manchester Trades Council explaining that the
Council had ceased to campaign for control by emphasising the good
example that the Jewish Tailors Union in Manchester had set for English
workers (*Manchester Evening News*, 28.1.1903). Chauvinism thus did at
times give way to economic self-interest, but it was not to disappear.

Eugenics and the National Efficiency Movement

Ideologically, there was another strand to the movement against Jewish
immigration also dominant in the movement for welfare reform – the
National Efficiency Movement. This was not a unified movement, but
rather a series of ideas taken up by a broad range of organisations. The
idea of efficiency was closely allied to 'eugenics' – an ideology based on the
theory that people's physical, intellectual and social attributes are the result
of inheritance. A third element in this ideological pantheon was 'Social
Darwinism', which viewed social progress as a struggle between races.
Britain's international dominance was seen to rest on the cultivation of the
fitness of the British race, and the fostering of national unity. Welfare
reform was seen as central to this project.

The catalyst which brought these ideas into prominence was the protracted struggle of the Boer War, which traumatised the British body politic because of the physical and military failing of the British soldiery which the war exposed. This led to a re-evaluation of the role of the state in promoting the health of the population (see Semmell, 1960; Searle, 1971). These ideas were extremely influential at the time, and found support across the entire political spectrum. A typical exposition can be found in a speech by Lord Rosebery, then leader of the Liberal Party, in 1902. He declared that 'The imperialism that grasping after territory, ignores the condition of the Imperial Race is a blind, a futile, and a doomed imperialism.' He urged action to provide suitable housing for 'citizens and subjects of the Imperial Race' and explained that a 'drink sodden population . . . is not the true basis of a prosperous Empire' (Semmell, 1960: 63). Elsewhere he advocated more widespread educational opportunities as a necessary basis of imperial strength.

The correlation between efficiency, nation, empire and welfare reform is absolutely dominant in this period. It is a clear indicator of the chauvinism of the social reforms which were to follow. For instance Karl Pearson, the eugenicist and self-proclaimed socialist, wrote that 'you cannot get a strong and effective nation if many of its stomachs are half-fed and many of its brains untrained'. It was the politician's duty to 'treat class needs and group cries from the standpoint of the efficiency of the herd at large'. He also wrote that 'This tendency to social organisation always prominent in progressive societies may be termed in the best and widest sense of the word – Socialism' (Semmell, 1960: 42–3). Similarly Earl Roberts, a Tory and one of the few popular heroes of the Boer War, wrote to *The Times* to express the need for a 'constructive policy on National Reform and National Defence'. Roberts considered these were two problems which were 'intimately connected' and 'a satisfactory solution of which had to precede any real strengthening of Imperial bonds' (Semmell, 1960: 221).

Two groups of people were singled out for repression in the debate over efficiency. One was women and the other was Jews. The role of women was to be reduced to that of breeding healthy children. In a lecture on 'The Woman's Question' in 1885 Pearson stated that 'Those nations which have been the most reproductive have, on the whole, been the ruling nations in the world's history . . . If child-bearing women must be intellectually handicapped then the penalty to be paid for race-predominance is the subjection of women' (Semmell, 1960: 47). He argued that educational reform should exclude women.

The position of Jews in all this was to be excluded from social reform by being excluded from the country altogether. They were considered eugenically unfit for entry. James Silver, President of the Brothers League, advocated immigration control to avoid grafting 'onto the English stock and diffused into English blood the debilitated, the sickly and the vicious products of Europe' (*Eastern Post*, 2.11.1901). Likewise, Pearson, the socialist, called for the exclusion from the workhouse and asylums of the 'congenital pauper and the insane', the 'deportation of "confirmed criminals"' and the barring of the 'undesirable alien' (Semmell, 1960: 48). It was a common theme amongst many socialists that England was eugenically doomed if it carried on sending its own citizens to the colonies while receiving Jews from Europe. An article in the *Clarion* declared that while the country was 'sending out her finer specimens of humanity' it was receiving in exchange people who were to be considered 'as so much poison injected into the national veins' (*Clarion*, 22.6.1906). Ben Tillett stated that 'for heaven's sake, give us back our own countrymen and take from us your motley multitude' (*London Evening News*, 19.6.1891). Medical practitioners wrote articles to substantiate these politics. The most prominent was Robert Rentoul. His two major contributions to the question was his pamphlet, *The Undesirable Alien From the Medical Standpoint* and his book *Race Culture or Race Suicide?*

Fabianism

Many aspects of the legacy of the Fabians are attacked by present day socialists – in particular their bureaucratic and gradualist approach to social change. What is less well-known is that their vision of a welfare state was eugenic, combining racism, nationalism and a hatred of the native 'unfit'. Their intellectual leaders, the Webbs, were anti-semites. At the time that the Jewish masses were fleeing pogroms in Eastern Europe, Beatrice Webb was writing in her essay 'East London labour' (1888) that 'the love of profit distinct from other forms of money earnings is . . . the strongest impelling motive of the Jewish race'. Sidney Webb wrote that he was in fear of 'national degeneration or, as an alternative, of this country gradually falling to the Irish and the Jews' (Semmell, 1960: 51). The Webbs were advocates of eugenics and efficiency. Their fellow Fabian, H.G. Wells, went as far as advocating 'the sterilisation of failures' (ibid.). Perhaps the simplest way of illustrating the Webbs' attitude towards welfare is to look at their advocacy of family allowances, which was based on fears about a declining birth rate. Their concern was not for women but for eugenics and nationhood. Sidney Webb argued for the endowment of motherhood on the grounds that 'once the production of healthy, moral and intelligent citizens is revered as a social service and made the subject of deliberate praise and encouragement on the part of the government it will, we may be sure, attract the best and most patriotic of the citizens' (ibid.). Given these sorts of politics, it is no wonder that the Fabians did not oppose the campaign against Jewish immigration.

The Liberals and the Aliens Act

In opposition the Liberals opposed the Aliens Act. In office they enforced it. The Act did not exclude 'Jews' by name – no more than modern legislation refers specifically to Black people. Instead it purported to restrict 'undesirable immigrants'. An 'undesirable immigrant' was someone who, *inter alia*, either (a) 'cannot show that he has in his possession or is in a position to obtain the means of supporting himself and his dependants' or (b) 'owing to any disease or infirmity appears likely to become a charge on the rates or otherwise a detriment to the public'. In other words English welfare was to be denied to the foreign sick and the foreign poor. This is a direct forerunner of the present Immigration Rules which prevent the entry of those who may have 'recourse to public funds' or may in any other way become a 'burden on the state'. In fact the 1905 Act was in one respect even more draconian than the present law. Thus the Aliens Act gave the Home Secretary power to deport 'aliens' not only following the recommendation of a court where there had been a criminal offence but also where a court of summary jurisdiction determined that within 12 months of arrival an alien 'had been in receipt of any such parochial relief as disqualifies a person from the parliamentary franchise or been found wandering without ostensible means of subsistence or been living under insanitary conditions due to overcrowding'. In the first four years of the Act's operation 1,378 people were deported (*Jewish Chronicle*, 24.6.1910). The numbers refused entry were much higher. For example, in 1909, 1,456 passengers were refused leave to land (see Zimmerman, 1911). A typical case was the refusal of entry of Elke Rubin and her children Mayer, aged 5, and Boruch, 3½. It was claimed that Mayer was mentally deficient and that 'in the event of the child being permitted to land in England he would necessarily become a burden on the rates by having to attend a special school for mentally defective children' (*Jewish Chronicle*, 2.8.1907). However the most frequent refusal on health grounds was trachoma – an eye disease. Trachoma played the same role in immigration control mythology as TB was to do in the 1960s – it was portrayed as a threat to the national welfare.

Social Policy and the 1906 Liberal Government

The relationship between immigration control and the social reforms of the 1906 Liberal government was not just ideological. The enforcement of the Aliens Act inevitably ensured that Jewish people excluded from the country were also excluded from the new social benefits. However, over and above this many of the Jews within the country were made ineligible for the new welfare schemes precisely because eligibility was made dependent on various immigration and nationality criteria. In other words, the Liberals did not simply legitimise the idea of state provision of welfare which later developed into the post-1945 welfare state, they also legitimised welfare as a nationalistic and racist concept. Two points need to be emphasised. First there was no real debate within Parliament (or outside) on the linking of welfare entitlement and immigration status. After the agitation for the

Aliens Act the righteousness of this sort of chauvinism was simply assumed. Second, because the issue was never really openly debated the discrimination against 'aliens' proceeded in a pragmatic *ad hoc* manner rather than with much coherency. Jews were not excluded from all Liberal social reform. However they were, to some degree or other, excluded from the two major pieces of social legislation on which the 1906 government has founded its historical reputation as a reforming government – the Old Age Pensions Act of 1908 and the National Insurance Act of 1911. It was probably not coincidence that both of these dealt with receipt of financial benefit, with the exclusion from the national insurance scheme being particularly vicious as it was contribution-based. Each Act will now be looked at in turn and in the next section we will examine developments after the First World War.

The Old Age Pensions Act, 1908

The 1908 Act introduced the first ever national scheme of state financed cash benefits. The pensionable age was fixed at 70. However there were two further requirements that prevented most Jews from receiving pensions (Section 2). First, they had to have been a British subject for 20 years and, second, they had to have been 'resident' in the UK for 20 years. This latter requirement was interpreted as meaning 20 years prior to pensionable age (see Barnes, *Hansard*, 19.6.1911). This combination of both a citizenship and a residency requirement is actually quite rare – most other contemporary and subsequent legislation just demanded one or the other. The combination of both tests was extremely onerous. The need for 20 years' citizenship was harsh enough. Moreover, as is shown below, there was, over the next decades, constant protest about the difficulties in obtaining naturalisation and there were particular protests over the length of time this took. Under the Naturalisation Act of 1870, later to be replaced by the British Nationality and Status of Aliens Act 1914, a person must have lived for five years in the UK before they could even apply for nationality – and then their claim could take several years to process. In the debate on the Pensions Bill there was even a suggestion by one MP, Arthur Fell, that no foreign-born person should be eligible for pension rights even if they had become naturalised. Fell wanted benefits to be confined to 'British-born subjects'. He voiced a nationalistic sentiment that has been heard throughout the rest of this century in respect of the welfare provisions of UK – namely that 'It might be that crowds of foreigners of the age of forty-five or fifty might come over here in the hope that, having resided in this country for the required time, they might get a pension' (*Hansard*, 6.7.1908).

The obstacles in obtaining citizenship were a sufficient deterrent to this. However, in addition there was the need for 20 years' 'residence' immediately prior to pensionable age. This requirement is remarkably similar to the criterion of 'ordinary residence' which permeates much modern welfare legislation and excludes Black people from it. There were regulations under the 1908 Act which attempted to define the meaning of 'residence' (Old Age Pensions Regulations 1908, No. 812). In any event, such a provision would have had a serious effect on Jewish men, amongst whom there was at this time something of a pattern of re-emigration, especially to the USA, in search of better conditions for maybe one or two years while the rest of the family stayed in the UK. The 20 years' residency provision was almost a 'loyalty test' – which, combined with the citizenship requirement, led Viscount Wolverhampton, in introducing the Pensions Bill in the Lords, to reassure any potential opposition that the Bill was confined to 'British subjects in every sense of the word' (*Hansard*, 20.6.1908).

In fact the naturalisation and residency requirements came in for two sorts of criticisms and were amended by the Old Age Pensions Act (Section 3) of 1911. First, the 20 years' residency was thought too harsh and was altered to 12 years' residency out of the last 20 prior to pensionable age. Typically, the reasons put forward for this did not take account of Jewish people at all but were mainly designed to protect the interests of those who went out and 'served' in the 'Dominions and Dependencies' until they were too old for pension rights in the UK (Hayes Fisher, *Hansard*, 19.5.1911). The second criticism related to the position of women. More accurately it related to the position of English women, as no one bothered about Jewish women being deprived of pension rights. Under the Naturalisation Act (Section 10) a woman who married an alien automatically lost her citizenship and acquired his. As a consequence, women who married aliens were no longer eligible for benefits that were contingent on nationality. This led to a kind of 'white feminist' backlash. Under the 1911 Act there was a major concession made to this protest by allowing women who had married aliens to claim pensions where the husband had died, or the marriage had been annulled, or there had been a two-year separation. This concession to white womanhood prefigures the 1980 immigration marriage rules (since altered) under which only British women having close ancestral connections with Britain could be joined here by their husbands.

The National Insurance Act

The National Insurance Act was in two main parts, which reflected the two main categories of benefit to be provided. One part dealt with unemployment benefit. Initially this did not discriminate against aliens. The other part made provision for national health insurance which gave entitlement to sickness, disablement and maternity benefit. It was this apparently highly progressive and innovative scheme of health insurance that was in fact discriminatory and was based on nationality and residential criteria for eligibility (Section 45).

Health insurance benefit was to be administered not generally through government agency but through 'approved societies' which were mainly the existing self-help friendly societies that were now to be put under the control of the Insurance Commissioners. However, people who were not British were not to receive their full entitlements unless they had joined an approved society by a designated date before the Act had come into force (4.5.1911) and had been resident in the UK for five years. Non-British citizens who could not fulfil these criteria but who became members of an approved society were not entitled to the full rate of benefit – this was entirely at the discretion of the society. Moreover there was a scheme whereby people who were not members of any approved society could pay their contributions into what was called the Post Office Fund. These people were known as 'deposit contributors'. Male non-British deposit contributors were only eligible for seven-ninths of the normal rate of benefit and women were only eligible for three-quarters. It was at this point that racism met sexism. As in the Pensions Act of 1911 there was an additional perverse concession to racism in that those British women who had married aliens and who otherwise would have lost their health insurance entitlement along with their nationality, were made eligible for full benefit where their husband was dead, the marriage was annulled or there had been a legal separation. The interests of alien – mainly Jewish – women were again ignored.

Under the National Health Insurance Act of 1918 all discrimination against non-British citizens in respect to health insurance was repealed (Section 23). However this was not because of any principled revulsion against linking welfare with immigration status, rather it was because it was practically difficult to enforce such discrimination. The government minister who introduced the 1918 Act, Sir E. Cornwall, stated that,

> I dare say some people will be rather alarmed at our proposals that [aliens] should receive ordinary benefits but I can assure the House that it is not from any love of aliens. It is simply a business proposition. We find the arrangements in the original Act very complicated and it costs a great deal more than if we gave them ordinary benefits. (*Hansard*, 22.11.1917)

Social Legislation after 1918

The major impetus for social reform in this country came from the Liberal government of 1906. The inter-war years saw a gradual development of welfare legislation. This legislation simply reinforced the link between entitlement and immigration status. This chauvinism indeed became more systematic in that it extended to municipal as well as national government and it included all manner of social legislation – not just that concerned with financial benefits. Moreover, the Labour Party, as it replaced the Liberals as the party of the working classes and achieved governmental power, also adopted a nationalistic position on welfare. A relatively significant change from the Liberal period was that the Jewish established leadership, the Board of Deputies, actually became alert to the danger and made some protests. This was for varying reasons – not least was pressure from Jewish workers that persisted since the campaign over the Aliens Act. In any event one member of the Board understood the matter correctly when in 1925 he said, 'This country in its treatment of aliens has been making a descent to Avernus, beginning with its restriction of alien immigration and from then proceeding to impose liabilities on aliens already here' (Joseph Prag, *Jewish Chronicle*, 20.3.1925). This, of course, is precisely what has happened since 1945 to Black people. Here now are some examples of social legislation in the decade after the 'great war' which were predicated on racist legislation.

Old Age Pensions

In 1919 the Board of Deputies sent a delegation to the Committee of Inquiry which was investigating the operation of the Old Age Pensions Act (*Jewish Chronicle*, 28.3.1919 and 25.7.1919). The Board, true to fashion, did not seek to break the link between welfare and immigration status. However it did propose that the dual requirement of citizenship and residency be substituted by simply a 20 years' residence obligation. The resulting legislation was extremely perverse on this issue. The Old Age Pensions Act 1919 retained the citizenship requirement but lowered it from 20 years to 10. At the same time it introduced for the first time a distinction between British-born citizens and naturalised citizens. The former still had to show only 12 years' residence out of the 20 preceding pensionable age. The latter had to again prove actual 20 years' residence. At the same time all disabilities remaining on English women who married aliens were removed for pension purposes.

Unemployment Benefits

As has been seen, under the National Insurance Act of 1911 no distinction was made between British citizens and others as regards unemployment benefit. However, after the war this altered dramatically. First, in 1919, the government authorised what were called 'out of work donations'. These seem to have been a one-off payment for those who had become unemployed after being engaged in war-work. However, the Board of Deputies reported that 'The Ministry of Labour has refused to extend out of work benefit to aliens' (*Jewish Chronicle*, 28.3.1919). Second and more significant was the fact that nationality was made a criterion for certain unemployment benefit under the National Insurance Act. Under the Unemployment Insurance, No. 2, Act of 1921, the Minister of Labour was given power to extend unemployment benefit payments from 16 weeks by another six weeks (Section 3). However the Minister stated that 'I have decided that benefit beyond 16 weeks should not be granted to aliens – other than British born wives or widows of aliens' (Dr T.J. Macnamara, *Hansard*, 16.3.1922). The Board of Deputies protested without avail and noted that 'Jewish Labour organisations are deeply concerned at the reply and are meeting to consider it' (*Jewish Chronicle*, 23.6.1922). Similar legislation was re-enacted for a period of years and each year the Board protested about anti-Jewish discrimination in welfare (e.g. *Jewish Chronicle*, 23.3.1923).

Widows, Orphans and Old Age Contributory Pensions Act, 1925

This was a contributory scheme providing financial benefit by way of pension for the wife or child of an insured man and for men and women aged between 65 and 70. Initially it was intended to add an amendment to this legislation excluding aliens. For once, a protest by the Board of Deputies had some success and the proposal was dropped (*Jewish Chronicle*, 23.9.1925). However a residential qualification was imposed instead. No benefit was payable where the uninsured person had been out of the UK for a period of two years prior to the claim – irrespective of how many years they had been paying into the scheme. This has echoes of the 'returning residents' clause under the modern Immigration Rules, whereby a non-British resident can be refused re-entry to the UK if they leave for more than two years. In both cases two years' residence is imposed as a form of 'loyalty test'.

Labour Exchanges Act 1909

Immediately the exchanges were set up, there were objections against Jews using them. One parliamentary question in 1910 inquired whether 'applicants at the Labour Bureaux are asked or required to declare their nationality, and whether where an applicant's alien origin is apparent from his speech, he is asked for proof of his naturalisation' (Captain Faber, *Hansard*, 15.3.1910). The Minister of Labour denied this. Later the same year a Bill was introduced by a group of Tories which would have made it unlawful for a labour exchange to send an alien who had been resident in the UK for less than six months for any job vacancy. It also would have made it a criminal offence for an alien not to disclose his or her nationality at a labour exchange (*Jewish Chronicle*, 8.7.1910). The Bill was withdrawn. However, 20 years later Margaret Bondfield, by now Minister of Labour in a Labour Government, virtually reintroduced it by the back door when she stated in the Commons

> As regards offers of employment it would obviously be impractical to ascertain the nationality of applicants in all cases. The exchanges are, however, instructed to do so if there is reason to believe that the applicant is not of British nationality and where in such cases the applicant is found to be an alien who has resided in the United Kingdom for less than six months he is not to be submitted for any vacancy if suitable British subjects are on the register. (*Hansard*, 25.6.1930)

All this is a reminder of the present Tory government proposals to ask all unemployment benefit claimants their national origins (*Guardian*, 10.11.1981) which has got as far as a pilot scheme in selected offices where the nationality of claimants was assessed on 'appearance, speech and accent' (*Guardian*, 5.2.1981).

Municipal Government

The linking of immigration status and welfare also permeated local government, for example, the London County Council. In 1919 the Board of Deputies protested against the refusal by the LCC to grant scholarships to foreign-born children. This exclusion also applied to naturalised British children (*Jewish Chronicle*, 25.6.1919). The following year the Board had to protest against LCC regulations that precluded aliens from employment by the authority. Again, this also applied to Jews who became naturalised British (*Jewish Chronicle*, 22.10.1920). By 1925 both the Board and the editorial columns of the *Jewish Chronicle* were attacking the LCC for proposing that aliens be excluded from all municipal housing (*Jewish Chronicle*, 20.3.1925). An insight into the overall politics of the Jewish establishment can be seen in the position of Stuart Samuel, a Liberal MP, who stated at a Board meeting that 'To refuse a scholarship to a bright child was to cause it to grow up under a sense of injustice and of dissatisfaction of the state and this policy would lead to driving them into the ranks of revolutionaries' (*Jewish Chronicle*, 20.3.1925).

Internal Controls 1905–25

The tightening of the link between immigration status and welfare entitlements inevitably led to the development of internal controls against Jews. These controls were enforced by the new so-called 'caring' agencies which were obliged to investigate the nationality and residence of applicants. For instance in answer to a parliamentary question on extended unemployment benefit, which was denied to aliens, the Minister of Labour stated 'On the form of application for uncovenanted benefit the applicant has to state whether or not he is a British subject and in all cases of doubt inquiry is made' (*Hansard*, 11.7.1923). All Jews thus became suspect.

The inter-war period also saw a strengthening of the real material link between immigration controls and internal controls. Jews were increasingly excluded from the country and therefore from all benefit schemes. In 1914, the Aliens Act was hardened by the Aliens Restriction Act and in 1919 there was a further tightening of the law with the Aliens Restriction Amendment Act. This new legislation made it more difficult for Jews to get into the UK – not least by removing all appeals procedures. However, it also gave the Home Secretary the power to deport aliens already here irrespective of any court order. The powers of deportation under the present Immigration Act derive from this period. The effect of this new development was the constant deportation of Jewish people. At a meeting of the Board of Deputies in 1920 one member spoke of 'the deportation of alien Jews which were going on and which . . . recalled the worst days of the Russian tyranny' and another 'urged the gravity of the deportations now being conducted by the police' (*Jewish Chronicle*, 21.5.1920). At one stage a rumour was sweeping the Jewish community that there was to be a mass deportation of all Galacian Jews (*Jewish Chronicle*, 28.3.1919, Board of Deputies report). Though this was unfounded it shows the fear of the Jewish community. Simultaneously, other regulations made under the 1919 Act imposed almost a state of siege on the Jewish community (see particularly the Aliens Order of 1920). All Jewish aliens were obliged to carry identity cards, to notify the authorities if they were absent from their home for two weeks, to keep out of designated 'protected areas' and to fill in a special register if they stayed overnight at a hotel. At the same time the police were given power to close clubs and restaurants 'frequented by aliens'. A *Jewish Chronicle* editorial correctly described this combination of external and internal control as amounting to a 'War on Aliens' (30.5.1919).

The Struggle over Naturalisation

One of the major pieces of institutionalised racism in the last few years has been the Nationality Act. This has jeopardized the security of Black people in the UK by making it extremely difficult to obtain British citizenship – and it is British citizenship which alone guarantees the right of abode in the UK. Another piece of hidden history is the battles over naturalisation waged by the Jewish community in the first half of the century. As early as 1907 the Board of Deputies was sending a deputation to lobby the Prime Minister on the difficulties of obtaining naturalisation. The main problem pressed was the cost. This was £5 per person which was as prohibitive to Jews as the present fees are to Black people (*Jewish Chronicle*, 2.8.1907). Over the next decades the Board was to protest against other obstacles which are also familiar today. A particular impediment was the excessive length of time applications took to process. In 1922 the Board reported that this was two years (*Jewish Chronicle*, 23.4.1922) and one MP gave an example of someone who had applied prior to 1914 and was still awaiting an answer in 1925 (*Jewish Chronicle*, 31.7.1925). Another difficulty was the English language tests imposed on what was predominantly a Yiddish-speaking community, with the Board constantly trying to enforce an exemption for Jews who had fought in the British army (*Jewish Chronicle*, 6.6.1919).

The acquisition of British nationality had a three-fold importance. First, British citizenship was the only individual protection that Jews had against the mounting wave of deportation. Second, non-naturalised Jews resident in the UK were liable to be refused readmission if they went abroad for an extended period. Black people are today under similar disabilities by virtue of the two year 'returning residents' rule. Third, social and welfare benefits were themselves increasingly tied to nationality. For instance, when in 1919 the Board sent a delegation to the Committee of Inquiry on the Old Age Pensions Act it had to explain how the difficulty in obtaining naturalisation was itself an obstacle to claiming a pension (*Jewish Chronicle*, 25.7.1919).

Sections of the English labour movement also took up the issues of naturalisation, but only under pressure from Jewish workers. At its 1902 conference the TUC passed a resolution moved by the Amalgamated Tailors (a predominantly Jewish union) calling for easier access to citizenship. After the Liberal reform programme of 1906 the TUC began linking the agitation for simpler naturalisation with welfare benefit entitlement. At its 1910 conference it passed a motion moved by the Compositors Union and seconded by the Tailors' Machinists Union. This called for both the lowering of the naturalisation fee to £1 and an amendment to the Old Age Pensions Act substituting the 20 years' residence and 20 years' nationality requirement by 20 years' residence and simply nationality. The high-point of trade union support came with a conference organised by the Labour Defence Council in 1925. This attacked both the naturalisation fees and measures of internal control such as identity cards, in equal measure. It pledged itself to assist 'all efforts to put an end to the injustices which aliens in general and members of the working class in particular are subjected' (*Jewish Chronicle*, 29.5.1925). However, this conference was held in Whitechapel at the United Ladies Tailors Hall and seems essentially to have been a Jewish initiative.

The 1945 Welfare State

The historical nexus of nationalism, immigration controls and state welfare policies before the Second World War should now be apparent. An obviously crucial question is the extent to which, and the manner in which, these same practices were embodied in the post-war welfare state. If we look at what is widely regarded as the founding document of the welfare state, The Beveridge Report, we find an explicit incorporation of pre-war assumptions of efficiency and eugenics. The report has gained a reputation for being based on universal and humanitarian values. In fact it rested on the most narrow kind of racial and sexual chauvinism. For instance, the argument in favour of child allowance was that, 'with its present rate of reproduction the British race cannot continue, means of reversing the recent course of the birth rate must be found' (paragraph 413). Women were to be reduced to baby-machines in the service of capitalism and British culture and were told that 'In the next thirty years housewives as Mothers have vital work to do in ensuring the adequate continuance of the British Race and British Ideals in the world' (paragraph 117). The NHS was not to be created out of any sense of caring but because 'the individual should recognise the duty to be well . . . as disease and accidents must be paid for in any case in lessened power of production and in idleness' (paragraph 426). In fact the main objection to both unemployment and sickness was that they resulted in 'lower human efficiency' (paragraph 457). The clearest example of Beveridge's own deep chauvinism can be seen in his essay 'Children's allowances and the race'. In this he stated,

Pride of race is a reality for the British as for other peoples . . . as in Britain today we look back with pride and gratitude to our ancestors, look back as a nation or as individuals two hundred years and more to the generations illuminated by Marlborough or Cromwell or Drake, are we not bound also to look forward, to plan society now so that there may be no lack of men or women of the quality of those earlier days, of the best of our breed, two hundred and three hundred years hence?

Beveridge's nationalist and racist views were not directly translated into clauses excluding people from entitlement to welfare benefits on the basis of immigration or nationality status. Mere presence in the UK was sufficient for benefit under the National Assistance Act 1948 and the National Health Service Act 1946. Indeed, Aneurin Bevan, the first Minister of Health, frequently made grandiose statements declaring the health service was free to all irrespective of nationality. Thus he asserted that he supported 'the right of aliens to make use of the National Health Service' (*Hansard*, 2.6.1949).

Nevertheless, exclusion was achieved through immigration controls. Such controls were aimed initially against 'displaced persons' and 'refugees' – words which were often simply a euphemism for Jews. Such controls were often legitimated by reference to the need to protect welfare services, in particular the National Health Service. The 1920 Aliens Order had already given immigration officers powers to exclude persons both where they were allegedly not in a position to support themselves or where 'for medical reasons it is undesirable that the alien be permitted to land' (para 3). These provisions were re-enacted in the 1953 Aliens Order. Whenever ministers were challenged about 'abuse of welfare', they emphasised that these powers were being used. In 1954 a Tory backbencher asked the Home Secretary, Major Lloyd-George, what steps were being taken to 'check the entry of obviously ailing persons who may be presumed to be coming here for free medical treatment' (*Hansard*, 11.11.1954). The minister replied that such passengers were 'referred by the immigration officer to the medical inspectors appointed under the Aliens Order and the decision to grant or refuse leave to land is taken by the immigration officer'.

The beginnings of Black immigration fuelled demands for new controls, since existing legislation was insufficient to exclude Commonwealth citizens, who were not technically aliens. Underlying the campaigns which led up to the 1962 Commonwealth Immigrants Act were the same arguments about eugenics and national efficiency which can be found in Beveridge and earlier debates about welfare. Black people were habitually depicted as carriers of disease. For instance, in 1961 the Labour candidate in a by-election in Moss Side in Manchester raised directly the question of immigration control and disease and said 'every nation is entitled to protect its health' and the Tory candidate immediately accused him of 'jumping on the Conservative band-wagon on this issue' (*Manchester Evening News*, 1.11.1961). Intermingled with these notions were arguments about 'miscegenation', that is, racial sexual intermingling. For instance Cyril Osborne

MP, a fanatical restrictionist, wrote that 'If unlimited immigration were allowed, we should ultimately become a chocolate-coloured, Afro-Asian mixed society. That I do not want' (*Spectator*, 4.12.1964). Parallel with all of this was continual ideological propaganda about Black people 'abusing' the benefits offered by the welfare state. For instance, in 1958, after massive organised riots against Black people in Notting Hill and Nottingham, 30 Tories and three Labour MPs tabled a parliamentary motion 'expressing growing concern over the continued influx of immigrants from the Commonwealth and Colonies, thousands of whom have immediately sought national assistance' (*The Times*, 28.5.1958). Immigration control was to be enacted precisely to deny Black people any benefit from the welfare state. For instance, Cyril Osborne, in the debate on the 1962 Commonwealth Immigrants Act, quoted with approval an editorial in the *Observer* which had asserted that 'British workers' were concerned about 'competing with immigrants for houses, hospital beds and social services' (*Hansard*, 16.11.1961). In fact the arguments against control were often just as chauvinistic – namely that it was better to use cheap Black labour for the welfare state than to exclude Black people from the state. A Tory Home Secretary (R.A.B. Butler) argued that 'our hospitals . . . would be in difficulties were it not for the services of immigrant workers' (ibid.) and an editorial in *The Times* stated that 'Britain's essential services could not carry on without immigrant labour' (14.11.1961).

Internal Controls Post-1945

A debate over the reintroduction of internal controls within welfare began as early as the late 1940s in the context of parliamentary attacks on the right of foreigners to use the welfare state, particularly in respect of the NHS and national assistance. Ostensibly this attack was against short-term visitors, the Tory MP, W. Smithers, being obsessive about this in respect of the NHS (e.g. *Hansard*, 17.2.1949). In fact, though, the real objection was to Jewish displaced persons. For instance one parliamentary question, by Lady Tweedsmuir, was as explicit as could be dared on this when it asked 'the Minister of National Insurance how many refugees in the United Kingdom since 1945 are receiving National Assistance' (*Hansard*, 30.6.1952).

These constant demands to limit benefits to the British did lead to one important piece of legislation. In the 1949 National Health Service Act power was given to the Minister of Health to make regulations excluding from free treatments people not 'ordinarily resident' in the UK (Section 17). The minister who hypocritically introduced this was Aneurin Bevan. Such regulations were not officially made until 1982 but it is significant that provision for internal controls was made as early as 1949.

The crucial development of internal controls within the welfare state occurred in respect to Black immigration. In fact internal controls against Black people began more or less simultaneously with immigration controls. This was part of the ideological offensive against Black people – depicting them as both diseased and as 'scroungers' on the welfare state. The political significance of such controls is not so much that they exclude some Black people from benefit dependent on their immigration and residency status, but rather that all Black people have to prove eligibility. Both NHS and supplementary benefit entitlement are clear examples of the recent historic development of this. We look briefly at the NHS first (see *From Ill Treatment to No Treatment*, Manchester Law Centre). As early as 1963 – just one year after the Commonwealth Immigrants Act – the then Minister of Health issued a 'Memorandum of Guidance to Hospital Authorities for Hospital Treatment for Visitors from Overseas'. In 1964 a similar circular was issued to GPs (ECM 473). Then in 1974 the DHSS published a further memorandum, 'The Use of the National Health Service by People from Abroad'. In 1979 the DHSS felt confident enough to issue another circular brazenly called 'Gatecrashers'. The consequence of this was that, for example, by 1976 Asian women attending ante-natal clinics at Leicester General Hospital were routinely required to produce passports as proof of eligibility, and the District Administrator said this had been going on for 10 or 15 years, that is before the first post-war immigration controls (Lord Avebury, House of Lords, 6.4.1976). One of the remarkable features of this internal control was that it was strictly illegal. As we have seen regulations legalising such conduct and making free hospital treatment dependent on residency tests were not enacted until 1982 (NHS, Charges to Overseas Visitors (No. 2) Regulations, 1982). The law in relation to supplementary benefit has gone through a similar historical development (see *The Thin End of the White Wedge*, Manchester Law Centre). As has been seen, the original national assistance scheme had no immigration criteria. In fact the secret internal instructions to DHSS officers – the 'A' code – contained a specific section called 'Aliens and Immigrants'. This imposed certain benefit restrictions on 'any claimant who appears to come from abroad'. It also made clear that the DHSS was to act as a spy for the Home Office. It said that

> The Supplementary Benefit Commission has agreed to notify the Home Office of claims for supplementary benefit by people whose admission to this country is subject to time-limit or some other form of control. It is then for the immigration authorities to decide whether the person's right to remain here is in any way affected.

All this was revealed in 1979 when Nasira Begum was refused benefit by the DHSS whilst fighting the Home Office to remain in the UK after the breakdown of her marriage. It would seem from the A code that internal controls of this nature had been in force since at least the Supplementary Benefit Act of 1966. After the Nasira Begum case specific Supplementary Benefit Regulations were introduced legalising the exclusion of 'persons from abroad' from normal benefit and thus legitimising the questioning of all Black people as to their status (SB, Aggregation Requirements and Resources, Amendment Regs, 1980).

Conclusion

This chapter has been deliberately polemical. It has argued that welfarism is intimately linked to immigration control and cannot be understood other than as a construct of the basest nationalism. Indeed the relationships of welfare throughout the entire 20th century have been premised on national chauvinism – and this is a direct reflection of the fact that agitation for greater and greater immigration control has been one of the most constant and salient features of 20th century English political life. In fact the English have developed an unquenchable thirst for such controls. So it is no coincidence that a racist notion of welfare prevailed in the decades preceding the post-1945 reconstruction and is triumphant at the present period of Thatcherite attack on the welfare state. Indeed, part of that attack is to discover new areas of welfare to be linked to immigration status. Likewise it is argued here that racism is not peripheral to the welfare state itself but is essential to it. It is essential precisely because the provision of welfare services is supposedly its *raison d'être* and yet this provision is based on the ideology of British racial supremacy. Today all this has come to be seen as 'reasonable' and 'natural'. The ideology of immigration control and its relationship to welfarism has become so much part of popular consciousness as to appear to have no history and to be timeless. This chapter has attempted to highlight this relationship and to locate it in time by placing it in its historical context. This is the context of the first half of the 20th century, and institutionalised anti-semitism against Jewish people.

References

Beveridge, Sir William (1942a) *Social Insurance and Allied Services*, Cmnd 6404. London: HMSO.

Beveridge, W. (1942b) *Children's Allowances and the Race, Pillars of Security*. London: Allen and Unwin.

Cohen, S. (1980) *The Thin End of the White Wedge*. South Manchester Law Centre.

Cohen, S. (1981) *From Ill-Treatment to No Treatment*. South Manchester Law Centre.

Cohen, S. (1984) 'From Aliens Act to Immigration Act', *Legal Action Group Bulletin*, September.

Independent Labour Party (1904) *The Problem of Alien Immigration, Tracts for the Time*. No. 4.

Rentoul, R. (1905) *The Undesirable Alien From the Medical Standpoint*. Liverpool.

Rentoul, R. (1906) *Race Culture or Race Suicide?* New York: Walter Scott.

Searle, G. (1971) *The Quest for National Efficiency*. Oxford: Blackwell.

Semmell, B. (1960) *Imperialism and Social Reform*. London: Allen & Unwin.

Webb, B. (1888) *East London Labour, Nineteenth Century* (vol. XXIV). No. 138.

Wilkins, W.H. (1892) *The Alien Invasion*. London: Methuen.

Zimmerman, A. (1911) 'The Aliens Act: a challenge', *Economic Review*, April.

3

Racism and the Discipline of Social Policy: a Critique of Welfare Theory

Fiona Williams

The aim of this chapter is to argue for the centrality of an anti-racist perspective in welfare theory and strategy.[1] My contention is that the discipline of social administration has been disinclined, or unable, to take account of the welfare experiences of Black people. Put differently, those who fought Beveridge's Five Giants – Want, Squalor, Idleness, Ignorance and Disease, hid the giants racism and sexism (and the struggles against them) behind statues to the Nation and the White Family. And the rallying cries from social administration of Poverty! Redistribution! Equality of Opportunity! Universalism! even Class Struggle! and Patriarchy! do not ring quite true from the standpoint of the Black experience of the welfare state.

In this chapter, I explore, first, the ways in which the different theoretical perspectives on welfare within the discipline of social administration approach the question of 'race'[2] and racism, looking at anti-collectivism and social reformism, and more extensively at the political economy of welfare and feminism. Second, in the light of the recent literature on 'race' and racism, and its implications for welfare theory and policy, I present a framework for understanding the relationship between racism and social policy, in terms of the historical development of the welfare state in the context of capitalism and imperialism, a context which places racist ideology and practice as an unsurprising outcome of some of the dominant characteristics of the welfare state, and in terms which imply changes to welfare theory and strategy if racism and the struggles against Black oppression are to be taken seriously.

Introduction: The Neglect of the Black Experience of Welfare

Very few recent social policy textbooks deal with Black experiences or general policies in relation to Black people: Mishra (1981, 1984), Klein and O'Higgins (1985), Hill and Bramley (1986), Jones et al. (1978), Loney et al. (1983) make scant or no reference to racism, or race-related policies. Nor

First published in *Critical Social Policy*, 20, 1987.

do those texts which seek to assess the theoretical perspectives in social policy give us any clue as to how any of these perspectives approach 'race' and racism: George and Wilding (1985), Taylor-Gooby and Dale (1981) and Taylor-Gooby (1985). Nor do those who offer us strategies for welfare apply the issue seriously: Mishra (1984), Deacon (1983), Walker (1984), Bosanquet (1983). Where 'race' is brought in, it is often, like gender, as a discrete issue, a dimension of inequality, an 'ethnic' or 'minority' group, a group with 'special needs' (Bindman and Carrier in Glennnerster, 1983; Deakin in Bean and MacPherson, 1983).

The model of integration from Rose and Deakin's *Colour and Citizenship* (1969) and that of cultural pluralism still tend to dominate social policy and social work writing even though there have been considerable developments in work on 'race' and racism and in spite of the fact that these models have faced extensive critiques (Sivanandan, 1976, 1978, 1980; Bourne, 1980; Gilroy, 1982; Hall et al., 1978; Centre for Contemporary Cultural Studies, 1982; Mama, 1984). In fact, it is possible to identify at least three other strands of thinking derived from 'race and class' studies which present alternative theoretical models for welfare and public policy. (I examine the strengths and limitations of these alternative models for social policy elsewhere [Williams, 1989])[3] In addition, there are an increasing number of accounts of struggles against Black oppression in welfare, especially from Black feminists (Bryan et al., 1985; Mama, 1984; Bhavnani, 1986; Black Health Workers and Patients Group, 1983; Ohri et al., 1982; Carby, 1982), but few of these have been drawn into the body of social policy literature. There are some exceptions, Cohen's excellent article explaining the links between nationalism and racism at the heart of the Welfare State (1985, in this volume): Gordon (1985), Jacobs (1985), Ben-Tovim et al. (1986), Doyal (1979), Doyal et al. (1981), Stubbs (1985). In many cases, writers on 'race' straddle a 'social policy/other specialism' divide: Brah – education; Cross and Solomos – youth studies; Gilroy et al. – cultural studies; as well as the unfortunate coupling of race with criminology of which Brown (1974) is one example. To some, this compartmentalism is one reason for the neglect. Others, like Ben-Tovim et al. (1986) suggest that the radical analysis of 'race' and racism by writers like Gilroy, Lawrence, Bridges and others, is at too grand a level, too sweeping in its analysis of state racism, too occupied with the most coercive of the state's actions – policing, immigration control – too dismissive of reform to further an understanding of public and social policy. The argument presented here is different: that it is as much the theoretical shortcomings of the discipline of social policy which inhibit an understanding of the Black experience of the welfare state.

How Theoretical Perspectives of Welfare Handle 'Race' and Racism

I shall look here at major approaches in welfare theory and examine how their theory and, where appropriate their practice, faces up to the question of 'race' and racism. They are categorised into four groups: anti-collectivism, social reformism, the political economy of welfare, and feminism. I shall deal briefly with the first two, although the points made here are developed elsewhere (Williams, 1989). There are two reasons for this: first because, as I argue, it is only on the basis of the last two that we can begin to construct an adequate theory of welfare that accommodates the Black experience of the welfare state; second, much work on racism exposes the inadequacies of the New Right, and, though less so, social reformism; yet there is an equal need for socialists and feminists to be self-critical about their own theories.

Anti-collectivism

In examining the relation between welfare and 'race' in the anti-collectivist approach, distinctions have to be drawn between neo-liberal philosophy, the writings of neo-conservatives like Scruton and Casey, and the practice of the New Right administration. For neo-liberals like Friedman and Hayek, the emphasis is on the freedom of the market and individualism. Friedman argues that the impersonality of the market overrides personal discrimination: people do not question the colour of the hand that grew the wheat in their bread (Friedman, 1962). Neo-conservatives, on the other hand, such as Scruton, Casey and Honeyford, have a particular theory of nation and race which focuses on cultural difference. The 'sense of nation' derives from a shared history, way of life, custom and overall sense of loyalty to 'one's own kind'. For Scruton et al., the threat to national unity comes from the cultural differences of the Black communities and their resistance to assimilating into British culture. Their solution is forced assimilation or repatriation (see Seidel, 1986). The methodological individualism of the neo-conservative approach rejects a structuralist view of racism. The neo-conservatives reject the idea that they are racists; they consider themselves only patriots, and manage to give intellectual respectability to racist ideas.

Several recent works have demonstrated the centrality of 'race' to the policies of the New Right (Hall et al., 1978; Solomos et al., 1982; Barker, 1981; Levitas, 1986; Parekh, 1986; Gordon and Klug, 1984). The themes of British 'nation' and 'culture' have been harnessed to an explanation of economic crisis with moral and political dimensions, in which the presence of Black people threatens national unity. Black cultures threaten British culture and Black youth threaten social stability and British democracy. Black communities, cultures and families are thus seen as pathological, bringing upon themselves the poverty and unemployment and racial violence they endure. These ideas pick up on 'common-sense' racism and are threaded into a justification for racist policies. Gordon has documented the stepping-up of racist processes in the welfare state, for example, the powers to enforce immigration laws have been extended to employers, to schools, colleges, DHSS offices, hospitals and local authority housing offices. In this way 'immigration and the welfare state have become intertwined' (Gordon, 1985: 94). However specific these racist policies are to the New Right and its associated ideology of nation and culture, it has also to be said that it is the severity and explicit justification of the racism which is unique rather than use of welfare policies and agencies to reinforce racist practice and immigration control. For this reason, I do not want to dwell on the racism of the New Right, but turn instead to the spectrum of social reformist ideas represented in the discipline of social policy.

Social Reformism

Here I look briefly at three examples of reformist thinking in the social policy literature: mainstream social administration which has been particularly influenced by the Fabian socialism of writers like Titmuss, the more recent radical variant of this represented by, for example, Walker and Townsend, and the work of a non-socialist social policy writer Pinker. Their views on the issues of 'race', nation and empire, and their relation to the welfare state are examined.

Mainstream social administration has largely marginalised the issue of 'race', and ignored the racism institutionalised within the practice and provision of the welfare state. The exploitation of unskilled and low-paid work after the Second World War, of men and women from the New Commonwealth went largely unquestioned by the labour movement and academics in social administration (Joshi and Carter, 1985). The subsequent hostility of a white working class whose historical concessions to racialist and racist ideology combined with a fear that post-war welfare capitalism was shortchanging them in relation to housing, in particular, produced appalling racism (Notting Hill 1958). Official, bureaucratic and public attitudes meant that the new immigrants' access to welfare provision – particularly housing and education – was not planned for and, by implication, was presumed not to exist. The reaction of the discipline of social administration to one of the most significant failures of the welfare state to provide for those in need, and one of the most startling examples, to use its own terms, of a lack of 'altruism', was fourfold: to ignore it, few social policy texts made reference to this denial of access; to categorise it as 'race relations', a separate problem, whose solution was that of changing the 'prejudices' of whites (Race Relations Acts) or the 'cultures' of Blacks (assimilation, integration, dispersion and so on); to produce empirical evidence to show how Blacks did not use many services after all (NISER, 1967); to subsume it under a general social problem – poverty or urban decline, or deprivation, or as a dimension of 'disadvantage'. More recently the issue of 'race' has become more visible, but generally in terms of 'minority groups' with 'special needs'. The reasons for this failure to acknowledge the gravity of racism in the welfare state lie in the very characteristics of the mainstream: its empiricism, its idealism, its inherent nationalism, and its belief in the welfare state as integrative, universalist and redistributive.

Social administration's emphasis on empiricism and pragmatism, on a policy-orientation, has led it towards an 'atheoreticalness', that is, a tendency to take certain things for granted. Amongst these have been: economic growth, the family and the sexual division of labour, and, importantly, institutionalised racism and an international division of labour which rests on the importation of cheap labour from underdeveloped countries. In addition, this policy-orientation has led to an acceptance of what Taylor-Gooby and Dale (1981) term 'the perspective of the state'. Successive governments had only seen Black immigrants as cheap labour. The state had overlooked their needs and social administration followed suit.

The empiricism and pragmatism of social administration were linked to a methodological idealism – a belief in change through ideas and rational discourse – which meant that in so far as any policies were favoured then they were anti-discriminatory legislation to change people's attitudes and the provision of evidence to show the irrationality of such attitudes (Rose and Deakin, 1969). An historical and material understanding of the roots of racism were excluded by this idealist orientation of the discipline.

Third, Fabianism's own roots grew in imperialist soil, heavily mulched with biological and cultural ideas of superiority of European over Black. The Fabian Society, including the Webbs, Shaw and Wells, all supported imperialism, and wove it into their programmes of welfare reforms – pensions, national insurance – by way of social imperialism (Semmell, 1960). Eugenicism, the belief in the elimination through control over breeding of the inferior or unfit also influenced the Fabians, especially in their 'endowment of motherhood' policy. Thus, nationalism, racial and cultural superiority were *linked* sentiments deeply embedded (though contested by some) in Fabian consciousness, so it is not surprising to find Darwinist echoes and nationalist pride in Titmuss' earlier works. In 1943 in *Problems of Population* he wrote, 'Western civilisation slowly evolved a higher way of life and it was our duty to help and guide the teeming millions of India and Africa to a more abundant life' (p. 9, quoted in Titmuss, 1943: 9); 'I only know that she is England, I am English and she is home' (quoted in Rose, 1981: 488), and that 'Altruism, the highest moment in the social relation of redistribution, is English' (ibid.: 489). It is, in part, this feature of social administration which Mishra identifies as 'ethnocentricism', a conviction that British is best that has led to its blindness to the international context of its welfare state and the racism of the welfare state's policies.

Fourth, the belief in the integrative power of the welfare state has contributed to the inability of mainstream Fabian social administration to fully acknowledge the Black experience of the welfare state. Equality, integration and universalism are linked themes in Fabian social policy. In relation to the NHS, Titmuss believed that equality of access to a universal service would create social harmony and national unity. He compared the NHS with the private medical system in the US where poor Blacks are excluded and stigmatized, in contrast to the British NHS, which would treat regardless of colour or class. Missing from this idealised picture was what we have come to term the oppressive social relations of welfare: that provision of welfare itself reinforces individualism, racism, sexism and the work ethic (London Edinburgh Weekend Return Group, 1979). The use of sterilisation and Depo-Provera on Black women (Bryan et al., 1985) reminds us that those eugenicist ideas are not far away.

In addition, it is the very concept of *universalism* which has come to be the defence of racist welfare practices. Ben-Tovim et al. (1986: 22) identify practices in local authorities where 'universalism in policy making which supports the view that everyone should be treated equally irrespective of already existing inequalities can, and does serve to maintain existing racial inequalities'. The traditional polarities within the social administration literature of universalism and selectivity, state and market, rich and poor, provide for extensive analysis of poverty, redistribution, the social division of welfare, but they inhibit an understanding of oppression – racial or sexual – particularly when set against the background of familism and nationalism strong in Fabianism. In so far as the problems of Black people became visible, they were submerged under generic problems of poverty, deprivation and urban decline, or ghettoised into the policy studies of race relations.

The strand of *Radical social administration* emerging from Fabianism with a greater awareness of the structural limitations to reformism, has only half acknowledged some of these problems. Alan Walker (1984) attempts to create a framework for the study of social and economic policy which, *inter alia*, focuses upon differences of status, power and rewards not just between classes, but sexes and 'races' too. However, his strategy makes little reference to how the eradication of racism could be achieved or to the link between immigration control and welfare. On the other hand, Peter Townsend's (1984) 500th Fabian Tract *Why are the Many Poor?* gives significant attention to the international context of poverty in Britain and the Third World, and the necessity to set solutions in terms of 'joint action internationally by trades unions, democratic socialist parties, professions, pressure groups' (1984: 34). Ultimately, however, these actions stress the transferring of planning and redistributive policies from a national to an international level, and underplay the specific material and ideological dimensions of racial domination and oppression within Britain.

As an example of *Non-socialist reformism* Pinker's work needs comment, because although some contemporary social reformists and Fabians have come to question the assumptions of familism, if not nationalism, Pinker sets out to defend them in relation to welfare. In *The Idea of Welfare* (1979) Pinker suggests there are boundaries to obligation and entitlement, in social welfare; Titmuss' 'altruism' is confined in most people to kith and kin and nation in that order, and the sense of internationalism in Titmuss' concept of the 'universal stranger', is misconceived. Indeed, it is also, in Pinker's view, the *internationalism* underlying Marxism and its concept of working-class solidarity, and the *internationalism* of classical economic theory and *laissez-faire* in the form of free trade between nations, which also flaw these doctrines. In contrast to the internationalism of left and right, he proposes a third model for welfare: mercantile collectivism. This was a 17th-century *nationalist* doctrine, where economic policies were aimed at national wealth creation necessary for the benefit of all citizens. Nation and welfare are thus interdependent. This concept of interdependence founds its modern form in the policies of Keynes and Beveridge, of which Pinker approves. Beveridge's welfare policies were firmly grounded in terms which related them to national efficiency and racial supremacy: 'housewives as Mothers have vital work to do in ensuring the adequate continuance of the British Race and British ideals in the world' (Beveridge Report, 1942: para. 117). In an essay on 'Children's Allowances and the Race' he stated 'Pride of race is a reality for the British as for other peoples' (quoted in Cohen, 1985 and this volume). As I show later this nationalism and racial pride, and its link with welfare reforms, were not coincidental but helped to set the racist cast of the welfare state where entitlement to welfare through nationality (or 'race'), and the use of welfare agencies to control immigration, went unquestioned and accepted.

I now turn to those theoretical approaches within the discipline of social administration – the political economy of welfare and the feminist critique – which should be more capable than the previous two approaches, of accommodating both Black people's experience of welfare and struggles against Black oppression embodied in welfare policy and practice. To do this, as I argue later, these approaches must be able to acknowledge both the specificity of the experience of racism as well as its centrality in the historical development of the welfare state. And they have to be reformulated according to the experiences of Black people as workers (including workers in the welfare state), as consumers of welfare and as those engaged in struggles over welfare.

First, I review the limited progress made by the literature within the political economy approach, and the slightly less limited progress made by the feminist critique. I then briefly evaluate three useful analyses of the relationship between 'race' and social policy emerging from the literature on 'race' and racism, before providing a framework for analysis which can accommodate the essential features of the Black experience and the struggles against Black oppression and can hopefully contribute a little to the necessary development of both the political economy and feminist perspectives of welfare.

Political Economy of Welfare

This approach offers an analysis of welfare based on the relations between class, capital and the state, and, as such, should be theoretically more capable of doing justice to the concept of institutionalised racism, at least in terms of the role of welfare in reproducing a reserve army of labour. In fact, there is little mention made of this, or of racism, in the Marxist theory of welfare standards (Gough, 1979; Ginsburg, 1979; Offe, 1984). Thus, although Gough states:

> Colonialism was used to 'open up' [the] markets to capitalist competition to protect them against depredations from other imperialist countries. In this way then a *world* capitalist system was established in the late nineteenth century. *Note that this too impinges directly on many aspects of the welfare state.* To take one example, since the war millions of migrant workers have been drawn to the industrial centres of Europe, so that now one in seven of all manual workers are immigrants . . . (1979: 29, my emphasis)

here the analysis stops. We never get to know the 'many aspects'.

Lesley Doyal (1979, Doyal et al., 1981) has been one writer in the political economy vein who has drawn attention to two particular ways in which welfare, imperialism and immigration are linked. First, her analysis of the 'political economy of health' examines the role of western medical technology and investment in the underdevelopment of health in the Third World and concludes that 'the historical form of capitalist expansion in the Third World has not only systematically undermined the health of the population, but has also created obstacles to the realization of effective health policies' (1979: 137). Second, she examines the role that Black immigrants and workers play in providing a cost-effective labour source for the NHS: 'these workers provide a critical source of cheap labour and their utilisation has always been an important component both in keeping down costs and in rationalising the labour process in health care' (1981: 54).

So far, then, these aspects are identified: the role of Black workers as cheap labour in the welfare state, and the development of welfare through imperialism in neo-colonialism. But there are many other welfare issues that a reading of anti-racist writers reveals and which are little mentioned so far in the political economy of welfare literature: the historical role of nationalism and welfare; the systematic neglect of the welfare needs of Black people; reproduction of a racial division of labour not only by employment within the welfare state, but through the institutional provision of welfare like education; the pathologising of Black families and cultures; the racial harassment of Black households; use of the heavier forms of social control in welfare: sterilisation, school units for disruptive children, taking into care, incarceration, and the use of welfare institutions to police state immigration controls; and, not least, the role of struggles against Black oppression within the welfare state.

It might be suggested that these writings have only emerged recently, however, it is also true that Sivanandan wrote his article on race, class and the state over 10 years ago (Sivanandan, 1976). It is probably more likely that Black radicals have been justifiably suspicious of the discipline of social policy, and do not contribute to its literature. After all, the policy-oriented studies of the 1960s and 1970s have, if anything, tended to reinforce, not alleviate, racism, and the welcome given by white radicals to such ground-breaking books as *The Empire Strikes Back* (CCCS, 1982) has been less than enthusiastic. Nevertheless, I would also suggest that some emphases in the political economy approach inhibit an acknowledgement of the Black experience of the welfare state: these cluster around the issues of the nature of class struggle, the power of the state and the limits of reforms, and the international division of labour. To some extent they also reiterate some criticisms made by the feminist critique of the political economy tradition (see Rose, 1981; Pascall, 1986).

Gough's analysis of the welfare state attempts to avoid the evils of a functionalist or conspiracy analysis of the welfare state, as a tool of ruling-class domination, by taking into account the role of the working-class struggle for welfare reforms. Two writers have suggested that in doing so he implies a *unitariness* of working-class struggle and purpose which fails to explain why many welfare struggles have resulted in gains for some sections rather than, or even at the expense of, others (Wilson, 1980; Taylor-Gooby, 1981). The white skilled male working class in the 1920s gained from National Insurance, for example, while 'aliens' and women were denied access. Jews, Irish, Black, women and the undeserving share a history of being denied welfare or it controlling them. The state's power to divide and rule and its need for an army of reserve labour is clearly one part of this, but it is not enough of an explanation, for it merely returns us to a functionalist analysis. What is also necessary is to examine more closely these class struggles, to deconstruct them and understand them in terms of the role that racism and nationalism have had in moulding the demands of the working class and in formulating the response from state and capital. It requires an assertion of the historical importance of struggles against Black oppression (often organised in the community as well as the workplace) and points to the need for the left to understand how struggles can and must reformulate class struggle.

Many accounts of the Black experience of welfare and the state give a clear picture of the state and capital continuing to oppress and exploit Black people, with the welfare state giving them a helping hand. The intertwining of immigration control and welfare agencies is one example. Most emphasise the controlling and repressive features of welfare (Amos and Parmar, 1984; Mama, 1984; Trivedi, 1984; Bryan et al., 1985). Furthermore, it is often the *limitations* of reform, especially in the present period, which Black accounts point to:

> We argue that in a context of emerging authoritarianism and a strengthening of repressive agencies, there is little hope that reformist strategies will fundamentally improve the material conditions which confront Black people in their daily struggle to survive in British Society. (CCCS, 1982: 35)

Some analyses of reforms in 'race' politics in the post-war period cast doubt on the supposition that these might have achieved anything at all for Black people (Bourne, 1980; Lawrence, 1982; Bridges, 1975; Solomos,

1985; Jacobs, 1985). All of these emphases sit uneasily with a discipline whose subject matter is reform and whose political economy approach insists upon a careful balancing of the gains of the welfare state with its controlling and bureaucratic features. This is not to say that Black people do not need or benefit from the welfare state, they do, but that the nature of the contradictions they face is qualitatively different and perhaps more stark, compared with the experiences of many white people. Thus, while Black people are among those who fight to retain the welfare state they do so, as Bryan et al. (1985) point out, from an unenviable position at the bottom of the welfare state's agenda. These contradictions are qualitatively different because of the specific ways in which racism is woven into welfare provision.

Ginsburg is one writer who attempts to avoid over-generalizing the concept of class struggle, and to point to the limits as well as the success of reforms. He provides a framework which examines in a detailed way the precise role played by sections of the working class and ruling class in struggles over housing and social security. Second, he begins an explanation of the 'duality' of the welfare state which connects the struggle, the gains and the needs of capital more clearly: 'the demands of the welfare state have produced important gains; but those demands have been processed and responded to in such a form that, far from posing a threat to capital, they have deepened its acceptance and extended its survival' (1979: 19). This is taken further by the authors of *In and Against the State* (LEWRG, 1979) who include racism as one of the ways in which the state reproduces the social relations of capitalism through the institutions of welfare. For them the important point is that class struggle has itself to be capable of visions and struggles which incorporate oppositional forms of social relations: collectivism, anti-sexism, anti-racism.

To begin to raise questions about racism means examining imperialism, neo-imperialism and international movements of labour. Bourne writes that 'the struggle against racism today has also to be a struggle against imperialism' (1980: 350). Most political economy analyses rests within the confines of Western Europe, perhaps influenced by a nostalgia amongst Marxists for a Eurocentric International. Anti-racist analysis must also be able to relate welfare strategy to immigration controls. Is the political economy approach for or against immigration controls? What is the relationship between economic growth in this country and the continuing global divisions between North and South? What role does the welfare state play in relation to the international division of labour? Apart from Lesley Doyal who deals with the last point (1979) the political economy approach has not been particularly forthcoming on these issues.

It is not only the Black experience but also the feminist critique of the welfare state which suggests that the symmetrical model of the welfare state as the outcome of pressure from above (bad) with pressure from below (good) needs further clarification. The political economy of welfare needs to open up its unified concept of class struggle, to re-examine the nature and impact of welfare reforms, to cast its net of contradictions wider and to situate the British welfare state in the context of imperialism, neo-imperialism and the international division of labour.

The Feminist Critique of Welfare

The feminist critique of welfare has criticised existing welfare approaches for their neglect of the specific oppression of women and gender divisions. In so far as it has done this, does it have a head start on the political economy approach in relation to racism? Yes and no. Though racism and sexism are both forms of oppression, they are not parallel. Gender refers to a biological difference between men and women upon which socially constructed differences (division of labour, aggressive/passive behaviour, etc.) are elaborated. 'Race' is a social and not a biological construct. Furthermore, the simultaneous experience for Black women of racism and sexism not only compounds the oppression, but reconstitutes it. Reproduction is a case in point. At a certain level (usually rhetorically, rather than practically, in Britain) within the ideology of familism the welfare state confers a '*positive*' value to women in terms of motherhood. No equivalent conferment exists for being Black – woman or man. Indeed, it is argued that, sometimes, racism reconstitutes the situation to such an extent that to be a Black mother is not simply negative (Black) plus positive (mother) it is double negative (the reproduction of more Blacks).

An example of where the assumptions of white feminists and their welfare strategies have been challenged by Black feminists is around the abortion campaigns of the 1970s. The 'right' to choose an abortion was seen as a demand only appropriate to white women whose fertility was taken for granted and approved. For Black women, the experience was one where their 'right to reproduction' was being questioned and sometimes controlled by a health service operating under a concern about 'black numbers', a racist view of Black female sexuality and a tradition of eugenicism. This tradition, it has been pointed out, was as strong in the feminist as in other political traditions (Josephine Butler, Charlotte Perkins Gilman, Eva Hubback, Marie Stopes, Christabel Pankhurst, though not Sylvia, were all touched by eugenicist ideas).

As feminists have often pointed out, it is women who encounter the welfare state most, thus it is most appropriate that the first challenges to white approaches to the welfare state should come from Black feminists, directed at the feminist critique of welfare (see also *Feminist Review* nos 17, 22 and 23). Essentially the criticisms of the white feminists' critique of welfare crystallise around three issues: the family, reproduction and sexuality, and the state.

The feminist critique of welfare is that, through its policy and practice, the welfare state upholds patriarchal relations in the family, it reinforces women as financially dependent on a male partner, as bearer and primary carer and cleaner, and it reinforces women's role as a reserve army of labour. Black feminists have explained that this 'familism' underpinning the welfare state has never fully applied to them and their families, and also that it is necessary to take issue with the feminist concept of the family as a 'site of women's oppression'. First, then, Hazel Carby challenges Elizabeth Wilson's (1980) interpretation of the immediate post-war period. Wilson's analysis is in terms of the state juggling with its priorities: on the one hand wishing to uphold the ideology of family life and women as mothers, but on the other aware of the needs of certain industries for (cheap) female labour. The solution, for many working-class women was found in part-time work which did not interfere with family responsibilities. However, even this was only possible because of the recruitment of Black immigrants to the labour market, many of whom were women (a factor often over-looked). Furthermore, these women, as Carby says:

> were recruited into the labour force beyond such considerations. Rather than a concern to protect or preserve the black family in Britain, the state reproduced common-sense notions of its inherent pathology: black women were seen to fail as mothers precisely because of their position as workers. (1982: 219)

To relate it to welfare: while one arm of the welfare state was busy exploiting Black women's labour in low-paid jobs with unsocial hours (auxiliary nursing, for example) another arm was refusing to meet their needs, for child care for example, and was blaming their difficulties upon the fact that they did such work. This 'pathology' of Black women and their families has been an important area of struggle for Black women, raising questions of the treatment of their children at school, over the numbers of and policies toward Black children in care, over allocation procedures in council housing and over mental health policies (see Bryan et al. 1985). Hazel Carby also queries the extent to which the ideology of femininity, which emphasises women's caring role in the home being extended to caring work in the social services, can be applied to Black women. She suggests that the racist image of *Black servant* is as strong as that of *carer*, in the acceptance of Black women in domestic, nursing and cleaning roles (Carby, 1982: 215). Furthermore, the role of state immigration policies in splitting up Black families is not seen as evidence of maintaining the sanctity of family life for many Black people. In other words, how far is the analysis of the family as 'the site of women's oppression' relevant for Black women? With racist and divisive state immigration policies, harassment from white families, fascist groups, from the police (Cherry Groce and Cynthia Jarrett), the Black family is neither socially privileged nor necessarily 'anti-social' but can become a basis for solidarity against racism (Bhavnani and Coulson, 1986). The family and community support for the strikes at Imperial Typewriters and Grunwicks are examples.

I have already mentioned the example of abortion in relation to repro-duction and sexuality. Sexuality is another area where the concept of patriarchy is questioned. Carby points out that while white female sexuality is cast in terms which are *sexist*, Black female sexuality, particularly in the myth of availability, is constructed in *racist* terms. Strategies over the issue of violence to women offer a case of what Black feminists have seen as white women's complacency regarding the racist nature of law and order and an undue faith in the state. Some of the demands from 'Reclaim the Night' marches in the late 1970s – some of which were marched through Black communities – were for greater police protection for women. Not only was this interpreted as an invitation to exert greater control on Black areas, and as a coupling of Black people with crime, but as a very specific sort of crime which plays into racist notions of Black male sexuality and white female sexuality.

The issue also raises questions about the state as Jenny Bourne writes:

> One can perceive in the WM [Women's movement] an ambivalence towards the state. Is it an instrument of oppression or is it a welfare state whence concessions can be won? . . . In their failure to understand the state, the women fail to side with the blacks; in failing to side with the blacks they play into the hands of the state. (1983: 12–13)

The contrast in the treatment of the state between some Black and white feminist writers is interesting. While at one level I would agree with Elizabeth Wilson and Mary McIntosh, who constantly urge us not to forget in our criticism of the welfare state, the benefits state provision can also bring: social security benefits, day care facilities (Wilson, 1980; McIntosh 1981 and this volume), at another level, this does not allow a sensitivity to the qualitatively different relationship Black women have with the state. For example, in examining the ban on the entry of male fiancés (1979–80), which the Conservative government rationalised on the grounds of 'protecting' young Asian women from the horrors of the arranged marriage system, Parita Trivedi says: 'We do not require the racist state to intervene on our behalf' (1984: 46) and she goes on to conclude: 'The state cannot – and will not – legislate in our favour. This much is clear' (1984: 48). The contrast between these two positions is resolved by Bryan et al. in their discussion of the effects of health cuts, in this way:

> For Black women, who are on the front line when it comes to health service attacks, the implications are very clear. Either we continue to fight tooth and nail for the preservation and improvement of the Health Service we have worked so hard to build; or we risk being ousted from our already unenviable position at the very bottom of the NHS agenda. (1985: 109–10)

Bhavnani and Coulson also try to resolve this problem by arguing that feminism must recognise that the *state deals with different women differently*,

> we are drawn to the need for fresh analysis of the relationship between the state and 'the family' and of how this differs for black and white people. This may lead us to an analysis, and some understanding, that the state may have different strategies for each group. (1986: 86)

In general they conclude that to consider racism as a central issue 'involves a fundamental and radical *transformation* of socialist-feminism' (ibid: 85).

The main criticism is that white feminism has over-generalised the concept of patriarchy and therefore failed to recognise the far greater significance (at times) of other forms of oppression. In addition, the representations of women in the Third World as primarily victims of patriarchal cultures (for example in Daly's *Gyn/ecology*, 1978), is criticised for failing to acknowledge the history of struggles by many such women against imperialism, class exploitation and racial oppression, as well as patriarchal oppression (Trivedi, 1984). In so far as the feminist critique of welfare has identified the processes and policies which reinforce aspects of women's oppression, then it is also necessary to continually acknowledge that racism within welfare provision is not just an added dimension, but one which can combine with sexism to produce a qualitatively different experience of oppression for Black women.

To conclude this section on welfare approaches; the individualism of anti-collectivism fails to register structural racism; the methods of the mainstream social administration approach – empiricism, idealism, policy-orientation, its perspective of the state and its goals – the elimination of poverty, redistribution, social harmony – have inhibited any more than a very marginal acknowledgement of racism. Further, the influences on Fabianism of familism and nationalism – extolled by Pinker – have reinforced this marginalisation. The political economy approach, while its framework offers the possibility for the analysis of some aspects of racism, has also neglected it. This has partly been the result of a concern to present a dialectical analysis of the welfare state which has had the effect of taking the unitariness of 'class struggle' for granted. It has also prevented a full appreciation of some of the more controlling features of the state. In addition, it has lacked an international perspective of global divisions which are necessary to the analysis of racism. Finally, the critical method of feminism has much in common with an anti-racist analysis, but in its assumption of a 'false universalism' of the family as the site of oppression, and patriarchy as the root of oppression, it has ignored the impact of racism on Black women. The limitations of all the approaches are perhaps more surprising given the development of recent theoretical and analytical work on 'race' and racism.

Theoretical Approaches to 'Race' and Racism – a Brief Summary

At this point, I make summary mention only of the main strands of literature around 'race' and racism in post-war Britain, in order to state which strand I believe to be the most fruitful for an analysis of 'race' and racism in the welfare state, and how it could be incorporated into the political economy and the feminist perspectives. Elsewhere (Williams, 1989) I discuss more fully the reasons for my choice, and the strengths and limitations of these and other approaches. Leaving aside the integrationist and cultural pluralist approaches and the important critiques of these, it is possible to pick out three approaches which have emerged from the more recent debate around the relationship of race to class, and which have particular significance for a study of the welfare state.

The first approach is represented by the work of John Rex who identifies Black workers as a separate class, an underclass, and suggests that this position is determined by their exclusion from the welfare and employment rights which the white working class take for granted. The second approach is represented by the work of Ben-Tovim and Gabriel who have attempted to move away from what they see as economistic and conspiratorial interpretations of racism generated from studies of the more repressive aspects of state policy, especially law and order. They suggest that racism as an ideology is autonomous from the mode of production. What is particularly significant for social policy is that their recent book, *The Local Politics of Race* (1986), with Ian Law and Kathleen Stredder, looks at racism and anti-racist policies in the local state and welfare state in these terms. The third approach is that found in the works of Hall et al. in *Policing the Crisis* (1979), and Lawrence, Solomos, Gilroy, Carby and others in the essays of *The Empire Strikes Back* (CCCS, 1982) and by Gilroy in his recent book *There Ain't No Black in the Union Jack*. (1987). Here, 'race' is seen as a 'modality' through which capitalism, in terms of both its mode of production and the reproduction of social relations, operates. It also affects the way class struggle is experienced and then formulated. In addition there is an historical dimension. Commercial colonial exploitation, military and economic imperialism, decline of the Empire, rise of independence movements, the importation of immigrant labour to Britain, all of these periods are marked by specific ways in which race was transformed by and reformulated production, exploitation and social relations. Neither class, class struggle, nor racism are fixed phenomena. But at the same time, it is within this history that the material and ideological roots of racism lie. This, then, is a 'moving picture' analysis of race and racism in its relationship to capitalism. Here, racism is not an autonomous ideology nor an ahistorical constant, but a materially rooted and changing set of ideas. It is this emphasis on an historical account of 'race' and racism and their shifting relationship to capital and class which is one distinguishing feature of this third approach, especially compared with Ben-Tovim and Gabriel (another is the differing emphasis on forms and purpose of struggle: Gilroy's particular stress is on the anti-capitalist political imperatives of Black expressive culture, contrasted with Ben-Tovim and Gabriel's stress on anti-racist campaigns within the local authority and political parties). While Ben-Tovim and Gabriel offer useful critiques of the practices and policies of the local state, and in so doing, fill an important gap, their account tends to limit the explanation for (and thus the alleviation of) racism to these practices and policies themselves. In my view, an historical, internationalist and materialist account is crucial to understand the links between social imperialism, immigration control and nationalism in the development of both Labourism and welfare capitalism. In addition it provides a broader framework to understand the sometimes contradictory relationship (and sometimes not) between the repressive areas of law and order on the one hand and the administration of welfare benefits and services on the other, *and* the range of struggles over them. Rex's important, but ungendered account of the exclusion of Black people from welfare rights offers a limited historical analysis of the impact of colonial heritage influencing the post-war white working class to hang on to their hard-won welfare rights for themselves. In emphasising, however, the *exclusion* of Black people from welfare rights, Rex tends to an uncritical view of those rights themselves, ignoring the extent to which exclusion was written into the earliest provisions of pensions, unemployment benefits and education grants. Thus, though the 'modality' approach seems to evade simple interpretation, it seems to me to be the best start so far to begin an analysis of the welfare state and 'race'; that is to say: how the various historical, political and economic features of the welfare state have been affected by 'race' and in their turn contributed to elements of 'race' and racism.

Towards a Framework for the Analysis of 'Race', Racism and Social Policy

I have argued so far that the major approaches within the literature of social policy have been flawed either by their inability, in the case of anti-collectivism and social reformism, or unwillingness so far, in the case of the political economy and feminist critique, to offer an understanding of the welfare experiences of Black people, or to link themselves with the theor-etical approaches which analyse 'race' and racism. I have also suggested on the other hand that, taken together, the political economy of welfare approach, the current debate between Black and white feminists and the 'moving picture' approach of Hall, Gilroy and others provides a useful framework within which to begin an analysis of the Black experience of welfare.

What is needed for social policy, then, as I suggested earlier, is an approach which is formulated according to the experiences of Black people as workers (including welfare workers), as consumers of welfare, and those engaged in struggles over welfare. It has to be based on an historical analysis of racism, imperialism and neo-imperialism, in their articulation with the main goals of the welfare state: accumulation, reproduction, control legitimation/repression. Class struggle, women's struggles and class conflict too must be deconstructed to understand their relationship – ideological and material – to racism, imperialism and neo-imperialism, and other forms of oppression. And our strategy for welfare must be informed and regenerated by the needs articulated by Black people themselves, both in Britain and internationally. I shall begin here to spell out such an approach which I hope may provide a basis for others to improve upon.

The Historical Cast of Welfare Reforms: Social Imperialism,
Nationalism and Immigration Control

Although relatively large-scale Black immigration is a post-war phenomenon, racism is certainly not, but neither still is the racism of the welfare
state. This last aspect took hold in two ways. Social imperialism was a
solution supported by Liberal and Labourist parties to the threat posed in
the 1880s and 1890s by an increasingly organised working class. It aimed to
subordinate class interests to those of nation and empire, and it succeeded
by linking these issues to social reform and by suggesting a necessary
interdependence. In this way trade unions, in so far as they were pressing
for welfare reforms, came to believe that such reforms were the fruits of
imperialist policy and were necessary to create national efficiency upon
which imperial power depended. This combined with a strong influence of
Darwinism and eugenics. There was thus an *apparent* material as well as
ideological basis for the working class to believe in imperialism and racial
supremacy. It also created a principled belief in entitlement to welfare
benefits *by nationality*, which readily built upon the already-existing
'deserving and undeserving' categorisation of the working class. Nationality
became written into all the early benefits – 1908 and 1911 Old Age
Pensions, 1918 National Insurance Act, municipal education and housing
in the 1920s (see Cohen, 1985 and this volume). It is also worth noting that
not only 'nation' but 'motherhood' too was an important theme in the
quest for national efficiency and maintenance of racial supremacy. But it
was strictly British white respectable motherhood which was encouraged.
(Davin, 1978). (Women too were excluded from many of these benefits on
a 'family wage' argument.)

The second way in which nationalism and welfare became intertwined was
through immigration controls. Demands from the trade unions and socialist
organisations for Jewish immigration control were based on anti-semitism
and the defence of jobs and welfare benefits. In addition the regulation of
immigration (1905 Aliens Act) was done through the welfare agencies like
the Labour Exchanges, and, like the Nationality Act, restriction from
benefits was expedited by the tightening of the Aliens Act. By 1919 all
Jewish aliens had to carry identity cards, report absences, keep out of
'protected areas', amongst other things (Cohen, 1985: 87, and in this
volume). As well as anti-semitism, racism was also part of pre-war policy
and sentiment. In 1919 at a time of rising unemployment the Ministry of
Labour sent secret instructions to labour exchange managers that unemployed Black seamen of British nationality should be kept ignorant of their
rights to 'out-of-work-donation' (Fryer, 1984: 299). Racist attacks took
place after demobilisation from the First World War by white mobs on
Black workers and families in South Tyneside, Liverpool and Cardiff.
During the Second World War, Caribbean workers who had responded to
the need for labour found vicious racism when they arrived (Sherwood,
1985; Ford, 1985). Somerset County Council automatically took into care

any illegitimate baby born to a British woman and fathered by a *Black* American GI (She Married a Yank, BBC TV). The point is that the ground was well laid by the trade unions, the welfare agencies and governments of all hues, for the exclusion and subsequent racist welfare provision to the new Black immigrants and their descendants. In many cases Black people had to organise for themselves, for example, in Liverpool in 1948 the Colonial People's Defence Committee organised for the welfare of Black seamen who were denied benefits when unemployed even when many were war veterans. Indeed, as Cohen points out, racism, immigration and internal controls were *intrinsic* to the welfare state before and after the Second World War.

The Role of Black Workers in Maintaining Lower Social Expenditure

The economic role Black immigrant workers played in maintaining profitability through low labour costs was the main reason for capitalism's need for commonwealth labour in the late 1940s. There are two aspects of this which are relevant to the welfare state: first the role Black workers have played in keeping down the 'relatively rising costs' of welfare provision, particularly in the health service, and, second, an ambivalence about the responsibility of the British welfare state to bear the social costs of Black workers.

The study by Doyal et al. (1981), clearly shows how, since the 1960s, the NHS has been dependent on overseas workers, both as contract labour and settlers, from the Caribbean, India, Ireland and Malaysia, at all levels of skills, though they tend to be concentrated in the lower grades and many of them are women. One-third of the doctors and 20 per cent of student nurses working in Britain in 1981 were born overseas. In the London hospital in the Doyal study, 84 per cent of domestics and 82 per cent of catering workers were from abroad. Further, in spite of immigration controls, the NHS has continued to recruit skilled overseas workers and until recently, by a number of anomalies, unskilled labour. Since there are limits to the scope for rationalisation of labour in such heavily labour intensive sectors as the health service compared with private industry, the availability of cheap labour has been particularly crucial in keeping costs down. On the other hand, where rationalisation and deskilling *have* taken place, this has been possible by the use of overseas nurses, concentrated in SEN training and less prestigious areas like the psychiatric and geriatric services. A further point related to the question of social costs being borne by the immigrants' country of origin is that many of the doctors and nurses have had their training paid for by their own – far poorer – countries, and the children of many of those women on contract labour are being cared for and educated in their own countries. In other words 'the need to reproduce labour power effectively while at the same time keeping down the costs of reproduction to capital as a whole . . . helps to explain the need for migrant labour both historically and today' (Doyal et al., 1981: 68).

The issue of social costs of immigrant workers was an important issue in the late 1940s as the government looked for new sources of labour. As Joshi and Carter (1984) point out, Commonwealth workers were cheaper than aliens because they were British citizens, and as such were deemed to have come 'individually and on their own initiative' and thus there was no need to make welfare provision for them. There was thus *no intention* to provide for them, and when Black immigrants *did* use the welfare services they were seen as scroungers. The juxtaposition of these two features are pinpointed by Jacobs when he says: 'black workers were acceptable as cleaners, porters, kitchen staff, even nurses and doctors, but never wholeheartedly as patients. They could build council houses but were not expected to live in them' (Jacobs, 1985: 13).

Social Reproduction and the Black Population

Gough sees social reproduction as one of the prime concerns of the welfare state. I have already noted an ambivalence about the responsibility for bearing social costs. In so far as it was accepted then what does it mean for Black people?

Reproducing a Racially Stratified Workforce The failure of the education system to provide 'equal opportunities' has particular poignancy for Black children. Schools in a number of ways play an important part not only in maintaining class divisions but racial and gender divisions too, contributing to the maintenance of a racially stratified workforce. Brah and Deem (1986) comment that the 'deficit model' of the aspirations, abilities and cultures of Asian and Afro-Caribbean children persists in educational thinking in spite of official policy having traversed the assimilation, integration and multi-cultural models. Young Blacks who dream of a better future are deemed as having 'unrealistic aspirations', and Asian girls are denied career opportunities because of assumptions about Asian culture and the 'passive' role of women therein.

The MSC's youth training programmes, caught between the conflicting ideologies of equal access, 'special needs', and social control and containment, are also reinforcing existing racial inequalities and structures as young Black people are filtered into the lower status Mode B schemes.

Rex (1984a) has also pointed out how the 1977 White Paper on Inner City Policy made racist assumptions about the occupational destinations of those living in the inner cities. It argued in effect that as the inner cities were revived and new industries developed, the present residents (mainly Black) would be unsuitable for the new jobs because of their lack of skills. The assumption is that Black people and their children can only work at unskilled levels (Rex, 1984a).

Second, I have already detailed with reference to the Health Service, how the welfare services themselves maintain divisions of labour along class, sex and race lines, where Black *women* in particular are employed in lower grades, in lower-paid work at unsocial hours. At the same time, it should also be said that the assumption that women do not work, or that their work is marginal, which is written into many aspects of social security legislation have particular *in*applicability to Black women. According to the 1981 Labour Force Survey, 23 per cent of white women worked full-time, compared with 42 per cent of West Indian women, and 25 per cent of Asian women. West Indian women in particular are more likely than both white and Asian women to be a head of household (quoted in Barrett and McIntosh, 1985).

Maintenance of the Non-working White Population but Limitation of the Black   Part of the social reproduction function identified by Gough (1979) is the maintenance of dependants, albeit in ways which often reinforce dependence and subordination. In cash terms this means pensions, invalidity and child benefits, etc.; in care terms it has meant in particular the promotion of motherhood and women's caring role in a whole range of ways. As detrimental as some of these policies are to a notion of women's equality, they have different meanings for Black women and their families. The emphasis has not been so much on the 'endowment' of motherhood and the maintenance of dependants, but on the *restriction* of motherhood and *limitation* and *control* of dependants. This is illustrated in two ways: immigration control and reproductive policies. Paul Gordon (1985) cites many examples of instances where normal rights afforded dependants through social security are denied to Black people, or where their having made claims renders them guilty of scrounging. More generally, the concern about 'numbers' surrounding the 1962 and 1971 Commonwealth Immigration Acts, was about '*dependants*': wives, children and grandparents, and the shift that the immigration laws mark from citizen to migrant worker is precisely about the denial of benefits to those dependants and therefore about their limitation. Refusal of admission to many immigrants is on the basis of dependants having to prove they have no recourse to public funds and can be maintained by a relative or friend already resident. (This doesn't apply to Commonwealth citizens with right to abode or pre-1973 settlers.) Gordon also points out that although the 1977 Child Benefit Act was hailed as progressive for the way it transferred money for children from fathers to mothers, it also had the consequence of withdrawing financial support for children living abroad but whose parent works here, as child tax allowances could be claimed in this instance but child benefits could not. The 'Sole Responsibility' rule of the 1971 Act also makes it difficult for single parents to bring their children into the country unless they have themselves solely maintained and *visited* them (Bryan et al., 1985: 157). The non-maintenance of Black dependants is reinforced further by the assumption that Asian cultures, in particular, are self-supporting and have no need for public provision. This underlies the lack of provision for elderly Black people. Yet, in one study 26 per cent of the Black elderly interviewed had *no* family in Britain (Bhalla and Blakemore, 1981).

This concern with 'numbers' has also centred around the fertility of Black families. A crop of studies in the 1960s was directed at future estimates of the numbers of Black children given the rate of fertility of Black families. Such concerns are heavily influenced by eugenicist ideas, and racist ideas about Black sexuality. It is not surprising, therefore, that the right of Black mothers to fertility is not always taken for granted as campaigns over the use of the long-lasting contraceptive Depo-Provera, abortion and sterilisation have shown (Bryan et al., 1985: 103–4). In general then, as mothers, Black women's experience is not the same as that of white mothers:

> Black women, as mothers, encounter other state agencies such as the DHSS, schools and so on in a very particular way; they may be asked to produce their passports before being considered eligible for benefit, or before their children are allowed to be enrolled in schools. (Bhavnani and Coulson, 1986: 84)

Social Control of Black Welfare Users

The modification of behaviour, attitudes and practices to work and family is a well acknowledged historical role of all aspects of the welfare state. And it has particular resonance with the poor, the residuum, the undeserving (Piven and Cloward, 1972). But it intersects with 'race' in a number of very particular ways.

Black Cultural Pathology   The characterisation of individuals, families or communities being to blame for their deprivation because of their way of life, their culture, has long been part of common-sense ideas in social work, education and health care. But deeply embedded notions of cultural and racial superiority, absorbed and reworked through different modes of racial domination gave rise in the post-war period to specific and often contradictory ideas of the deficiencies of Afro-Caribbean and Asian families and cultures. They are particularly persistent in education, social work and health care. Hazel Carby points out that Black children are seen to fail at school either because their Asian mothers are too passive and withdrawn and stay in the home, or because their Afro-Caribbean mothers are too assertive and go out to work (Carby, 1982). Illnesses such as rickets are seen as resulting from unsuitable diets rather than the need for a policy for Vitamin D to be put into chapati flour or ghee. The problems of adolescents are translated in terms of their parents' maladaptive childcare practices. The Black Health Workers and Patients Group point out that 40 per cent of all Black people in NHS beds are psychiatric patients, and that 'multi-culturalism' has affected psychiatric diagnosis in such a way as to reinforce racism: 'the "hysteric" young Asian women in dread of arranged marriage .. the vicious and violent Afro-Caribbean male youth, perhaps already implicated in the social psychosis of Rasta . . .' (1983: 32). This last example points to another variation in social control: potential danger and the need for containment.

Danger, Containment and Incorporation   Hall et al. (1978), Solomos (1985), Gilroy (1982) have all shown how policies on law and order, youth and unemployment have been constructed upon the image of Black youth in the 'urban ghetto' as a potential danger, in terms of increased crime and political instability. This has emerged particularly since the 1970s and the economic crisis, and the identification of Black unemployed youth as part of the 'enemy within'. It is not only through law and order that containment policies are practised. In 1980 the ILEA provided £1.6 million for disruptive units in schools. Increasingly, evidence and suspicion mounted that there were disproportionate numbers of Black children being sent to them (as with the earlier incidence of ESN classes and schools), such that Black parents in Haringey demanded that the provision be stopped (Carby, 1982: 205). According to the Black Health Workers and Patients Group (1983) Section 136 of the 1959 Mental Health Act, which empowers the police to remove to a place of safety someone judged to be dangerous to themselves or others, is three or four times more likely to be used on Black people than white. Further, Black people are more likely to be offered drug or ECT treatment than therapy (Mama, 1984). Bryan et al. (1985) also claim that attitudes of cultural pathology and lack of access to housing and childcare facilities lead to the likelihood of Black children being taken into care in the event of homelessness or domestic violence. Indeed, as Jacobs (1985) points out, in the event of allocation, Black tenants are more likely to find themselves on more heavily controlled and policed estates. The 1981 riots crystallised a rationalisation of such policies for the right. But it should also be noted that the threat of political instability has also led to the voicing of a different approach – most notably by Lord Scarman. He is against the tough law and order approach and argues for one of consensus through community consultation, as well as for the injection of money into deprived areas. This has been criticised as soft social control and incorporation by some:

> Increasingly the effect of state funds on our community has been to neutralise its militancy; political mobilisation has come to be seen as a salaried activity — accountable not to the Black community but to the state which pays them. Their brief, however unwitting, is to keep the lid on the cauldron, and their existence is seen as proof of the government's 'concern' to soften the effects of its own institutionalised racism. (Bryan et al., 1985: 179)

Others argue that such policies at least expose the contradictions, and create openings and opportunities for anti-racist struggle and debate (Hall, 1982).

Internal Controls   A third form of control adopted by the welfare state is that of policing the immigration control laws, which I have already described as having an important historical dimension. Gordon and Newnham (1985) instance case after case since the mid-1970s where housing departments, hospitals, schools and colleges, and DHSS offices all played a part in reinforcing controls by refusing services and benefits to those they deemed ineligible, arbitrarily checking immigration status (asking for passports) and informing the immigration authorities of suspects. The overall effect of inhibiting access to social services to Black people is clear.

Struggles Against Black Oppression

What do these struggles tell us about the welfare state and how it should be changed? 'We have been among the first to question the overall power of the Welfare State to record, control and intervene in our lives' (Bryan et al., 1985: 110). Many of the community struggles over, for example, high suspension rates amongst Black children in schools, over the need for the NHS to recognise sickle-cell anaemia, over child care, over homelessness, over the SUS law and deportation, have often involved mainly, though not exclusively, Black *women*. They point to an experience where the welfare state, in setting us up, puts us down as well. And where that process involves racism it is particularly controlling, subordinating, blaming and punishing.

If the welfare state is the result of pressure from above and pressure from below, then Black people get squeezed out altogether. But now Black struggles are applying the pressure in different ways in different places. Not just from the workplace, but from the *community*, not just knocking at the door, not asking for more when it is opened, but addressing the question of *human need* and reclaiming *culture*. There is some similarity here with women's struggles. Where women have demanded a reassessment of the relationship between production and reproduction, struggles against Black oppression raise a further dimension: the relationship between welfare policies, the state and the *international division of labour*. It is this internationalism – of connecting to the oppression and exploitation in the Third World, to the global division between North and South – which perhaps raises the greatest challenge to socialism in general and to welfare strategy in particular.

How are these issues of community struggle, human need and culture, and internationalism raised by struggles against the welfare state's role in the oppression of Black people?

Struggles at Grunwick's, Imperial Typewriters and Chix linked workplace to community, for it was from the Black communities that financial and organisational support was forthcoming when the trade unions and welfare agencies failed. The organisations of Black parents against suspensions, harassment, violence and even murder in schools (Manchester, Burnage High School) are significant and important welfare struggles which, while they focus on *specific* racial aspects, also challenge central issues concerning form and control in state provision. These examples underline the historical importance of community as a site of struggle over welfare and make important links between it and the workplace struggle which have often been overlooked in an account of class struggles around the welfare state. A further example is the suggestion by Paul Gilroy that there was a 'continuity of protest which links the 1981 riots with the Health Service strike which followed them' (1987: 37).

Second, in challenging not simply the question of access to welfare, but the entire basis of welfare and the form of its provision, such struggles are about the politics of need – challenging the state's and the administrators', and agency's definition of need: if your access to health care is determined by the need for a doctor or nurse who speaks your own language, then this becomes not a 'special' but a basic need. Struggles in pursuit of equal opportunities, positive action and anti-racist education policies, monitoring of local authority housing and employment, reviewing appointments procedures, creating race relations units, race awareness training, all have in common the recognition of white racism as the problem, institutionalised within the structure of society. Increasingly, there has also to be a recognition that none of these policies guarantees much without a significant transfer of power to the Black community, an acknowledgement that it is the struggles in the Black community which have forced these institutionalised responses, as well as the need to mobilise the white working class to combat white racism. This mobilisation can and does take place over welfare issues, for example, in the recent campaign for non-racist social security benefits. At the same time, there can be within these policies, important challenges to the concepts of race relations policy. For example, Avtah Brah's discussion of the need for anti-racist schooling (Brah and Deem, 1986) presents a nine-point strategy that involves reclaiming *culture* as 'an oppositional force which stands in a complex relationship with the material conditions of society' (Brah and Deem, 1986: 76). Her strategy extends far beyond multi-culturalism, to include, *inter alia*, examining the wider curriculum, challenging the racial divisions within the education hierarchy, making the study of racism compulsory within teacher training. Another example is the challenging of racism institutionalised in social work practice where disproportionate numbers of Black children are taken into care. The Association of Black Social Workers and Allied Professionals has put forward the need and right of a Black child to a Black parent or surrogate. While this is an important move to counter notions of Black family pathology and assert the strengths Black families have to offer, it has been seen as a misguided response by others. Paul Gilroy (1987) argues that the assumption that only Black parenting can enhance positive Black identity rests in the end on a simple notion of racial essentialism, or 'ethnic absolutism' which matches but does not counter the cultural and national essentialism of the New Right. It also raises questions about the potential and limitations of Black professionalism (see Stubbs, 1985).

Finally, as an example of the importance of an internationalist perspective there is the way in which immigration control is related to the historical and contemporary international movement of labour, and forms of exploitation. The relevance of this to anti-racist struggle can be illustrated in two ways: first, anti-imperialism and support for Third World movements informs many struggles against Black oppression. For example, the exposure of the use of Depo-Provera, unwarranted termination and sterilisation on Black women in this country, made immediate links to the use of Third World Black women as guinea-pigs in contraceptive drug trials. Gilroy expresses this internationalism in the following way:

> The need to develop international dialogues and means of organisation which can connect locality and immediacy across the international division of labour is perhaps more readily apparent to black populations who have recent experience of migration as well as acute memories of slavery and international indenture. (1987: 68)

Second, there is an important critique of the export of western forms of 'aid' and technology which have developed out of western development of welfare to the Third World. The most obvious example is the export of drugs and medical technology which are unable to deal with, and sometimes reinforce the ill health in these countries (Doyal, 1979) (education offers another example). Finally, the significance of an internationalist perspective to the future of the welfare state in Britain has been raised by Rose (1986). The international movement of capital and production to some Third World economies, accompanied by high unemployment in the West, has thrown doubt upon the possibility of the future of a welfare state based on full male white employment. The old accommodation of capital's and labour's interests in the need for the welfare state to guarantee a social reproduction no longer holds so fast, and the focus of struggles against exploitation turns upon the young female factory workers in the Third World. Racism, then, is not a simple parochial problem of practice and provision, but one with international implications.

Conclusions[4]

In the first part of this article I examined the causes for the neglect of 'race' and racism in welfare theory. All four approaches – anti-collectivism, social reformism, the political economy of welfare and feminism were found wanting to greater and lesser degrees. Nevertheless, the political economy and feminist analysis of welfare, taking into account the Black feminist critique of it, have within social policy the greatest potential for understanding the Black experience of welfare. Second, I suggested which approaches to 'race' and racism could help us to examine the relationship between 'race' and welfare. I have attempted to provide a framework to do just that in this final section. I have shown that the Black experience of the welfare state is at one and the same time both *specific* and *central*. It is specific in the sense that 'race' joins together with some of the existing characteristics of the welfare state (social control, for example) to produce policies or practices which are race-specific (Black pathology, for example). On the other hand, racism must be central to our analysis of the welfare state because of the way the welfare state is so heavily implicated in the exploitation and oppression of Black people, as an employer of cheap Black and immigrant labour, as executor of the state's racist immigration laws, as depriver of provision, or provider of second-class provision, as controller and container of political unrest. The struggle for better welfare provision has to reckon with these more oppressive aspects of social welfare.

I have also shown that this racism has operated in specific ways over the historical development of the welfare state, but with a certain consistency which makes the present relationship of 'race' to welfare not simply a post-war, or 'crisis' phenomenon but the emergence, in particularly harsh form, of a nationalism and racism intrinsic in the provision of welfare. I have suggested that the constellation of imperialism with patriarchal capitalism also found its way into the demands of the working class for welfare reforms at the turn of the century by way of the all-party platform of social imperialism. The nationalist and often racist assumptions of the welfare state come not only from 'above', but from 'below' too, in the labour and social reformist movements.

By contrast, anti-racist writing and struggles around welfare issues have demonstrated not only the importance of the Black community as part of the class struggle over welfare, not just that anti-racist struggles of Blacks and whites raise in new ways the meaning of welfare needs from the standpoint of the Black experience, but also the necessity for an *inter-nationalist* and anti-imperialist approach to welfare strategy. This requires welfare theory and strategy to take seriously questions of immigration controls, of the international division of labour, and of the transnational economic order whereby the rich North exploits the resources and labour of the poor South. These struggles have also pointed to an experience of the British state as overwhelmingly racist in its policies for Black people. While law and order and immigration controls operate in different ways for different Black groups, the result is a form of oppression that intersects with, and transforms, other forms of oppression like that of gender. Welfare theory and strategy must be able to acknowledge not only that the state deals with different groups differently, but that the difference is sometimes one of severity and intransigence. This acknowledgement does not mean moving backwards to the functionalist equation of the welfare state = social control, it means moving forward, basing our analysis on the political, economic and feminist analyses of welfare but with greater knowledge of the specific experiences of different sections of the working class – Black people and women in particular – so that our understanding and strategies can be transformed according to their needs and priorities. In this sense, the political implication of my argument is not, as some suggest that the New (or not-so-new) Social Movements have displaced the notion of class and the need for class struggle. It is that the forms and priorities of these 'New' Social Movements must transform and regenerate class and class struggle. Nor should the grandeur of these new priorities – such as reassessing the international division of labour as well as the relations of production and reproduction and the sexual division of labour – paralyse us into inaction; it means that, as feminists, socialists, academics and practitioners we have to be much more critical of our traditions, our strategies and our visions.

Notes

I would like to thank those who have commented on several drafts of this article. They are: Avtar Brah, Miriam David and Ahmed Gurnah. I am particularly indebted to Bob Deacon and Sidney Jacobs for their constant support, and their detailed comments.

1. In writing this I have been aware of the limited capacity I, as a white person, have in interpreting the experiences of racism in the welfare state. The imperative for this work came originally from a socialist-feminist commitment to anti-racism and anti-imperialism, several years' experience in two African countries, the indirect experience of racism towards those close to me, and the demands of Black students for a more relevant social policy analysis.

2. I have followed the recent convention of putting 'race' in quotation marks to distinguish it from any biological connotation the word otherwise has. However, I recognise it is not ideal, and can sometimes be taken as a euphemism for 'Black people'. I have used it here for want of a less loaded abstract noun. In addition, racism can extend beyond Black people to Jewish and Chinese people and gypsies. Several historical references are made here to anti-semitism, but in the main my contemporary references concern racism directed at Black people of Afro-Caribbean and Asian origins.

3. See Williams (1989). These critiques are greatly expanded in this work.

4. As a retrospective postscript, some 10 years after this article was originally written, I would refer readers to attempts to escape from the straitjacket of fixed categories: Williams (1992 and 1995).

References

Amos, V. and Parmar, P. (1984) 'Challenging imperial feminism', *Feminist Review*, 17.

Barker, M. (1981) *The New Racism: Conservatives and the Ideology of the Tribe*. London: Junction Books.

Barrett, M. and McIntosh, M. (1985) 'Ethnocentricism and socialist feminist theory', *Feminist Review*, 20.

Bean, P. and MacPherson, S. (eds) (1983) *Approaches to Welfare*. London: Routledge.

Ben-Tovim, G., Gabriel, J., Law, I. and Stredder, K. (1986) *The Local Politics of Race*. London: Macmillan.

Bhalla, A. and Blakemore, K. (1981) *Elders of the Ethnic Minority Groups*. London: All Faiths For One Race.

Bhavnani, K. and Coulson, M. (1986) 'Transforming socialist-feminism: The challenge of racism', *Feminist Review* 23.

Bhavnani, R. (1986) 'The struggle for an anti-racist policy in education in Avon', *Critical Social Policy*, 16.

Black Health Workers and Patients Group (1983) 'Psychiatry and the corporate state', *Race and Class*, 25(2).

Bosanquet, N. (1983) *After the New Right*. London: Heinemann.

Bourne, J. (1980) 'Cheerleaders and ombudsmen: the sociology of race relations in Britain', *Race and Class*, 21(4).

Bourne, J. (1983) 'Towards an anti-racist feminist', *Race and Class*, 25.

Brah, A. and Deem, R. (1986) 'Towards anti-sexist and anti-racist schooling', *Critical Social Policy* 16.

Bridges, L. (1975) 'The Ministry of Internal Security: British urban social policy 1968–74', *Race and Class*, 16(4).

Brown, J. (1974) *A Theory of Police–Immigrant Relations*. Cranfield Institute of Technology

Bryan, B., Dadzie, S. and Scafe, S. (1985) *The Heart of the Race. Black Women's Lives in Britain*. London: Virago.

Carby, H. (1982) 'Schooling in Babylon and white woman listen! Black feminism and the boundaries of sisterhood', in CCCS, *The Empire Strikes Back: Race and Racism in '70s Britain*. London: Hutchinson University Library.

Centre for Contemporary Cultural Studies (CCCS) (1982) *The Empire Strikes Back: Race and Racism in '70s Britain*. London: Hutchinson University Library.

Cohen, S. (1985) 'Anti-semitism, immigration controls and the welfare state', *Critical Social Policy*, 13.

Davin, A. (1978) 'Imperialism and motherhood', *History Workshop Journal No. 5*.

Deacon, B. (1983) *Social Policy and Socialism. The Struggle for Socialist Relations of Welfare*. London: Pluto Press.

Doyal, L. (1979) *The Political Economy of Health*. London: Pluto Press.

Doyal, L., Hunt, G. and Mellor, J. (1981) 'Your life in their hands: migrant workers in the NHS', *Critical Social Policy*, 1(2).

Ford, A. (1985) *Telling the Truth: The Life and Times of the British Honduran Forestry Unit in Scotland 1941–44*. London: Karia Press.

Friedman, M. (1962) *Capitalism and Freedom*. Chicago: Chicago University Press.

Fryer, P. (1984) *Staying Power: The History of Black People in Britain*. London: Pluto Press.

George, V. and Wilding, P. (1985) *Ideology and Social Welfare*. London: Routledge & Kegan Paul.

Gilroy, P. (1982) '"Steppin" out of Babylon – Race, Class and Autonomy', in CCCS, *The Empire Strikes Back: Race and Racism in Contemporary Britain*. London: Hutchinson University Library.

Gilroy, P. (1987) *There Ain't No Black in the Union Jack*. London: Hutchinson.

Ginsburg, N. (1979) *Class, Capital and Social Policy*. London: Macmillan.

Glennerster, H. (ed.) (1983) *The Future of the Welfare State*. London: Heinemann.

Gordon, P. (1983) 'Medicine, racism and immigration control', *Critical Social Policy*, 7.

Gordon, P. (1985) *Policing Immigration. Britain's Internal Control*. London: Pluto Press.

Gordon, P. and Newnham, A. (1985) *Passport to Benefits? Racism in Social Security*. London: CPAG and Runnymede Trust.

Gordon, P. and Klug, F. (1984) *Racism and Discrimination in Britain. A Select Bibliography 1970–83*. London: Runnymede Trust.

Gough, I. (1979) *The Political Economy of the Welfare State*. London: Macmillan.

Hall, S. (1982) 'The lessons of Lord Scarman', *Critical Social Policy*, 2(2).

Hall, S., Critcher, C., Jefferson, T., Clarke, J. and Roberts, B. (1978) *Policing the Crisis*. London: Macmillan.

Hill, M. and Bramley, G. (1986) *Analysing Social Policy*. Oxford: Basil Blackwell.

Jacobs, S. (1985) 'Race, empire and the welfare state: council housing and racism', *Critical Social Policy*, 13.

Jones, K., Brown, J. and Bradshaw, J. (1978) *Issues in Social Policy*. London: Routledge & Kegan Paul.

Joshi, H. and Carter, B. (1984) 'The role of labour in the creation of a racist Britain', *Race & Class*, 25(3).

Klein, R. and O'Higgins, M. (eds) (1985) *The Future of Welfare*. Oxford: Basil Blackwell.

Lawrence, E. (1982) 'Just plain commonsense: the "roots" of racism', in CCCS *The Empire Strikes Back: Race and Racism in '70s Britain*. London: Hutchinson University Library.

Levitas, R. (1986) *The Ideology of the New Right*. London: Polity Press.

London Edinburgh Weekend Return Group (LEWRG) (1979) *In and Against the State*. London: Pluto Press.

Loney, M., Boswell, D. and Clarke, J. (1983) *Social Policy and Social Welfare*. Milton Keynes: Open University Press.

McIntosh, M. (1981) 'Feminism and social policy', *Critical Social Policy*, 1(1).

Mama, A. (1984) 'Black women, the economic crisis and the British state', *Feminist Review*, 17.

Mishra, R. (1981) *Society and Social Policy*. London: Macmillan.

Mishra, R. (1984) *The Welfare State in Crisis*. London: Wheatsheaf.

National Institute for Social and Economic Research (NISER) (1967) *Social Costs of Immigrants*.

Offe, C. (1984) *Contradictions of the Welfare State*. London: Hutchinson.

Ohri, A., Manning, B. and Curno, P. (eds) (1982) *Community Work and Racism*. London: Routledge & Kegan Paul/Association of Community Workers.

Øyen, E. (ed.) (1986) *Comparing Welfare States and their Futures*. Aldershot: Gower.

Parekh, B. (1986) *The New Right and the Politics of Nationhood*, in G. Cohen et al. *The New Right: Image and Reality*. London: Runnymede Trust.

Parma, P. (1982) 'Gender, race and class: Asian women in resistance', in CCCS, *The Empire Strikes Back: Race and Racism in '70s Britain*. London: Hutchinson University Library.

Pascall, G. (1986) *Social Policy. A Feminist Analysis*. London: Tavistock.

Pinker, R. (1979) *The Idea of Welfare*. London: Heinemann.

Piven, E. and Cloward, R. (1972) *Regulating the Poor: The Function of Public Welfare*. London: Tavistock.

Rex, J. (1984a) 'Black marks for a White Paper', *Guardian* 15 Feb.

Rex, J. (1984b) 'Social policy and ethnic inequality', paper given at the SAA Annual Conference, July.

Rose, F. and Deakin, N. (1969) *Colour and Citizenship*. Oxford: IRR/Oxford University Press.

Rose, H. (1981) 'Re-reading Titmuss: the sexual division of welfare', *Journal of Social Policy*, 10(1).

Rose, H. (1986) 'Women and the restructuring of the welfare state', in E. Øyen. *Comparing Welfare States and their Futures*. Aldershot: Gower.

Seidel, G. (1986) 'Culture, nation and race in the British and French New Right', in R. Levitas (ed.), *The Ideology of the New Right*. London: Polity Press.

Semmel, B. (1960) *Imperialism and Social Reform*. London: George Allen & Unwin.

Shaw, G.B.S. (ed.) (1900) *Fabianism and the Empire*. London: The Fabian Society.

Sherwood, M. (1985) *Many Struggles – West Indian Workers and Service Personnel in Britain, 1939–45*. London: Karia Press.

Sivanandan, A. (1976) 'Race, class and the state', *Race & Class*, 17(4).

Sivanandan, A. (1978) *From Immigration Control to Induced Repatriation*. London: IRR.

Sivanandan, A. (1980) *Imperialism in the Silicon Age*. London: IRR.

Solomos, J. (1985) 'Problems, but whose problems? The social construction of Black youth unemployment', *Journal of Social Policy*, 14(4).

Solomos, J., Findlay, B., Jones, S. and Gilroy, P. (1982) 'The organic crisis of British capitalism and race: the experience of the 1970s', in CCCS, *The Empire Strikes Back: Race and Racism in '70s Britain*. London: Hutchinson University Library.

Stubbs, P. (1985) 'The employment of Black social workers: from ethnic sensitivity to anti-racism?' *Critical Social Policy*, 12.

Taylor-Gooby, P. (1981) 'The state, class ideology and social policy', *Journal of Social Policy*, 10(4).

Taylor-Gooby, P. (1985) *Public Opinion, Ideology and State Welfare*. London: Routledge & Kegan Paul.

Taylor-Gooby, P. and Dale, J. (1981) *Social Theory and Social Welfare*. London: Edward Arnold.

Titmuss, R. (1943) *Problems of Population*. London: Association for Education in Citizenship/English Universities Press.

Townsend, P. (1984) *Why are the Many Poor?* Fabian Pamphlet 500. London: Fabian Society.

Trivedi, P. (1984) 'To deny our fullness: Asian women in the making of history', *Feminist Review*, 17.

Walker, A. (1984) *Social Planning: A Strategy for Socialist Welfare*. Oxford: Basil Blackwell and Martin Robertson.

Williams, F. (1989) *Social Policy, A Critical Introduction: Issues of Class, Race and Gender*. London: Polity Press.

Williams, F. (1992) 'Somewhere over the rainbow: universality and diversity in social policy', in N. Manning and R. Page (eds), *Policy Review*, 4: 200–19. Canterbury: Social Policy Association.

Williams, F. (1995) 'Race/ethnicity, gender and class in welfare states: a framework for comparative analysis', in *Social Politics: International Studies in Gender, State and Society*. University of Illinois, USA, Vol. 2, No. 2, pp. 127–59.

Wilson, E. (1980) 'Marxism and the welfare state', *New Left Review*, 122.

4

'Us' and 'Them'? Feminist Research, Community Care and Disability

Jenny Morris

As a disabled feminist I have often been angered by the way that feminist research and theory has excluded disabled women. There is one particular area of concern for feminists – the development of social policy on 'community care' – where a failure to identify with the experience of disabled women has had a significant detrimental effect, both in terms of the validity of the research itself and also in terms of disabled people's civil rights.

Both disability and 'community care' are issues of fundamental interest to women yet the feminist concern with 'community care' has been partisan in that it is almost entirely from the point of view of non-disabled and younger women. The experience and interests of disabled and older women are missing from the terms of debate, from the research and from the development of theory. In order to understand how this has come about, it is necessary to go back to the origins of feminism's concern with 'community care'.

Feminist Theory on the Family

The feminist concern with 'community care' policies is integrally linked to feminism's central concern with women's position within the family. During the 1970s and 1980s, feminist academics developed theoretical analyses of the family and of the welfare state and the interrelationship between the two was particularly apparent in the boom in research and theorising on the issue of 'carers'. Feminists exposed the way that the state exploits women's unpaid labour within the home and the extent to which the policies of caring for elderly and disabled people within the community depend on women's role within the family.

A key concern for feminists was to assess what social policies should be supported and campaigned for. Research and analysis was particularly

First published in *Critical Social Policy*, 33, 1992; based on a chapter in the author's book, *Pride Against Prejudice: Transforming Attitudes to Disability*, published by The Women's Press.

directed at the question of whether, and under what conditions, 'care in the community' could be supported or whether alternative types of policy would further women's interests. A theoretical basis for the debate (from a socialist feminist point of view) was set by Mary McIntosh in a contribution entitled 'The welfare state and the needs of the dependent family' (McIntosh, 1979).

Capitalism, according to McIntosh, depends on a family household system in which

> a number of people are expected to be dependent on the wages of a few adult members, primarily of the husband and father who is a 'breadwinner', and in which they are all dependent for cleaning, food preparation and so forth on unpaid work chiefly done by the wife and mother. (1979: 155)

This system also enables women – whose main role is unpaid caring work within the family, supported by the male wage – to be used as a reserve army of labour when required by socio-economic and technological developments.

The key issue for non-disabled feminists is that this family household system is based on women's economic dependence on men. Mary McIntosh, Elizabeth Wilson and other feminists also identified that the state has an important role to play in perpetuating and strengthening this family system and women's dependency within it (Wilson, 1977). It followed from this recognition of the role of the state that, if a feminist strategy was to be aimed at freeing women from their economic dependence, campaigns around equal pay and equal employment opportunities were not enough; it was also crucial to resist state policies which perpetuated women's role of providing unpaid labour within the home.

As McIntosh concluded, there were two aspects to the strategy which needed to be developed to address women's role within the family. 'What is called for' she said, 'is political struggle for state recognition of the needs of both sexes and all unwaged individuals, combined with a transformation of the dependent household so that women can participate in production on the same basis as men' (McIntosh, 1979: 170–1).

In respect of women's needs as 'unwaged individuals', the work of Hilary Land and others drew attention to the way in which the social security system perpetuated women's economic dependence on men. Various campaigns were waged around specific issues in an attempt to win financial support for women in their own right rather than as wives. This strategy was articulated by the adoption by the British Women's Liberation Movement in 1974 of the 'fifth demand' – that of legal and financial independence.

Feminists also attacked the family as the context in which women provide unpaid care. In the late 1960s and early 1970s the caring function which feminists primarily focused on was child care. From the late 1970s, however, feminists started to turn their attention to the caring tasks which are carried out within the family other than child care – the care of people with physical and/or sensory impairments, of older people and people with learning difficulties or mental health difficulties. This was partly prompted by the fact that during the early 1980s a radical Conservative government enthusiastically took up the issue of 'community care' in its task of bringing about a radical restructuring of the relationship between the state, the individual and the family.

Feminists and 'Community Care'

Caring for people who needed some level of support in their daily lives outside of large-scale institutions had been slowly developing as a social policy since the 1950s when such ideas had started to be applied to people who were in psychiatric hospitals and asylums. Initially, however, the concept of community care was more along the lines of smaller residential establishments within communities to replace the large, isolated asylums which were a legacy from the 19th century. Furthermore, for mentally ill people the 'care' that made living outside institutional care possible was primarily the development of certain drugs and also a changing attitude as to what type of treatment was required. It was only when, in the 1980s, the 'care in the community' philosophy started to be applied to those who needed physical help with daily tasks, and there was a recognition that most of such care could (and did) take place within families, that researchers and policy makers started to address the issue of who performed these caring tasks.

A piece of research on the care of 'mentally handicapped people' published by Michael Bayley in 1973, had significantly advanced the debate, identifying the necessity to distinguish between 'care in' and 'care by' the community (Bayley, 1973). Bayley asserted that if community care policies were to be effective, a variety of different forms of professional services would have to support the care provided by families. Most people who required physical care had in fact always had that care provided by families, but the late 1970s and 1980s saw a development of policies which were aimed at getting those who were in institutional care out into the community and preventing those within the community from having to go into institutional care. The provision of domiciliary services, respite care and day care (to supplement family care) were recognised as a necessary part of community care.

Policy debates during the 1960s and 1970s had been primarily informed by ideas on institutions and the damage that institutional life did to individuals – ideas which emanated from a variety of sources, from the theoretical work of Erving Goffman to the empirical work of Peter Townsend. However, the development of community care policies in the 1980s has been more determined by the Conservative government's desire to diminish individuals' 'dependence' on the welfare state and to emphasise the family's responsibilities for caring. In such a context, feminists and socialists have been concerned to develop analyses and strategies which not only defend the welfare state, but which also promote the interests of women and the working class.

In the context of all this, the feminist research on carers has been very productive in that it has drawn attention to the work which women do within the home, which was very little recognised by policy makers and yet is vital to the development of community care policies – and particularly crucial to the Conservative desire to encourage 'family care' rather than 'state care'.

Mary McIntosh's 1981 article in *Critical Social Policy* sets out the general terms of the debate which feminists developed during the 1980s (McIntosh, 1981, and this volume). Although, in the context of the Tory ideological and financial onslaught on state benefits and services, much feminist energy of necessity has had to go into defending the welfare state, McIntosh argues the importance for feminists of getting our strategic priorities clarified. 'The problem', she says, 'is whether to press for equality with men, usually in terms of legal, political and citizenship rights, or to press for greater support and respect for women in their role as housewives and mothers.' In other words, 'Should we become more fully proletarian-ised or should we seek better conditions of dependence on husbands or on state benefits?' (this volume, p. 19). McIntosh is arguing from a Marxist perspective, but the same question (albeit posed in different terminology) is integral to any type of feminist analysis because of the importance that feminism gives to the role of the family in creating and maintaining women's dependence on men.

Like many feminists, therefore, McIntosh comes down firmly in support of the first strategy – that of placing women on the same footing as men – because this would undermine the dependency relationships within the family. As she writes, 'Women's liberation depends upon the radical trans-formation of [the] family' (this volume p. 21). The main tactic which McIntosh focuses on in this article is the demand for disaggregation in the social security and taxation system (i.e. the abolition of the treatment of the married couple as one unit for taxation and social security purposes), the motivation being that 'all women will have rights to full social security and that all men will lose the right to state back-up for keeping their wives in dependence' (this volume p. 21). It is no coincidence, however, that in a bracketed aside McIntosh states 'we should be mounting a much stronger criticism of present ideas of "community care" and fighting new forms of institutional care that avoid the problems earlier radicals have pointed to' (this volume, p. 16). If women's dependence on men and their concomitant lack of economic independence as individuals is grounded in their caring role within the family, then it is but a short step to arguing that women should not do this caring and that such caring tasks should be performed outside the family.

The logic of a feminist strategy on community care policies seems inevitable. As Janet Finch says in an article published in 1984,

> We are clear what we want to reject: we reject so-called community care policies which depend on the substantial and consistent input of women's unpaid labour in the home, whilst at the same time effectively excluding them from the labour

market and reinforcing their economic and personal dependence upon men. (Finch, 1984: 15)

Finch takes issue with socialists such as Alan Walker (Walker, 1982) who holds the view that non-sexist modes of community care could possibly be developed through both the expansion of domiciliary services and a challenge to men's attitudes to caring. She argues that even if state provision expanded so that adequate care was provided by paid carers, the family will still remain the setting for community care, and since the family is the location of women's oppression, women's dependence would remain unchallenged.

This leads Finch to ask the question, 'Can we envisage *any* version of community care which is not sexist?' (1984: 7). Feminists researching on informal carers have generally agreed with her when she asserts that she cannot. The case is a strong one; all the evidence is that caring for adults within the home places a greater burden on women and that this caring role is a crucial part of women's dependence. Moreover, as Hilary Graham discusses, the association of 'caring for' with 'caring about' plays an important part in the social construction of what it is to be a woman in western society (Graham, 1983).

In the context of this analysis, feminists have difficulty supporting community care policies. This creates a dilemma. Either feminists have to support residential care or, as Finch says, conclude that alternative ways of 'looking after highly dependent people' cannot be developed without fundamental social, economic and cultural transformation (Finch, 1984: 16).

Finch admits that it may be that 'the only intellectually honest position . . . is to admit that non-sexist caring policies are *not* possible without such a transformation and – until it happens – we must abandon the quest for them, fight other battles, and accept that women will carry on caring' (1984: 16–17). However, she feels that this position lacks appeal and comes down in favour of the residential alternative.

> On balance, it seems to me that the residential route *is* the only one which ultimately will offer us a way out of the impasse of caring; collective solutions would, after all, be very much in the spirit of a socialist policy programme, and a recognition that caring *is* labour, and in a wage-economy should be paid as such, in principle should overcome some of the more offensive features of the various 'community' solutions. An additional bonus would be for the creation of additional 'real' jobs in the welfare sector. (1984: 16)

Finch goes on:

> Working through precisely how such care could be provided in a way which does not violate the relational aspect of caring, nor individual autonomy and identity, and would actually be popular with those for whom it was provided, seems a difficult but a possible programme for both feminists and socialists concerned with this area of social policy. There is a particular urgency about this task, given the rising numbers of elderly people in the population between now and the end of the century. (1984: 16)

Gillian Dalley has taken up this challenge. In *Ideologies of Caring*, published in 1988, she argues strongly against community care policies and in favour of new forms of residential 'collective' care. She starts from the position that community care policies

> appear to be premised precisely on principles to which feminists are opposed – that is, upon the primacy of the family and the home-bound status of women within it. They are exact contradictions of the collectivist solutions to the problems of caring which feminists would propose. (Dalley, 1988: xii)

Dalley not only criticises the failure to provide sufficient resources to enable a good quality of life within the community, but also argues that 'care in the community' is actually against the interests of both women and those people who they are supposed to benefit.

She therefore advocates non-family-based solutions to disabled and older people's accommodation and personal care requirements, concluding, 'This much is certain then: the familial model of care which currently dominates is based on premises which are unacceptable to feminists and (often) to those who are themselves dependent on care' (1988: 137). Dalley's solutions are to pursue 'alternative' forms of non-family care. For adults in need of physical care, the form of care that she has in mind is primarily residential care (whereas, interestingly, she assumes that non-disabled children will remain living with their parents but that 'collective' provision would take the form of after-school play schemes and day nurseries for pre-school children). This new type of residential care, according to Dalley, would be very different from current residential establishments because the underlying philosophy would be that of mutual concern.

> In physical terms there may be little difference – numbers of biologically un-related individuals live together under the same roof, characterised by some need for care and other support. In one, however, there is a lively integrated community of individuals participating freely and fully in the social life of the group and having relationships with others outside the group, where carers and cared for collaborate. In the other, at worst, there is a collection of separate isolated, often apathetic individuals warehoused together, serviced by a staff which works in poor and exploiting conditions, having little concern for those in its charge. (1988: 121)

Disabled and older people experience daily the inadequacies of 'community care' and would agree with everything that feminists such as Finch and Dalley say about the isolation, poverty and sheer hard work which too often characterises both their lives and that of people who support them. However, disabled and older people as individuals and through their organisations have almost without exception put their energies into achieving a better quality of life *within* the community (taking this to mean outside residential care) and have thus maintained a (critical) support of community care policies – whilst recognising that the Conservative government may have some questionable motivations for promoting such policies. For those disabled people who have resisted residential care as the solution to their housing and personal care needs and insisted on their rights to live within the community, the approach of feminists such as McIntosh, Finch and Dalley to care in the community policies is very alarming. Are we right to be alarmed or should we be putting our efforts into demanding better forms of residential care, as they suggest?

'Us' and 'Them'

We can go a long way towards answering this question when we recognise that for feminists writing and researching on carers, the category 'women' does not generally include those who need physical assistance. When Janet Finch asked the question 'Can we envisage any version of community care which is not sexist?' she went on to say, 'If we cannot, then we need to say something about how we imagine such people *can* be cared for in ways which we find acceptable' (1984: 7, italics in original). In order to understand how she, and other feminists, answer this question it is necessary to recognise who Janet Finch means when she says 'we' and whether 'we' are included in the term 'such people'.

The latter term refers to 'people (of whatever age, although this perhaps is an experience most common in old age) whose physical needs require fairly constant attendance or, at least, the constant presence of another person' (1984: 7). Throughout Finch's writing and that of other feminists on community care policies it is clear that the term 'we' quite definitely does not include 'such people'. When Finch and others are assessing what policies would be acceptable to 'us' she means what policies would be acceptable to non-disabled feminists.

Much of the research that feminists have engaged in on caring explicitly separates out non-disabled women from disabled women. Gillian Dalley, for example, refers to 'women and dependent people' as if they are two completely separate groups, whose interests, what is more, are in conflict (Dalley, 1988). She introduces her book by saying 'This book is about dependent people and the women who usually care for them' (1988: 1). This separation of 'women' from disabled and older people (who are treated as genderless unless their gender, as in Clare Ungerson's research [1987], is of significance to the carer) is evident in most of the feminist research on caring and has major implications for the questions and issues which feminists consider important. Finch and Groves, for example, identified the equal opportunity issues around community care as those concerning the sexual division of labour between men and women as carers (Finch and Groves, 1983). In none of the pieces of research is there any analysis of equal opportunity issues for disabled and older women.

This separating out of disabled and older women from the category of 'women' comes about because of a failure of the feminist researchers concerned to identify with the subjective experience of 'such people'. The principle of 'the personal is political' is applied to carers but not to the 'cared for'. This general tendency is articulated by Clare Ungerson's account of why the issue of caring is of personal significance to her. She writes:

> my interest in carers and the work that they do arises out of my own biography. The fact that my mother was a carer and looked after my grandmother in our home until my grandmother's death when I was 14 combines with the knowledge that, as an only daughter, my future contains the distinct possibility that I will sooner or later become a carer myself. (1987: 2)

Lois Keith, a disabled feminist, commented on Ungerson's inability to see *herself* (and not just her mother) as potentially a person who may need physical care:

> Most of us can imagine being responsible for someone weaker than ourselves, even if we hope this won't happen. It is certainly easier to see ourselves as being needed, than to imagine ourselves as dependent on our partner, parents or children for some of our most basic needs. (Keith, 1990: v)

Ungerson's failure to identify with the interests and experiences of those who need care is then carried over into her feminist analysis. Thus she writes, 'the second set of reasons for writing this book is that it accords with and is fed by my own commitment to women-centred issues and to feminism'. She goes on to identify what are the 'women-centred' issues around community care. 'It has almost reached the dimensions of banality to claim that most carers are women', she says,

> Nevertheless, given the accuracy of that statement, it seems to me necessary to explore the full implications of the fact. If most carers are women, do women carers feel that what they do is particularly compatible with their female identity? Do men carers feel emasculated? How do women carers feel about caring for men? How do men carers feel about caring for women? There is more to a feminist approach to knowledge than in the documentation of the role of women in a set of social processes; while this is important, it is also necessary (and even exciting) to use issues of sex and gender to illuminate those very social processes. The topics discussed in this book are always considered from a gendered perspective; in other words, I have tried throughout to think about the issues by asking the question, do sex and gender make a difference? (1987: 2)

Like most feminists who have written on this subject, Ungerson fails to incorporate into her analysis the fact that, not only are most carers women (although, as I shall discuss later, not such a large proportion as feminists have assumed), but so are most of those who receive 'care'. Her analysis of social processes involved in the issue of caring must remain incomplete while she considers only one part of the caring relationship and, far from being exciting, research such as hers is profoundly depressing from the point of view of disabled and older women who are yet again marginalised – but this time by those who proclaim their commitment to 'women-centred issues'. Even Suzy Croft (1986), who started to challenge the concepts of independence and dependence, still failed to break out of the analytical straitjacket which divides 'women' from disabled and older people.

Feminist research on carers is a valuable application of the principle 'the personal is political' and I do not underestimate the importance of the higher public profile of the needs of carers which this research has helped to bring about. However, the failure to include the subjective experience of disabled and older people has meant that the feminist analyses and strategies stemming from the research have a number of limitations. Most importantly it has resulted in a choice being posed between 'care in the community' *or* residential care, which is in many ways a false dichotomy. It is also evident that, not only are the attempts to encompass the interests of disabled and older people merely token gestures, but that the interests of carers have not been fully addressed either.

Gillian Dalley's 'Collectivism'

Although Mary McIntosh and Janet Finch were fairly explicit in their espousal of residential care and their rejection of community care policies, neither they nor most other feminists have developed this position much further; they have, in fact, tended to accept that women will carry on caring and that the most that feminists can hope for, this side of the revolution, is better domiciliary support services and respite and day care. However, as discussed above, Gillian Dalley presents a more fully developed feminist critique of community care, arguing for the development of social policy based on the principle of collectivism rather than that of familism and possessive individualism which she says motivates current community care policies.

Most disabled people would thoroughly endorse Dalley's promotion of the principles of collectivism and mutual support – individualism and self-help are not principles which do much to ensure a good quality of life for disabled people. We would also welcome her insistence that disabled and older people should 'be in a position to be responsible for his or her life choices' (Dalley, 1988: 115). The problem is that she has reached a decision about which policies should be supported and which abandoned without allowing our voices to be heard.

Like most of the feminist research on community care, Dalley has made no attempt to study the subjective experience of those who are cared for. Instead she undermines our support of 'care in the community' by claiming that either we are merely giving voice to familist ideology or that our organisations are unrepresentative. I want to examine exactly how Dalley ignores our views in order to demonstrate some of the consequences of failing to identify with the subjective experience of those who need assistance.

One of Dalley's reasons for arguing against community care policies is that she believes that these policies are not necessarily supported by 'dependent people'. In arguing this, she refers to a report of the Social Services Select Committee of the House of Commons Report on community care and 'adult mentally ill and mentally handicapped people' which stressed that 'there is still a need felt by many who are dependent for asylum in the sense of haven or refuge, away from the stresses and rigours of the world'. Dalley goes on:

It may be that many of those stresses and rigours are caused by the prejudice and heartlessness of non-disabled people and that such attitudes should be contested; it is hardly just though to expect the objects of that prejudice and heartlessness to fight that battle themselves from such an unequal and exposed position. It is important, therefore, to recognise the needs and wishes of dependent people themselves; practitioners and policy-makers may be overly susceptible to what the Select Committee report calls 'the swing of the pendulum of fashionable trends and theories'. (1988: 6)

On such a basis, Dalley insists that community care policies are not necessarily what 'dependent people' want.

Unfortunately, the only evidence that she produces to back this up with is from non-disabled people. The only time she cites the opinion of a disabled person, she quotes him out of context to support a position which he would never have agreed with. In advocating group living for disabled people, Dalley quotes Bernard Brett (whom she describes as 'heavily dependent') on the subject of the advantages of having more than one person providing personal care. 'Nothing is quite as corrupting for all concerned as being completely dependent on too few people', he says.

This also tends to exhaust the helpers, who feel under too much strain, and can lead to the risk of various kinds of abuse. I can promise you, there are few less pleasant things than to be cared for by somebody who is constantly tired and under too much strain. This makes life tense, unpleasant and unfulfilled. (quoted in Dalley, 1988: 120)

Far from advocating some kind of residential, group living situation (which is how Dalley uses this quote), Bernard Brett was describing a set-up where he had bought his own house, let rooms in it to non-disabled lodgers and employed a number of different carers. Like many disabled people, Bernard Brett described residential care as 'a form of living death' and like most non-disabled people he aspired to, and achieved, a home of his own (see Shearer, 1982: 37–48).

Bernard Brett was not, of course, receiving 'family care'. He was instead able to choose to pay (in cash and in kind) those who provided assistance to him. However, feminists such as Dalley and Finch have dismissed this as an option to support, arguing that even where assistance within the home is provided by a paid carer that carer is still likely to be a low-paid, low-status woman and, although this is also true for care workers employed in residential establishments, residential workers are more likely to be able to campaign for better pay and conditions. They also, as discussed above, see the removal of caring for disabled and older people from a family setting as a crucial part of undermining non-disabled women's dependency.

Dalley dismisses the demands that have been made by disabled people and their organisations for good quality services to enable them to live in their own homes. She insists that either such demands are merely expressions of dominant ideology or that they are made by organisations which are not representative of what she calls 'dependent people' as a whole.

She argues that 'Propounders of the familist ideal favour it [community care policies] because for them it embodies notions of the family as haven, as repository of warm, caring, human relationships based on mutual responsibility and affection and thus a private protection against a cold, hostile, outside world' (1988: 25). When disabled and older people express an aversion for residential care, according to Dalley, this must be set in the context of the strength of the ideology of the family. 'Where institutional or residential care is available, it is regarded as second-best precisely because it differs in conception so markedly from the family model of care' (Dalley, 1987: 12). We are invited to treat people's preference for living in their own homes as a kind of 'false consciousness' arising from what Dalley identifies as the 'familist' ideology which pervades our culture.

There is no recognition here that disabled people have often been denied the family relationships that she takes for granted. Insult is then added to injury by the assumption that for a disabled person to aspire to warm, caring human relationships within the setting where most non-disabled people look to find such relationships is a form of false consciousness. We are to be denied not only the rights non-disabled people take for granted, but when we demand these rights we are told that we are wrong to do so.

The other way of undermining disabled people's opposition to residential care – an insistence that our organisations are not representative – should be familiar to feminists. Anti-feminists often seek to undermine feminism by claiming that most feminists are white, young and middle class. Dalley echoes this sort of divisiveness by quoting a critic of the Independent Living Movement.

> The core constituency of the independent living movement is young, male and 'fit' as opposed to 'frail', whereas a major feature of the social reality of disablement is the elderly female, lacking in robustness and living far from the supportive confines of university campuses [where the American ILM originated]. It may well be that the disadvantages and needs of an elderly arthritic in an urban slum have more similarity to the problems of her able-bodied neighbours than to the values of the movement for independent living. (G.H. Williams, quoted in Dalley, 1988: 117)

It is certainly true that the ILM both in the USA and internationally is dominated by men. However, to use this fact to undermine the very principles and aspirations of the movement is to deny the basic human rights for which the movement stands. Dalley refers to the 'heterogeneity of dependency' by which she means that personal assistance requirements are found in a number of different situations, depending on age, type of disability, gender, personal circumstances and so on. This does not mean, however, that the aims of the ILM are only relevant to young, middle-class, white men. Such men are merely demanding what young, middle-class, white, non-disabled men take for granted. The economic and social advantages of this latter group normally enable them to achieve such things – and this is why it is common for white, middle-class young men to react with such a sense of outrage and injustice when their social and economic privileges are suddenly threatened by disability. Why shouldn't those of us whose class, race, age, gender and disability mean that we are denied such advantages, insist on the same rights?

Given non-disabled feminists' inability to identify with the subjective experience of such people, perhaps they should be wary of prescribing the kind of care that would be best for disabled and older people. Dalley, however, is not inhibited by this. Dismissing the demands of the Independent Living Movement, she advocates new forms of collective provision on the grounds that it is only by removing caring and servicing functions from a family setting that the sexual division of labour (in both the private and public sphere) will be fundamentally undermined. A sceptical disabled feminist may comment that if communal living is such a liberating force for women, then perhaps non-disabled women should try it first before imposing it on disabled and older women whose lack of social, economic and political power makes them all too easy a target for enthusiasms and fashions in social policy.

Dalley illustrates her case by arguing that a group home would make it possible for a 'bed-bound' young mother to develop an 'ungendered' role. Such a woman, says Dalley will not expect to 'take up a domestic role vis-à-vis housework and child-rearing as she would (because of normative attitudes at large) if she were able-bodied' (1988: 122). Others would perform this role for her and the advantage of a 'collective' setting, according to Dalley is that her role would be performed by men or women, depending on who was employed.

Such a solution to accommodation and personal assistance needs would be firmly rejected by disabled mothers like Sheila Willis, who I interviewed when writing *Pride against Prejudice: Transforming Attitudes to Disability* (Morris, 1991). Her clear aim after learning that she had multiple sclerosis was to remain living in her own home continuing her role of a mother caring for her daughter. Sheila rejected the word 'bed-bound': 'What me? *Bound* to a bed?' During the last two or three years of her life, she spent most of the time on her bed, organising and taking responsibility for not only her own household but also setting up a voluntary organisation which would provide physical help to other disabled people. A feminist for 15 years, her role as a mother and her ability to run her own home were intensely important to her; to deny this would be a denial of her fundamental human rights – and those of her daughter.

Gillian Dalley goes further than most feminist researchers in opposing community care policies but both their and her perspective is fundamentally limited by the common failure to consider the subjective experience of those who need assistance to be a necessary part of the research. Almost all the feminist research on carers treats those who are 'cared for' as passive recipients of that care, and in so doing they also fail to fully address the experience of carers. One (partial) exception to this is

Jane Lewis and Barbara Meredith's research on daughters caring for mothers (Lewis and Meredith, 1985). Although this research, like others, failed to study the experience of those cared for, Lewis and Meredith had a clear concept of the active role which mothers played in the relationship and the importance of this for determining the nature of the caring role (see their Chapter 4). They were thus able to focus more clearly on the needs of carers. By analysing the relationships between mothers and daughters, and the various factors influencing those relationships (for example both parties' contacts with others), they were able to distinguish positive experiences of caring from more negative ones. This then enabled an identification of the factors which need to be addressed to mitigate the negative experiences of caring (see their Chapter 7).

Unfortunately, however, most feminist research has not properly addressed both sides of the caring relationship. As Lois Keith says:

> In wanting to show how difficult and unrecognised the work of the carer is, many have thought it necessary to portray those who may be in need of care as passive, feeble and demanding. And so deep-rooted are our prejudices about both disabled and elderly people, that no one really seems to have noticed the damage this can do. It merely confirms what most of us believe about disabled people anyway – that they are more or less helpless and need to be looked after by others. In this debate, they are continuously presented as 'the other', the non-person. They are rarely seen as having valuable lives in the way their able-bodied carer or partner does. (Keith, 1990: v)

Different Questions, Different Answers

Feminists cannot claim to have developed a full analysis and adequate strategies on the issue of community care policies until the subjective experiences of disabled and older people are included within the research. Nasa Begum, a disabled feminist, recently carried out a piece of qualitative research into 10 disabled women's experience of receiving personal care which illustrates some of the ways that this subjective experience can be incorporated into a feminist analysis of 'community care' (Begum, 1990). Unfortunately, however, this research is very unusual in that, generally, the feminists who have access to the funds to carry out research are neither disabled nor old and have, so far, not been able to identify with the subjective experience of those who are.

Disabled feminists (were they properly represented within the academic and research community) would raise different questions when carrying out research on community care and would not be faced with the stark choice which Finch has posed between community care or residential care.

Instead of focusing on the 'taking charge of' part of Hilary Graham's definition of 'caring about' (Graham, 1983: 13), such research would focus more clearly on the reciprocity involved in caring relationships and the threats to that reciprocity. We would do this because it is the loss of reciprocity which brings about inequality within a relationship – and disabled and older people are very vulnerable within the unequal relationships which they commonly experience with the non-disabled world.

There has been very little attention paid to disabled and older people's experience of physical and emotional abuse within caring relationships. Such abuse occurs within both residential and community care and takes place in the context of physical and economic dependence where the person being cared for experiences a fundamental inequality in their relationship with those providing physical care. This is an issue which affects both disabled men and women but as Nasa Begum points out, 'Women with disabilities are particularly vulnerable when the practices and assumptions which shape current provision fail to recognise that the nature of the personal care relationship is such that it can legitimise and endorse oppression' (Begum, 1990: 41). It is particularly unfortunate that feminism's concern with the various forms of abuse experienced by non-disabled women has generally failed to incorporate the experience of disabled women.

We need to ask whether people want to receive physical care from someone they care about and who cares for them. For someone like Clare Robson, who has multiple sclerosis and lives with her lover and her children, the answer is clear:

> I know that I am loved and that I love her. I feel very privileged and secure. I never, ever, anticipated a relationship that was so wonderful and loving. Obviously there are difficulties. There are, in effect, three of us – me, her and the MS – and we have to take account of the uninvited guest, the squatter. (Morris, 1991: 164)

On the other hand, Simon Brisenden identified that where there are no other options than dependence on a relative or partner then this can be 'the most exploitative of all forms of so-called care delivered in our society today for it exploits both the carer and the person receiving care. It ruins relationships between people and results in thwarted life opportunities on both sides of the caring equation' (Brisenden, 1989: 9–10).

Research needs to examine what makes 'caring for' in a 'caring about' relationship possible in a way which meets the interests of both parties. Many disabled people have clearly identified that 'caring for' in a 'caring about' relationship cannot work unless there is real choice based on real alternatives. Such a choice cannot exist where the only alternative to assistance by a partner or relative at home is residential care.

Where the choice is between unsupported (or minimally supported) 'family care' and residential care, the physical and emotional suffering incurred by both parties to a caring relationship is often enormous. This is starkly apparent, for example, in the case of one of the respondents in Patricia Owen's study where it was only the provision of services within the home which prevented a disabled mother from being restrained against her will within residential care away from her 3-year-old daughter (Owen, 1987: 21–3). Surely feminists should be supporting strategies which would promote adequate support to people who wish to remain outside, or leave, residential care, rather than washing their hands of community care policies because of the way that such policies currently bolster women's dependency within the family.

Feminist research which incorporated the experiences of disabled and older people might also raise the question of the meaning of the word 'home', separating this out, in a conceptual and political sense, from the feminist critique of the family. Disabled feminists should be able to assert their right to live in their own home without being accused of supporting the oppression of women within the family. Indeed, non-disabled feminists in other contexts have insisted on women's rights to a home (for example, Watson, 1986) yet in their opposition to community care policies and their aim of undermining the family and women's dependence within it, they are in danger of denying one group of women the right to a home.

Feminist research on caring insists that most carers are women. 'In general', says Hilary Graham, 'caring relationships are those involving women; it is the presence of a woman – as wife, mother, daughter, neighbour, friend – which marks out a relationship as, potentially at least, a caring one' (Graham, 1983: 15). Disabled feminists would point out that in fact we now know that there are 2.5 million male carers and 3.5 million female carers, although women are more likely to be full-time carers (Green, 1988) and that it is of fundamental concern to (particularly heterosexual) disabled women to challenge the assumption that men will not 'care for' in a 'caring about' relationship.

This assumption is often experienced as oppressive by disabled women, confronted by health and social services professionals who undermine the ability of such women to sustain heterosexual relationships. For example, it seems to be common for married women entering Spinal Injury Units, particularly if they are tetraplegic, to encounter a negative attitude towards the chances of their marriages surviving their disability. One woman's husband was told by her consultant that '75% of marriages go bang and to get rid of our double bed. I am sure this stayed with him and did not give our personal life a chance. He left 15 months after I came home' (Morris, 1989: 83).

Hilary Land has raised the issue of men caring in the context of the increasing trends towards early retirement/redundancy amongst men in the 55–64-year-old age group. 'This means', she says, 'that one important legitimate reason not to care, namely that priority should be given to their paid work, is being removed very rapidly from growing numbers of middle-aged men' (Land, 1989: 155). If such men are carers they are most likely to be caring for their wives. In 1986, 46 per cent of British women in the 45–64 age group reported long-standing illness and for 28 per cent their illness limited their activities (*General Household Survey*, 1989: 147). We need to know more about the experiences of the significant number of women in both this age group and in older age groups who rely on their husbands for care.

However, it is also of significance that roughly the same levels of long-standing illness are found amongst men in these age groups, which must mean that there are many households where both partners require some level of care. Indeed, among the elderly population there is evidence that significant numbers of carers are also in need of care. In this situation we need to know what factors enable or prevent women from getting the care they need.

Feminist research has tended to draw very distinct lines between carers and those who are cared for. This means that the extent to which older and disabled women are also carers is obscured. Lois Keith, in criticising the feminist research on carers, is writing from the perspective of having 'made the overnight transition from someone who was essentially a carer – a wife, mother of two young children, part-time teacher – to someone who was, in addition to these roles, sometimes in need of care' (Keith, 1990: v). Research on women who have experienced spinal cord injury found that 'women are primarily the carers within a family and most of us continue in this role. Yet too often it is assumed that we will be the passive recipients of care' (Morris, 1989: 188). Pam Evans, herself disabled and whose husband has ME, has a positive experience of a reciprocal relationship 'He looks after me, and I look after him, in complete equality and peace – it's what marriage is in its true sense, a harmonious way of living and a bastion against all external conflicts and demands' (Morris, 1991: 167).

The failure of feminist researchers and academics to identify with the subjective experience of those who receive care has meant that they have studied caring situations where there are seemingly very clear distinctions between the person who cares for and the person who receives care. Their assumptions have led them to seek out carers and the most common source of identifying potential interviewees is organisations (statutory authorities and voluntary organisations) to whom people have identified themselves as carers. However, a situation in which one party to a relationship has a clear identity as a carer while the other is clearly cared for can only represent one type of caring relationship – and may, in fact, not be the most common. If we focused not just on the subjective experience of those identified as carers but also on the other party to the caring relationship we may find that in some situations the roles are blurred, or shifting. We may also want to expand our definition of caring for, to encompass not just physical tasks but also the emotional part of caring for relationships. Research carried out by disabled feminists would, therefore, focus not so much on car*ers* as on car*ing*.

In their insistence that provision and control over personal assistance services are a human right, disabled people and their organisations are actually mounting a fundamental attack on the family – an attack which non-disabled feminists should be supporting rather than undermining. Simon Brisenden's 'Charter for personal care' rejects the way in which disabled and older people are forced to look for support from their relatives and partners, arguing that we should receive the financial support to enable us to make free choices about the kind of personal assistance we require (Brisenden, 1989). Such a demand is not unrealistic, as has been shown by the introduction of the Independent Living Fund in Britain in 1988 and direct payments legislation in 1996 which provide a grant (albeit a means-tested one) to cover the cost of personal care, has shown. Non-disabled feminists would serve us better by joining with us in promoting such policies rather than assuming that the only way to mount an attack on women's caring role within the family is to consign us to residential care.

Disabled people would join with non-disabled feminists in rejecting the way that 'community care' too often means 'family care'. But we would assert our own political demand – a demand for the right to live within the community in a non-disabling environment with the kind of personal assistance that we would choose. In doing this, we are not only pursuing the human rights of disabled and older people but also launching an attack on the form that caring currently takes. Such a strategy should therefore also be clearly supported by feminists who wish to undermine women's dependency within the family.

References

Bayley, M. (1973) *Mental Handicap and Community Care*. London: Routledge & Kegan Paul.

Begum, N. (1990) *The Burden of Gratitude*. Warwick: University of Warwick and SCA.

Brisenden, S. (1989) 'A charter for personal care', *Progress*, 16, Disablement Income Group.

Croft, S. (1986) 'Women, caring and the recasting of need', *Critical Social Policy*, 16: 23–39.

Dalley, G. (1987) 'Women's welfare', *New Society* 28 Aug.

Dalley, G. (1988) *Ideologies of Caring – Rethinking Community and Collectivism*. London: Macmillan.

Finch, J. (1984) 'Community care: developing non-sexist alternatives', *Critical Social Policy*, 9: 6–18.

Finch, J. and Groves, D. (eds) (1983) *A Labour of Love – Women, Work and Caring*. London: Routledge & Kegan Paul.

General Household Survey 1986 (1989) London: HMSO.

Graham, H. (1983) 'Caring: a labour of love', in J. Finch and D. Groves (eds) *A Labour of Love – Women, Work and Caring*. London: Routledge & Kegan Paul.

Green, H. (1988) 'Informal carers', *General Household Survey 1985*, Supplement A, HMSO.

Keith, L. (1990) 'Caring partnership', *Community Care* 22 Feb. suppl. pp. v–vi.

Land, H. (1989) 'The construction of dependency', in J. Lewis Bulmer and D. Piachaud (eds), *The Goals of Social Policy*. London: Unwin Hyman.

Lewis, J. and Meredith, B. (1985) *Daughters Who Care*. London: Routledge.

McIntosh, M. (1979) 'The welfare state and the needs of the dependent family', in S. Burman (ed.), *Fit Work for Women*. London: Croom Helm.

McIntosh, M. (1981) 'Feminism and social policy', *Critical Social Policy* 1, and this volume pp. 13–26.

Morris, J. (1989) *Able Lives – Women's Experience of Paralysis*. London: Women's Press.

Morris, J. (1991) *Pride Against Prejudice – Transforming Attitudes to Disability*. London: Women's Press.

Owen, P. (1987) *Community Care and Severe Physical Disability*. London: Bedford Square Press/NCVO.

Shearer, A. (1982) *Living Independently*. CEH and King's Fund.

Ungerson, C. (1987) *Policy is Personal*. London: Tavistock.

Walker, A. (ed.) (1982) *Community Care: The Family, the State and Social Policy*. Oxford: Blackwell/Martin Robertson.

Watson, S. with Austerberry, H. (1986) *Housing and Homelessness: A Feminist Perspective*. London: Routledge & Kegan Paul.

Wilson, E. (1977) *Women and the Welfare State*. London: Tavistock.

5

Institutional Discrimination against Disabled People and the Campaign for Anti-discrimination Legislation

Colin Barnes

Evidence showing that disabled people have a significantly poorer standard of living to that of non-disabled people is now overwhelming and beyond dispute (Barnes, 1991; Martin and White, 1988; Thompson et al., 1990). Disabled people and their organisations have identified institutional discrimination as the principal cause of the problem, and anti-discrimination legislation as the best way of dealing with it. During the last 10 years there have been several abortive attempts to get such legislation on to the statute books (Barnes, 1991; Bynoe et al., 1991; Oliver, 1985). Hitherto successive Conservative governments have blocked the introduction of these bills arguing that there is little if any evidence of widespread discrimination against disabled people.

Behind the opposition to anti-discrimination legislation lie the assumptions of the traditional individualistic medical view of disability explaining the difficulties encountered by disabled people in terms of individually based functional limitations. This has led to the assertion that there are few specific examples of discrimination against disabled people. This explanation does not correspond with the views of disabled people and their organisations, who argue that most of the problems they encounter are socially created and that discrimination is an everyday occurrence. This chapter will articulate these arguments and explain why, in late 20th-century Britain, disabled people are demanding legal protection from institutional discrimination.

Definitions and Terminology

Traditional explanations for the extreme economic and social deprivations experienced by disabled people rest on the assumption of the individual medical model of disability. Official bodies such as the World Health

First published in *Critical Social Policy*, 34, 1992.

Organisation (WHO) and the Office of Populations Censuses and Surveys (OPCS) employ functional assessments of disability based on a threefold distinction between impairment, disability and handicap. 'Impairment' refers to a defective limb, organ or mechanism of the body, 'disability', is the resulting lack of function, and 'handicap' denotes the limitations on daily living which ensue from disability (see Martin et al., 1988; Wood, 1981).

Relying upon able-bodied assumptions about the experience of disablement, these definitions individualise and medicalise the problems associated with living with an impairment. Because they remain close to medical classifications of disease they ensure that individuals with impairments are perceived as primarily responsible for the economic and social difficulties they encounter during the course of their daily lives. It is not surprising, therefore, that they are rejected by disabled people and their organisations; that is organisations controlled and run by disabled people themselves such as the British Council of Organisations of Disabled People (BCODP) and Disabled People's International (DPI) (Davis, 1986; Finkelstein, 1985; Oliver, 1990).

They, along with a growing number of professionals and policy makers – especially outside Britain, have recognised that the principal cause of the disadvantage experienced by disabled people is not impairment, but restrictive environments and disabling barriers; a perspective generally referred to as the social model of disability (Oliver, 1986, 1990). Thus, 'disability' represents a complex system of social constraints imposed upon people with impairments by a highly discriminatory society – to be a disabled person means to be discriminated against. The problem is compounded for disabled members of the lesbian and gay communities, Black people and women with impairments (Campling, 1981; Conference of Indian Organisations, 1987; Lesbian and Gay Committee, 1990; Lonsdale, 1990; Morris, 1989).

Moreover, in the same way that gay men, lesbians, racial and ethnic minorities, and women have identified the power of language in the promotion of homophobia, heterosexism, racism and sexism, so too disabled people are sensitive to the way words perpetuate disablism: attitudes and policies which perpetuate inequality between disabled and non-disabled people. In order to counter discriminatory language the BCODP and the DPI have actively promoted a twofold classification, similar to that first developed by the Union of the Physically Impaired Against Segregation (UPIAS) in 1975, which redefines impairment and disability. Hence:

Impairment - is the functional limitation within the individual caused by physical, mental or sensory impairment.
Disability - is the loss or limitation of opportunities to take part in the normal life of the community on an equal level with others due to physical and social barriers.

'Disabled people', therefore, refers to all those with impairments, regardless of cause, who experience disability as social restriction; whether those restrictions are due to inaccessible built environments, the inability of the general public to use sign language, the lack of reading material in braille, or hostile public attitudes to people with non-visible impairments such as epilepsy or sickle cell anaemia (Oliver, 1990). Consequently, discrimination is not simply a question of specific examples of individuals discriminating against individual disabled people, although this is not an uncommon view. It is institutionalised within the very fabric of our society.

Following recent studies of sex and race relations in Britain (Ginsburg, 1988; Gregory, 1987; McCrudden, 1981), institutional discrimination is a complex form of discrimination which operates throughout society and is supported by history and culture. Historically, disabled people have been viewed with a variety of emotions including suspicion, ridicule and pity (Thomas, 1982). Until fairly recently they have been excluded almost completely from all aspects of community life (Scull, 1984). Indeed, our culture is replete with disablist imagery and language which keeps the traditional fears and prejudices which surround impairment alive (Biklen and Bogdana, 1977).

Institutional discrimination is evident when the policies and activities of all types of modern organisation result in inequality between disabled people and non-disabled people. It is embedded in the excessive paternalism of contemporary welfare systems and is apparent when they are systematically ignoring or meeting inadequately the needs of disabled people. It is also evident when these agencies are regularly interfering in the lives of disabled people as a means of social control in ways, and/or to an extent not experienced by non-disabled people. It incorporates the extreme forms of prejudice and intolerance usually associated with individual or direct discrimination, as well as the more covert and unconscious attitudes which contribute to and maintain indirect and/or passive discriminatory practices. Within this frame of reference direct, indirect and passive discrimination are not easily distinguishable concepts but are intertwined in most contents. It is, therefore, a descriptive concept related to outcome (Barnes, 1991; Oliver and Barnes, 1991).

Institutional Discrimination in Contemporary Britain

The Education System

Mainly because of traditional negative assumptions surrounding impairment, disabled children and young people are still not legally entitled to the same type of schooling as their non-disabled counterparts. Following over a century of largely state-sponsored education most British schools, colleges and universities are not prepared to accommodate students with impairments in a mainstream setting. Hence, more than a third of those under 16 (Meltzer et al., 1989) and almost nine-tenths of those in the older age groups (Smith, 1990; Stowell, 1987) have little choice but to accept segregated 'special' facilities which on the whole do not provide them with the essential skills either to get a job or live independently as adults (BCODP, 1986).

The widespread segregation of disabled children is not due to over-crowding in mainstream schools. Since the 1970s the number of children in the school population as a whole has dropped by almost a fifth, yet while 2,962 ordinary schools have closed the figure for 'special' schools is only 177 (DES, 1990). It is not a lack of resources which is the problem, it is an unwillingness to change. In 1989 Local Education Authorities (LEAs) in England and Wales spent £820 million on special education; most of it went on segregated schooling rather than integration (CSIE, 1989). Since 1981, 15 LEAs have increased the numbers of disabled children they send to special schools – and some have done so by more than 25 per cent (Swann, 1991). In addition, there has been a considerable expansion in post-16 provision during the 1980s, yet fewer than one in five colleges of further and higher education have a policy on the admission of disabled students; and those which have specialise in 'special' and 'low-level' courses (Stowell, 1987).

There is also substantial evidence that in academic terms the learning experience for disabled children in separate school environments compares unfavourably with that of non-disabled children in mainstream classes (DES, 1986, 1989a, 1989b). Much of the further education provided for disabled students concentrates on 'social training', 'general life skills' and specialist impairment-related skills rather than employment training (Stowell, 1987). Further, although all non-disabled young people aged 16 or 17 are eligible for a place on a Youth Training (YT) course, disabled young people can be refused on the basis that their employment prospects are minimal (Glendinning and Hirst, 1989).

As a result, the lack of qualifications, unemployment, social isolation and dependence on services are especially high among disabled young people (Barnes, 1990; Hirst, 1987; Kuh et al., 1988; Martin et al., 1989; Prescott Clarke, 1990; Walker, 1982). Indeed, by producing educationally and socially 'disabled' young adults in this way the 'special' education system perpetuates the misguided belief that disabled people are somehow inadequate, and in so doing legitimates discrimination in all other areas of social life – particularly in employment.

The Labour Market

In all modern societies work is essential for an individual's economic and social well-being (Fagin and Little, 1984). But in conjunction with educational and environmental factors attitudes and practices which discriminate against disabled people's employment are entrenched in the British labour market. They are conspicuous in the policies of employers who discriminate openly against workers with impairments, and employment agencies, both public and private, when they direct disabled people into low-status occupations (see for example Graham et al., 1990; Fry, 1986; Mainstream, 1990).

Consistently, official statistics show that disabled people are three times more likely to be out of work than non-disabled people. At every age disabled workers are unemployed longer than non-disabled workers. During the 1980s proportionately three times as many disabled people as non-disabled people were out of work for two years or more. When disabled people do find employment it is usually low skilled, poorly paid work with poor working conditions and few opportunities for advancement. Only 12 per cent of the disabled workforce hold professional or managerial jobs compared with 21 per cent for non-disabled workers (DE, 1990; Prescott Clarke, 1990). Furthermore, most of the management posts in organisations specialising in the employment of disabled people such as 'Remploy' and 'Outset' are held by non-disabled people (Dutton et al., 1990; Hurst, 1990; Mainstream, 1990). Generally, disabled workers earn much less than non-disabled workers. Disabled men in full-time work earn almost a quarter less than non-disabled men, and disabled women earn a third less than disabled men (Martin and White, 1988). This level of inequality accelerates the downward spiral of multiple deprivation in which the majority of disabled people find themselves.

The Social Security System

More than three-quarters (78 per cent) of Britain's 6.2 million disabled people (54 per cent of whom are below retirement age) have to depend on social security benefits in order to survive. Additionally, they are substantially poorer than their non-disabled neighbours because their basic living costs are much higher. Because disabled people live in a non-disabled environment they have to spend more on making their homes accessible, on personal and domestic assistance, and on food, clothing and travel. Inevitably, these costs increase as impairment increases. Government sources say the extra costs of impairment average at £6.10 per week (1988 prices) (Martin and White, 1988). Independent estimates show it to be much higher. The Disablement Income Group (DIG), for example, put the figure at £69.92 (Thompson et al., 1989). All agree that disabled people have a much lower standard of living than non-disabled people.

Moreover, the present disability benefit system is highly discriminatory and effectively discourages those who struggle for personal autonomy and economic independence. People with similar impairments receive vastly different amounts according to the cause of their impairment, their work record, their age, their marital status and even their country of residence prior to claiming. For example, an unemployed disabled man on a war pension can get up to four and a half times a week more in benefits than someone with a similar impairment who has never worked, and who has not lived in Britain for the previous 20 years (Disability Alliance, 1990a).

All disabled claimants have to emphasise their limitations instead of their strengths to doctors, social workers and/or other professional 'experts' before benefits are paid (Wood, 1990). In addition, disability benefits do not cover impairment-related costs for those in work. Consequently, disabled workers have less disposable income than their non-disabled colleagues. Moreover, since most of the jobs available to disabled people are low paid many have little choice but to endure unemployment (IFF, 1990). The inevitable outcome is an existence characterised by excessive poverty and enforced dependence.

Health and Social Support Services

Disabled people's dependence on the non-disabled community is compounded by the present system of health and social support services, most of which are dominated by the interests of the professionals who run them, and the traditional assumption that people with impairments are unable to take charge of their own lives (Wood, 1990; Davis, 1990). Independent living means disabled people have access to and control of a range of community-based services which empower them to identify and pursue their own lifestyle. However, because of the poverty which comes with impairment disabled people have no choice but to use services provided by local authorities' Social Services Departments. Most of the money spent on these services goes on institutional type care and professionals' salaries (Gray et al., 1988; Oliver, 1990; Wolfensberger, 1989). Neither give disabled people the same level of autonomy and independence as non-disabled people.

Official figures suggest that approximately 422,000 disabled people live in institutions (Martin et al., 1988). Of these, 20 per cent are below retirement age and most of them are in old people's homes, psychiatric and geriatric hospitals, or in ordinary hospital wards (Royal College of Physicians, 1986). Before disabled people living in the community can have access to essential services like personal and domestic assistance they must have their individual and family circumstances assessed by 'professional experts': doctors, social workers and the like. 'Case' or 'care managers' are then appointed to organise and co-ordinate services (HMSO, 1989); control does not rest with the person receiving the service. Disabled people's opportunities for economic and social integration are severely restricted by the absence of relevant information, appropriate technical aids and a comprehensive personal assistant service. Consequently, the majority are forced to rely on informal unpaid helpers; this usually means women family members or friends (Martin et al., 1989). Current services, therefore, not only fail to provide disabled people with opportunities to live independently in the community, but also deny them the dignity of independence within the context of personal relationships and the family home.

The Built Environment

The spiral of dependence is intensified further by a hostile physical environment. Though personal mobility has become increasingly important for all sections of the community, particularly with regard to employment, disabled people are confronted with inaccessible homes, inaccessible transport and inaccessible buildings.

Although there are now over 4.25 million disabled people with 'mobility related impairments' in Britain (Martin et al., 1988) there are only around 80,000 accessible homes. Moreover, a substantial proportion of these are set apart from 'normal' housing estates in 'special needs housing ghettos' where disabled people are cut off from their families, their friends and the non-disabled community as a whole (Rowe, 1990). Most of Britain's buses, taxis and trains are inaccessible to disabled people (DPTAC, 1989). 'Special' transport systems such as 'Dial-a-Ride', for example, are usually segregated and inferior to those available to non-disabled people. In London, Dial-a-Ride services are so limited that users can only get one return journey every ten and a half weeks (Nichols, 1991). A wide variety of public and private buildings are inaccessible and disabled people's needs are still ignored by town planners and architects. A recent study by the influential Research Institute for Consumer Affairs found that steps, heavy doors, inaccessible toilets and other barriers continue to prevent disabled people from doing even routine daily tasks like shopping without someone else's help (*Which*, 1989).

Leisure and Social Life

Along with unemployment, a lack of money and a heightened and unnecessary dependence upon others, environmental factors are a major factor in the exclusion of disabled people from the type of leisure and social activities which non-disabled people take for granted. Many pubs, restaurants, art galleries, theatres, concert halls, cinemas and sports stadia are inaccessible to disabled people (Carnegie Council Review, 1988). There is also widespread ignorance (Dillon, 1990) and sometimes prejudice (Harper, 1990) against disabled people among those who work in the entertainment industry. Books and newspapers are rarely published in accessible forms for people with visual impairments, and television and film companies continue to produce programmes which ignore the language of the deaf community (Barnes, 1991). In several concert halls lone disabled people have to be accompanied by a non-disabled steward, some theatres and cinemas do not allow people who use wheelchairs in without a non-disabled companion, and others do not allow them in at all (Crouch et al., 1989).

Enforced dependence and discrimination in the leisure industry means that many disabled people have few friends and experience extreme social isolation (Barnes, 1990; Hirst, 1987; Martin et al., 1989). This is not helped by the distorted view of disability presented through the media: newspapers, television and the advertising industry. On the whole, disabled people are ignored by the press and TV companies, so diminishing their role in society, but when they are depicted it is usually in ways which perpetuate the traditional prejudices and fears surrounding impairment (Barnes, 1991, 1992; BRU, 1990; Wertheimer, 1988). Probably the best example is the way in which charity advertisers present disabled people as pitiable and pathetic in order to raise money (Campbell, 1990).

The Political System

Much of this can be explained with reference to the fact that until fairly recently disabled people have not had a credible collective voice with which to articulate their views. Consequently, successive governments have been able to successfully avoid and even deny the extent of institutional discrimination against disabled people. Indeed, research on the political participation of disabled people in the 1987 general election shows that many did not even appear on the electoral register. Others, notably blind and deaf people, did not have access to the political information necessary to make an informed choice. Inaccessible transport and physical access to polling stations prevented still more from exercising their democratic right to vote (Fry, 1987; Ward, 1987). Traditional organisations and charities claiming to represent disabled people are prevented from being actively involved in politics because of their charitable status. Furthermore, there is no opportunity within the present party system for politicians to get disability issues as perceived by disabled people on to the political agenda (Oliver, 1990).

Additionally, successive governments have been reluctant to support organisations of disabled people which accurately reflect disabled people's views. In 1990, the British Council of Organisations of Disabled people (BCODP), the national umbrella organisation of organisations of disabled people received only £30,000 from central government. The Royal Association for Disability and Rehabilitation (RADAR), on the other hand, the national equivalent for traditional organisations for disabled people and disability charities got £233,000 (*Hansard*, 24 April 1990, cols 160–4). Unlike charities and traditional organisations for disabled people, which are controlled and run by non-disabled people, organisations of disabled people are controlled and run by disabled people themselves. Historically, the former have purported to represent disabled people's interests to government and have been used and supported by them for this express purpose. In general, they lack direct contact with disabled people and are very inadequately accountable to them (Large, 1981).

Government Policy and Disabled People

A great deal of the responsibility for the persistence of institutional discrimination against disabled people rests with a succession of British governments since 1945. While there is a growing consensus throughout the democratic world that disabled people have the same basic human rights as non-disabled people, and that it is the responsibility of governments to ensure that they are able to secure a standard of living comparable to that of their fellow citizens, this has not occurred in the United Kingdom. This is particularly disturbing since Britain was one of the first western nations to establish the notion of rights for disabled people in law with the setting up of the welfare state in the 1940s, and because almost everything that has happened since has been a gradual but significant retreat from this position. Further, although the British government endorsed the United Nations Programme of Action Concerning Disabled Persons in 1982, to date it has failed to introduce policies which will enable disabled people to achieve a comparable lifestyle to that of non-disabled people (Bynoe, 1991).

The Education Act 1944 introduced the principle that disabled children should be educated alongside their peers, and the Disabled Persons (Employment) Act 1944 attempted to secure employment rights for disabled workers. However, non-enforcement of these tentative rights, coupled with the subsequent gradual but intensifying drift from rights-based to needs-based policies, has served to underline the significance of the traditional individual medical approach to disability, the very opposite of what is needed (Barnes, 1991; Oliver and Barnes, 1991). This is evident in each of the areas mentioned above.

With regard to education, while reiterating the principle of integration the Warnock Report (1978) and the 1981 Education Act both explicitly underlined and emphasised the importance of the concept of Special Educational Needs within the education system as a whole. This is a policy which has not only been used to justify the continued and widespread segregation of a substantial proportion of the student population, but also the exclusion of minority languages and cultures from the mainstream sector, in particular the language and culture of the deaf community (Reiser and Mason, 1990).

The introduction of the employment quota scheme with the Disabled Persons (Employment) Act 1944 secured employment rights for disabled people. Yet the reluctance of subsequent governments to enforce it along with their overt predilection for voluntary policies of persuasion, have failed to provide disabled people with meaningful employment and, at the same time, emphasised the traditional divisions between disabled and non-disabled workers. The quota scheme specifies that all firms employing more than 20 workers must employ 3 per cent of their workforce from the disabled persons' employment register. The maximum fine for employers who break the law was set in 1944 at £100; it has never been updated. Although the overwhelming majority of employers ignore the quota scheme, there have only ever been nine prosecutions and the last was in 1975 (Lonsdale, 1986). Moreover, negative presumptions concerning disabled people's work potential are constantly reinforced by the Department of Employment's half-hearted attempts to persuade employers to employ individual disabled workers. Policies such as 'Fit for Work' and the 'Code of Good Practice on the Employment of Disabled People' (Warnock, 1978) stick closely to the traditional medical view of disability. The latest edition of the 'Code' has been seen by less than a fifth of all employers, and of these only a third felt that it had heightened the 'employability' of disabled workers (Morrell, 1990).

Although government sources have at last publicly acknowledged that disabled people and their families receive significantly lower incomes than those of the rest of the population (Martin and White, 1988) recent changes to the disability benefits system will not change this situation. Throughout the 1980s disabled people have seen the value of disability allowances reduced as a succession of Conservative governments have tried to cut social security spending. The long awaited disability benefits review of 1990 will only help a small number of disabled people in a very limited way and offers no help whatsoever to those who are above retirement age (Disability Alliance, 1990a).

Equally important, the 1988 social security reforms signalled a significant erosion of disabled people's rights, as well as an intensification of un-necessary bureaucratic regulation and control. Under the old supplemen-tary benefit system disabled people were legally entitled to 10 additional allowances for impairment related costs as well as lump sum payments for major items such as furniture and household equipment. Disabled people now have to apply for means tested discretionary grants or loans from two cash-limited funds, the Social Fund and the Independent Living Fund (Disability Alliance, 1990a; Glendinning, 1991).

A similar situation exists with regard to health and social support services for disabled people. While the systematic withdrawal of statutory rights can be traced back to the 1948 National Assistance Act, it has intensified greatly in recent years. Although the 1948 Act imposed a duty on local authorities to provide a range of services for disabled people it also allowed them to designate responsibility for provision to charities. This led to a huge variation in both the quality and the availability of local services in different parts of the country. Moreover, contrary to the views of some non-disabled observers (Topliss and Gould, 1981) the 1970 Chronically Sick and Disabled Persons Act did little to change this situation (Keeble, 1979; Oliver, 1990). The subsequent growth in the number of professionals employed in the disability and 'caring' industries during the 1970s also served to reinforce the traditional view that disabled people are incapable of accepting the responsibilities and rights of citizenship.

The 1980s have seen a further retreat from the notion of rights as a result of policy makers' apparent preference for voluntary rather than statutory run services. While the introduction of the 1986 Disabled Persons (Services, Consultation and Representation) Act promised meaningful collaboration between service users and providers, there is widespread disregard for the law by local authorities. For example, Section 10 of the Act required local authorities to consult with organisations of disabled people when planning services. Government research shows that most have chosen to speak to voluntary organisations for disabled people and charities; many simply do not bother – only one London borough can boast 'a positive stance' toward disability organisations (Warburton, 1990). Further, it has recently been announced that key sections of the 1986 Act which would have secured the right of disabled people to have an advocate should they need one, given them the right to ask local authorities for services, and the right to have a written statement following their needs assessment are not to be implemented (*Hansard*, 22 March 1991).

Additionally, disabled people's right to an independent lifestyle will still be inhibited by inaccessible homes, inaccessible transport, and an inaccessible physical environment. Although there is a chronic shortage of accessible homes there are no government plans to remedy this situation in either the public or the private sectors, and segregated 'special needs' housing remains central to the government's community care plans (HMSO, 1989). Even though the Department of Transport support in principle fully accessible buses, taxis and trains, it is generally agreed that it will be well into the next century before they are anything approaching the norm rather than the exception. At present there is no legislation which compels transport providers to make their vehicles accessible. Additionally, although recent amendments to the building regulations clearly acknowledge disabled people's rights of access to public buildings, such measures have not and will not eradicate discrimination in the built environment. This is especially relevant in the leisure industry where inaccessible buildings play a significant role in the exclusion of disabled people from mainstream recreational activities like concerts, plays and sporting fixtures.

This continual denial of equal rights for disabled people by a succession of British governments is especially unacceptable when other disadvantaged groups in the British Isles have some protection under the law, and when legislation to combat institutional disablism is increasingly common throughout the western world. In mainland Britain the Sex Discrimination Act (1975) and the Race Relations Act (1976) prohibit discrimination on the grounds of gender and race, and in Northern Ireland the Fair Employment (Northern Ireland) acts (1976 and 1989) outlaw discrimination in employment on religious grounds. America, Australia, Canada, France and several other European states now have laws specifically aimed at removing the restrictive environments and disabling barriers which confront disabled people (Bynoe, 1991). Indeed, the overtly unequal treatment accorded disabled people in Britain has promoted an almost universal demand from disabled people and their organisations for similar legislation; it is a demand which is unlikely to diminish.

The Political Emancipation of Disabled People and the Campaign for Anti-discrimination Legislation

Within the British context the roots of disabled people's fight for equal rights can be traced back as far as the last century with the formation in the 1890s of the British Deaf Association and the National League of the Blind (Pagel, 1988). But the movement really took hold during the 1960s with the struggle for independence by a group of disabled residents in residential institutions, and the setting up of the DIG by two disabled women in 1965 to lobby Parliament for improved disability benefits. The proliferation of disability organisations in the ensuing decade and the lack of progress in securing a comprehensive disability income resulted in the formation of an umbrella organisation known as the Disability Alliance (DA) in 1975.

Largely due to the influence of non-disabled professionals, both the DIG and the DA have concerned themselves primarily with the financial needs of disabled people. This is an approach rooted in the traditional assumption that disabled people are economically and socially dependent on the non-disabled community. It is a strategy which perpetuates this myth by ignoring the root causes of disabled people's dependence, that is, their widespread and systematic exclusion from the mainstream economic and social life of the community (UPIAS, 1976). Organisations controlled and run by disabled people favour a more radical approach commensurate with that of the Independent Living Movement (ILM) in the USA (Finkelstein, 1991; Oliver, 1990).

From the mid-1970s onwards, organisations of disabled people such as UPIAS, formed in 1974; the Liberation Network, who functioned mainly through the publication of a magazine entitled *In From the Cold* between 1979 and 1983; and the early disabled women's movement in the form of 'Sisters Against Disability', have all shared the same basic goals: securing equal rights for disabled people and the removal of negative discrimination in all its forms. These goals were later adopted by the handful of organisations which came together to form the BCODP in 1981. A member of Disabled People's International (DPI) from the outset, the BCODP now includes 82 organisations representing over 250,000 disabled individuals.

Self-organisation and developments at the international level precipitated a significant intensification of the campaign for equal rights during the 1980s. In 1985 the Voluntary Organisations for Anti-Discrimination Legislation (VOADL) was established. The formation of VOADL is important because it signalled the decisive coming together of organisations of disabled people, such as the BCODP, along with a number of the traditional organisations for disabled people like RADAR and the Spastics Society. VOADL's existence is a clear indication of the growing strength of the disability movement in Britain; hitherto several organisations for disabled people had advised British governments that discrimination was not a problem, and that anti-discrimination legislation was unnecessary (notwithstanding that in 1979 the Silver Jubilee Access Committee had identified a number of 'blatant acts of discrimination against disabled people', and that the official committee which investigated these claims came to the conclusion that discrimination was widespread and that laws to prevent it were essential [CORAD, 1982]). Nevertheless, in spite of this apparent unity of purpose there remain crucial differences between the inherently paternalistic approach of these organisations and the emancipatory philosophy of the BCODP (Oliver and Barnes, 1991).

In addition to being at the forefront of the campaign for disabled people's rights the BCODP and its member organisations have produced a range of policy initiatives which have transformed the lives of many disabled people in Britain. These include policies which enable people with impairments to throw off the shackles of unnecessary bureaucratic regulation and control; to earn a living rather than live off the state; to achieve personal autonomy to a degree comparable to that of their non-disabled peers; and to expand their role as consumers. These initiatives have firmly established the BCODP as the only truly representative voice of disabled people in Britain (Barnes, 1991; Hasler, 1991; Oliver, 1990).

The BCODP's success has also prompted an increasing number of disabled individuals to adopt a collective disabled identity and take a more direct approach to political participation. Much of the inspiration for this radicalisation stems from America, in particular the strategies adopted by the Civil Rights Movement and the ILM. In the USA the Civil Rights Movement of the 1960s had an enormous influence on the securing of disabled people's rights, and the manner by which those rights were secured. When traditional legal channels were exhausted, disabled Americans employed other techniques of social protest including organised boycotts, sit ins and street demonstrations (Oliver, 1990).

However, the excessive paternalism of the welfare state coupled with the absence of a strong British Civil Rights tradition has caused disabled people in Britain to be relatively cautious in their choice of tactics. But this situation has changed dramatically over the last three or four years. Despite the enormity of the environmental barriers confronting them they have been taking to the streets in increasingly large numbers to protest against institutional discrimination in all its forms. Since the 'Rights not Charity' march of July 1988 there have been a growing number of demonstrations and civil disobedience campaigns by disabled people and their supporters up and down the country on a range of issues including: inaccessible transport, an inaccessible environment, the exploitation of disabled people by television companies and charities, and the poverty which accompanies impairment. In order to focus the public's attention on these and other injustices disabled people are now prepared to risk public ridicule, arrest and even imprisonment (Barnes, 1991; Hasler, 1991; Oliver, 1990).

What disabled people and their organisations are demanding is the introduction of comprehensive anti-discrimination legislation which; first, establishes a suitable framework for the enforcement of policies which would ensure the meaningful integration of disabled people into the main-stream economic and social life of the community, such as the employment quota scheme for example, and, second, provide public confirmation that discrimination against disabled people for whatever reason and in whatever form is no longer acceptable. In other words, legislation which emphasises social rights rather than individual needs and focuses on the disabling society in which we live, and not on individual disabled people.

However, as the experience of Black people and women in Britain clearly demonstrates, legislation alone is not enough. The abolition of institutional discrimination is not a marginal activity, but one that strikes at the very heart of social organisations in both the public and the private sectors. It would be impossible to confront such a problem without becoming embroiled in political debate and taking up seemingly radical positions on a wide range of issues. It is imperative, therefore, that individuals and enforcement agencies remain independent of government influence and control. As Gregory (1987) has shown, one of the key factors in explaining the relative failure of the Sex Discrimination Act (1975) and the Race Relations Act (1976) to remove sexism and racism in Britain, is the semi-autonomous status of the Equal Opportunities Commission and the Commission for Racial Equality. Their semi-autonomy has become a double edged weapon in the hands of unsympathetic governments; because they are independent, they can be ignored; because they are not independent, they can be subdued through government control of funds and appointments. Hence, both organisations have been compelled to focus on policies of education rather than enforcement, an approach which is a proven failure.

Therefore, for anti-discrimination legislation to be truly effective disabled people must have access to the kind of medical and other information which historically has been used to justify their economic and social subordination. Hence an essential addition to legislation would be laws facilitating freedom of information which go beyond providing access to data held on computers and in local authority files. Closed medical cabinets would need to be opened and the unofficial documents which are kept as ways of avoiding information disclosure would need to be made available.

There will also be a need for some kind of formal mechanism able to offer disabled people meaningful individual and collective redress. This can only be achieved by the adequate funding and resourcing of the national network of organisations controlled and run by disabled people themselves. In the face of fierce opposition from a variety of sources it is these organisations which have put the issue of institutional discrimination on to the political agenda, and it is these organisations which are best suited to ensure its eventual eradication.

However, as Oliver (1990) has noted, none of these policies by themselves are likely to prove successful. First, anti-discrimination legislation without freedom of information and a supportive network of disabled people will simply benefit the legal profession. Second, access to information by itself will almost certainly expose disabled individuals to further professional mystification and exploitation. Third, support for organisations of disabled people without an appropriate framework which guarantees basic human rights will effectively neutralise the only collective voice that disabled people have in Britain. But an integrated policy similar to that suggested above would provide a mechanism by which institutional discrimination can be addressed effectively and, given time, eliminated altogether.

Conclusion

It is now apparent that traditional explanations and solutions for the disproportionate economic and social deprivations experienced by people with impairments are no longer acceptable. Disabled people and their organisations have identified hostile environments and disabling barriers – institutional discrimination – as the primary cause of the problem. This chapter has demonstrated how institutional discrimination is manifest in the core institutions of British society, and how, as a result, disabled people are forced to endure an existence characterised by excessive poverty and an unnecessary dependence upon others. Clearly, government policies in the post-1945 years, particularly during the 1980s, have failed to address this problem effectively. In the light of this disturbing situation disabled people have responded with the formation of their own organisations, the formulation of policies which enable them to achieve a comparable lifestyle to that of non-disabled people, and a call for comprehensive anti-discrimination legislation together with an appropriate mechanism to enforce it. The impact of these developments has had a profound effect on traditional organisations for disabled people; so much so that they now acknowledge the extent of institutional discrimination, and support openly the campaign for laws with which to tackle it. Although differences within the disability lobby remain, all are agreed that institutional discrimination against disabled people can be addressed only by changing organisational, social and individual behaviour and that this requires legal prescription.

However, cynics might argue that institutional discrimination is so entrenched within our society that any serious thoughts of its eradication by whatever means are both utopian and unrealistic. Such people need to be reminded that contemporary society is neither utopia nor the real world, it is a socially created world. Institutional discrimination, in common with everything else in our world, is little more than a social creation, and as such can be socially eradicated. While the policies outlined above might not eradicate it overnight, they will certainly make a significant contribution to its demise.

References

Barnes, C. (1990) *Cabbage Syndrome: The Social Construction of Dependence*. London: Falmer.

Barnes, C. (1991) *Disabled People in Britain and Discrimination: A Case for Anti-Discrimination Legislation*. London: Hurst & Co in association with the British Council of Organisations of Disabled People.

Barnes, C. (1992) *Disabling Imagery and the Media: A Code of Practice*. Derbyshire: British Council of Organisations of Disabled People.

BCODP (1986) *Disabled Young People Living Independently*. Derbyshire: British Council of Organisations of Disabled People.

Biklen, D. and Bogdana, R. (1977) 'Media portrayal of disabled people: a study of stereotypes', *Inter-racial Children's Book Bulletin*, 8(6–7): 4–9.

BRU (1990) *Images of Disability on Television*. London: Broadcasting Research Unit, City University.

Bynoe, I. (1991) 'The case for anti-discrimination legislation', in I. Bynoe, M. Oliver and C. Barnes (eds), *Equal Rights for Disabled People*. London: Institute for Public Policy Research.

Campbell, (1990) 'Developing our image – who's in control?' Paper presented at the 'Cap in Hand' Conference, February.

Campling, J. (1981) *Images of Ourselves*. London: Routledge & Kegan Paul.

Carnegie Council Review (1988) *After Attenborough: Arts and Disabled People*. London: Bedford Square Press.

Conference of Indian Organisations (1987) *Double Bind: To be Disabled and Asian*. London: Conference of Indian Organisations.

CORAD (1982) *The Committee on Restrictions Against Disabled People*. London: HMSO.

Crouch, G., Forester, W. and Mayhew Smith, P. (1989) *Access in London: A Guide for Those Who Have Problems Getting Around*. London: Robert Nicholson Publications.

CSIE (1989) *Integration and Resource: Financing Mainstream Education for Children with Disabilities or Difficulties in Learning*. London: Centre for Studies on Integration and Education.

Davis, K. (1986) *Developing Our own Definitions – Draft for Discussion*. Derbyshire: British Council of Organizations of Disabled People.

Davis, K. (1990) 'Old medicine is still no cure', *Community Care*, 8: 14.

DE (1990) *Employment and Training for People with Disabilities: Consultative Document*. London: Department of Employment.

DES (1986) *Report by HMI Inspectors on a Survey of Science in Special Education*. London: Department of Education and Science.

DES (1989a) *Report by HMI Inspectors on a Survey of Provision for Pupils with Emotionall Behavioural Difficulties in Maintained Special Schools*. London: Department of Education and Science.

DES (1989b) *Report by HMI Inspectors on the Effectiveness of Small Special Schools*. London: Department of Education and Science.

DES (1990) *Statistics on Education: Schools*. London: Department of Education and Science.

Dillon, E. (1990) Reviews, *Access by Design*, 51.

Disability Alliance (1990a) *Social Security Bill: Government Proposals for Changes in Benefits for People with Disabilities*. London: Disability Alliance.

Disability Alliance (1990b) *Disability Rights Handbook, 15th Edition*, April. London: Disability Alliance.

DPTAC (1989) *Public Transport and the Missing Six Millions: What Can be Learned?* London: Disabled Persons Transport Advisory Committee.

Dutton, P., Mansell, S., Mooney, P., Edgar, M. and Evans, E. (1990). *The Net Exchequer Costs of Sheltered Employment*. Sheffield: Department of Employment, Employment Services.

Fagin, L. and Little, M. (1984) *The Forsaken Families*. London: Penguin.

Finkelstein, V. (1985) Paper given at the World Health Organisation Meeting 24–25 June, Netherlands.

Finkelstein, V. (1991) 'Disability: an administrative challenge? (The health and welfare challenge)', in M. Oliver (ed.), *Social Work: Disabled People and Disabling Environments*. London: Jessica Kingsley.

Fry, E. (1986) *An Equal Chance for Disabled People: A Study of Discrimination in Employment*. London: The Spastics Society.

Fry, E. (1987) *Disabled People and the 1987 General Election*. London: The Spastics Society.

Ginsburg, N. (1988) 'Institutional racism and local authority housing', *Critical Social Policy*, 24: 4–19.

Glendinning, C. (1991) 'Losing ground: social policy and disabled people in Great Britain', *Disability, Handicap and Society*, 6(1): 3–21.

Glendinning, C. and Hirst, M. (1989) *After 16 – What Next?* Family Fund, Joseph Rowntree Memorial Trust, York.

Gray, A., Whelan, A. and Normand, C. (1988) *Care in the Community: A Study of Services and Costs in Six Districts.* York: Health Economics Consortium, University of York.

Graham, P., Jordan, D. and Lamb, B. (1990) *An Equal Chance or No Chance?* London: The Spastics Society.

Gregory, J. (1987) *Sex, Race and the Law.* London: Sage.

Hansard (1990) April 24, Cols 160–4.

Hansard (1991) March 22, Cols 252–3.

Hasler, F. (1991) 'The international year of disabled people', *Disability Now*, January: 5.

Harper, M. (1990) 'Storm as pub bans disabled skittles team', *Mail on Sunday*, 25 November: 14.

Hirst, M. (1987) 'Careers of young people with disabilities between ages 16 and 21', *Disability, Handicap and Society*, 2(1): 61–75.

HMSO (1989) *Caring for People: Community Care in the Next Decade and Beyond.* London: HMSO.

Hurst, R. (1990) Notes taken from minutes of British Council of Organisations of Disabled People meeting held on 6 January at Manchester Town Hall, Manchester.

IFF Research (1990) *Evaluation of Jobclub Provision for People with Disabilities.* Sheffield: Department of Employment, Employment Services.

Keeble, U. (1979) *Aids and Adaptations.* London: Bedford Square Press.

Kuh, D., Lawrence, C., Tripp, J. and Creber, G. (1988) 'Work and work alternatives for disabled young people', *Disability, Handicap and Society*, 3(1): 3–27.

Large, P. (1981) 'Enabling the disabled', Paper given to the Royal College of Physicians, London.

Lesbian and Gay Committee (1990) *Disability Review*, March no. 12.

Lonsdale, S. (1986) *Work and Inequality.* London: Longman.

Lonsdale, S. (1990) *Women and Disability.* London: Macmillan.

Mainstream (1990) *Workmates: A Study of Employment Opportunities for Disabled People.* London: Mainstream.

Martin, J., Meltzer, H. and Elliot, D. (1988) *The Prevalence of Disability Among Adults.* London: HMSO.

Martin, J. and White, A. (1988) *The Financial Circumstances of Disabled Adults Living in Private Households.* London: HMSO.

Martin, J., White, A. and Meltzer, H. (1989) *Disabled Adults: Services, Transport and Employment.* London: HMSO.

McCrudden, C. (1981) 'Institutional discrimination', *Oxford Journal of Legal Studies*, 2: 303–67.

Meltzer, H., Smythe, M. and Robus, N. (1989) *Disabled Children: Services, Transport and Education.* London: HMSO.

Morrell, J. (1990) *The Employment of People with Disabilities, Research into the Policies and Practices of Employers.* Sheffield: Department of Employment, Employment Services.

Morris, J. (ed.) (1989) *Able Lives: Women's Experience of Paralysis.* London: The Women's Press.

Nichols, V. (1991) Personal communication.

Oliver, M. (1985) 'Discrimination, disability and social policy', in M. Brenton and C. Jones (eds), *The Yearbook of Social Policy, 1984/5.* London: Routledge & Kegan Paul.

Oliver, M. (1986) 'Social policy and disability: some theoretical issues', *Disability, Handicap and Society*, 1(1): 5–18.

Oliver, M. (1990) *The Politics of Disablement.* London: Macmillan.

Oliver, M. and Barnes, C. (1991) 'Discrimination, disability and welfare: from needs to rights', in I. Bynoe, M. Oliver and C. Barnes (eds), *Equal Rights for Disabled People.* London: Institute for Public Policy Research.

Pagel, M. (1988) *On Our Own Behalf.* Manchester: Manchester Coalition of Disabled People.

Prescott Clarke, P. (1990) *Employment and Handicap.* London: Social and Community Planning Research.

Reiser, R. and Mason, M. (1990) *Disability Equality in the Classroom: A Human Rights Issue.* London: Inner London Education Authority.

Rowe, A. (ed.) (1990) *Lifetime Homes: Flexible Housing for Successive Generations.* London: The Helen Hamlyn Foundation.

Royal College of Physicians (1986) *Physical Disability in 1986 and Beyond.* London: Royal College of Physicians.

Scull, A. (1984) *Decarceration,* 2nd edn. London: Polity Press.

Smith, A. (1990) *Opportunities for Students with Disabilities.* London: The Public Information Unit, The Labour Party.

Stowell, R. (1987) *Catching Up: A Survey of Provision for Students with Special Educational Needs in Further and Higher Education.* London: National Bureau for Handicapped Students.

Swann, W. (1991) *Variations Between LEAs in Levels of Segregation in Special Schools, 1981–1990: Preliminary Report.* London: Centre for Studies on Integration and Education.

Thomas, D. (1982) *The Experience of Handicap.* London: Methuen.

Thompson, P., Buckle, J. and Lavery, M. (1989) *Not the OPCS Survey: Being Disabled Costs More than They Said.* London: Disablement Income Group.

Thompson, P., Lavery, M. and Curtice, J. (1990) *Short Changed by Disability.* London: Disablement Income Group.

Topliss, E. and Gould, B. (1981) *A Charter for the Disabled.* Oxford: Blackwell.

UPIAS (1976) *Fundamental Principles of Disability.* London: Union of Physically Impaired Against Segregation.

Walker, A. (1982) *Unqualified and Underemployed.* Basingstoke: Macmillan, National Children's Bureau.

Warburton, W. (1990) *Developing Services for Disabled People.* London: Department of Health.

Ward, L. (1987) *Talking Points: The Right to Vote.* West Country: CMH.

Warnock, M. (1978) *Special Educational Needs: Report of the Committee of Enquiry into the Education of Children and Young People.* London: HMSO.

Wertheimer, (1988) *According to the Papers: Press Reporting on People with Learning Difficulties.* London: Values into Action.

Which (1989) 'No entry', *Which,* October: 498–501.

Wood, P. (1981) *International Classification of Impairments, Disabilities and Handicaps.* Geneva: World Health Organization (WHO).

Wood, R. (1990) 'Care of disabled people'. Paper Presented at the Seminar on The needs and Resources of Disabled People, held on 3–4 December at the Policy Studies Institute, London.

Wolfensberger, W. (1989) 'Human service policies: the rhetoric versus the reality', in L. Barton (ed.), *Disability and Dependence.* London: Falmer Press.

6

'Constructing Women': Women's Sexuality and Social Policy

Jean Carabine

The Social Construction of Social Policy

This is a general chapter concerned with examining the relationship between women's sexuality and social policy. Central to this work is an analysis of the social construction of social policy as it relates to sexuality. This chapter will focus on the impact of heterosexuality and its interaction with ideologies surrounding motherhood and the family.

Extensive research showed this to be an area not looked into by either mainstream or feminist commentators on either social policy or sexuality. Existing feminist material on women and social policy, male and female sexuality and social control suggests a plexus of interrelations which both influence and structure, not only each other, but also male/female power relationships generally. Given this, I was concerned with the question: what are the implications of this for social policy analysis? Although feminists had written about sexuality and social control and women and social policy – all had failed to make the crucial link between women, sexuality, social policy and social control.

One explanation of this is the way in which sexuality is commonly seen as something which is private and personal, and as something beyond our control. Many of us think of our sexualities as privatised, as something we have always experienced, and something experienced as individuals – from childhood through puberty to adulthood.

Every day, as women, we are confronted with the relationship between our sexuality and social policy – like when we are deemed unfit mothers because we are single women or lesbians and have our children taken from us; or are considered 'unfit' to have children because we are not in a relationship with a man or when we fail to get work or promotion because it is known that we lesbians; or where we have to deny our sexuality because we work with young girls. Or as young women or girls we are often perceived only in terms of our sexuality rather than in terms of our potential or other attributes (Lees, 1986: 15). This is part of our common

First published in *Critical Social Policy*, 34, 1992.

shared experience. Yet, despite this we do not tend to think about social policy and popular ideas about sexuality as affecting us, for instance as affecting the number of heterosexual or lesbian women in Britain. If there were different policies or the same policies were constructed differently – would there be more lesbians?

Women, depending on their sexual identity, 'race', class, age and being differently bodied may experience social policies differently, but all will be affected by ideas about what is appropriate and acceptable sexuality.

Views about what is 'natural' and 'normal' sexuality abound in society. For example, it is commonly felt that it is 'normal' to be heterosexual but abnormal to be homosexual; or that it is 'normal' for women to be married or in a monogamous heterosexual relationship. Similarly, it is generally considered 'natural' for children to have both a mother and a father. Single-parent families or same-sex parents are thereby categorised as deviant, for example, Section 28 and 'pretended family relationships', teenage motherhood and more recently 'virgin' births. Central to views about what is 'natural' and 'normal' sexuality is the ideology of hetero-sexuality which in turn influences prevalent ideas about sexuality.

Ideas About Sexuality

Prevalent ideologies concerning sexuality, such as those coming from the religious, psychoanalytical and socio-biological traditions, influence common-sense and institutional ideas about what is both 'normal' and appropriate sex and sexuality. For example, as in religious ideas about sex being for procreation (Parrinder, 1987: 25) rather than pleasure, or marriage as a sacrament, sex as sinful, or the concern in religious ideas with the morality of sex – homosexuality, lesbianism, masturbation as immoral and sinful (see Bullough, 1987: 52). It is this concern with morals and ethics (and the control of immorality) which is reflected in much of today's legislation and social policy. Consequently, that which is considered ethically and morally wrong in Christian thinking is often equated with that which is legally forbidden (Moss, 1981: 25). For example, much of British legislation on homosexuality is influenced by Judeo-Christian views about sodomy and has resulted partly, at least until recently, in lack of provision for lesbianism in criminal and legal codes. Similarly, while matters such as homosexuality, contraception, AIDS, age of consent, prostitution, insemination by donor, abortion, marriage and divorce are the subject and concern of laws and social policies, they are also considered legitimate areas of church interest.

Second, because Christian beliefs, over time, have come to be closely associated with morals and morality, their influence is much more insidious and implicit throughout the whole of social policy. For example, unaccept-able sexual behaviour is seen as immoral and sinful, these ideas perpetuate as is evidenced by revitalised ideas of homosexuality being presented as immoral, evil and as the 'gay plague' within the context of AIDS and Section 28 (see *Marxism Today*, June 1988: 22–9).

The popular belief is that the family, and therefore traditional morals, are under threat from an increasing divorce rate, an increase in the proportion of married women working, surrogate mothers (West, 1984: 417–20; Marshall, 1986: 1), 'virgin' births, AIDS 'carriers', homosexuality and 'pretend family' relationships. Section 28 is evidence of a moral panic over not only the promotion of homosexuality but also lesbian motherhood and parenting, as is the recent furore over 'virgin' births (*Guardian*, 12 March 1991) and powers in the Human Embryology Act 1991 to restrict single women and lesbians access to 'treatments' including donor insemination and *in vitro* fertilisation. What is being evidenced in the 'moral panics' response is a revitalisation of ideas which relate sexuality, or at least certain expressions, acts and behaviour, to morality, ethics, sin, sickness and disease.

The socio-biological influence has left us with a legacy of sex as unavoidable, as given, an uncontrollable urge needing to be expressed. The belief is that we need to have sex regularly, especially in the case of men, otherwise there will be a dangerous build up of sexual desire. These ideas can be seen in social policy responses in cases of child sexual violence and rape in the family. Often the fact that a man (husband/father) is having 'marital' problems is accepted in mitigation in cases of incest by the courts (Viinnikka, 1989: 149). Similarly, the woman (mother/wife) is often blamed for the sexual assault of the child because she, for whatever reasons, was not sexually available to her husband/partner. It is believed natural for men to want sex more often than women. Male sexuality is active and aggressive, essential to male identity and masculinity.

Women's sexuality, in comparison to men's sexuality, is presented as something which is oppositional, but complementary. Women are not active but the passive receptacles of men's sexuality; they do not possess a sexual drive which requires fulfilling in the same way as men's. However, lesbians do not fit this model. Lesbians are, therefore, threatening because they are seen as 'not real' women, but as pseudo-men, sexually autonomous and sexually independent of men.

Not only is sexuality heterosexual, it is natural to want heterosexual sex. It is unnatural to be homosexual. In socio-biological thinking, lesbians and gay men can not help the origin of their sexuality – they are born that way, sometimes resulting in a liberal tolerance of homosexuality. This liberal tolerance was central to the populist response to the Sexual Offences Act 1967 and Section 28 (of the Local Government Act 1986) which resulted in it being seen as a threat to the civil liberties and human rights of people who were gay because they were 'born that way'.

In psychoanalysis, male sexuality is also seen as active, dominant, strong, and men as controlling, superior, independent and hard while female sexuality is repressed and passive and women are weak, inferior, soft, emotional and dependent (Baker-Miller, 1974: 367). Again, normal healthy sexual development is heterosexual development and homosexuality is perceived as an illness and a failure in social learning (Weeks, 1985: 149). In psychoanalytical work there has been an emphasis in the work on lesbianism on the mother–child dynamic rather than on lesbianism as sexual and erotic (Richardson, 1981: 31).

Neither is the essentialist perspective unaffected by issues of 'race' and class. For example, in ideas that the working classes and Black people were sexually rampant and immoral (Weeks, 1981: 33) and less able to control their sexual 'urges'. This is evidenced in popular attitudes towards child sexual violence and rape, for example, that the majority of assaults are perpetrated by working-class or Black men (Driver, 1989: 33–4).

The influence of racism adds another, very different, dimension to the way in which Black women's sexuality is seen. Black women, particularly African and Afro-Caribbean women, are seen as 'bursting' with an uncontrollable and insatiable sexuality, promiscuous and loose, needing to be civilised and to learn an appropriate sexuality. Asian women are simultaneously seen as passive victims and as exotic and sexual beings. Black women's sexuality is explained in terms of their nature and biology (Bryan et al., 1985: 46).

These normative values about sexuality are also replicated, asserted and reasserted in social policies through the ideology of heterosexuality.

Defining Social Policy

Definitions of social policy which go beyond traditional approaches (such as Walker, 1983 or Mishra, 1977) focus on resources and distributional effects in terms of ideological and material outcomes rather than on the impact of ideas about sexuality, ideas which are so central to society that they cut across the political spectrum and are accepted as both 'natural' and common sense. Certainly writers have examined the impact of ideology and of normative values on social policy, in both general and specific terms relating to politics, class, economics and more recently, gender and 'race' (see George and Wilding, 1985; Manning, 1985; Showstack-Sassoon, 1987; Dalley, 1988; Land, 1989; Qureshi and Walker, 1989). However, absent from all of these and other works is an analysis of the effect of normative ideas about sexuality on the formulation, implementation and practice of social policy. These writers, along with many feminist writers, have accepted the universality and normality of heterosexuality. Not only have they failed to question the impact of heterosexuality on the construction of social policy but much previous work on social policy reinforces heterosexual norms and relations. Feminist work, for instance, on the significance of the family and informal caring could be criticised for its focus on the heterosexual family. However, recently there have been exceptions to this, for example, Williams (1989) and Dominelli (1991). Failure to acknowledge the powerful influence of prevalent ideas about sexuality on social policy has resulted in the predominance of studies which are concerned with 'welfare' in resource or distributional or ideological terms but where ideology is materially based. They ignore other possible impacts of social policy which serve to reinforce societal norms about women's role and behaviour. In this chapter, therefore, I adopt a definition of social policy which allows the critical examination of heterosexuality and the ideologies of sexuality on the development, construction and implementation of social policy in Britain.

Social control is often exercised extra-legally, that is through more informal means than the law (Rubin, 1984: 292), for example, through medical, religious or media reinforcement of 'norms', as well as through state legislation. It would seem sensible, therefore, to include a definition of social policy which includes those institutions outside of direct state legislature: for example, marriage, heterosexuality, motherhood and the family along with non-state/private agencies and institutions. This recognises that a variety of groups and organisations are involved in developing and advancing social policies. These groups include women; feminists and non-feminists, Black and white, lesbian and heterosexual, young and old and differently bodied. These groups are not meant to be mutually exclusive; women may fall into one or more of these categories.

The definition of social policy which I adopt in this chapter would thus expand Walker's (1983) to incorporate,

> the analysis of the implicit as well as explicit intentions and assumptions of the state and non-state policies. This would entail a critical examination of the impact and influence of prevalent ideas about sexuality (both institutional/professional and commonsense). In particular, it would focus on the centrality of the ideology of heterosexuality and the way in which it interacts with the ideologies of motherhood and the family as well as how this ideology is promulgated by both state and non-state agencies, organisations and institutions alike. Such an analysis would be concerned not only to identify the processes by which this interaction and promulgation takes place but also to posit explanations as to the functions and impact of these ideologies. (Carabine, 1992)

Social policy is also a means of regulating women's sexuality. This control is exercised, however, in a number of ways, for example, at an explicit level through legislation and statutes, as in Section 28, in Paragraph 16 (Guidelines) to the Children's Act 1990 (although now amended), or the control of prostitution. Social control is also exercised, and perhaps most significantly, at an implicit level through the assumptions contained in social policies. The most important aspect of the role of social policy in the determination of sexuality is where social policy assumes a 'normal' set of relations such that heterosexuality is taken for granted without being asserted or the need for interventionist approaches. The public and private welfare system depends on traditional ideas and expectations about women as mothers and carers (soft, nurturing) publicly inactive who stay at home all day and who are economically dependent on men (are passive) and of men as publicly physically, sexually and economically active (go out to work) and dominant (are the head of household and have certain 'rights' as fathers and husbands). These are also bound up with notions of what constitute masculinity and femininity; male and female sexuality.

It would seem, as with sexuality, that women in social policy are defined in relation to men. The idea of women's dependency (whether on men or the patriarchal state) in social policy mirrors women's expected lack of autonomy in heterosexual relations and sexual self-definition and self-determination. This is not to suggest that women are powerless in defining their own sexuality but that when they do, as with lesbians, they are usually penalised.

Thus, women who seek sexual self-definition are often ostracised. Women who have a number of sexual partners may be labelled 'slags' or 'tarts'. Bound up in ideas of women's sexuality is evidence of double standards. So women are either virgins or whores, ladies or tramps and good or bad. These ideas appear in the social policy field, for example, notions about good mothers and bad mothers; proper mothers are heterosexual and married, bad mothers are unmarried, Black, teenagers and/or lesbian.

The experiences of all women are not the same, and this is particularly true in the determination and implementation of social policy (McRobbie, 1982: 52; Bhavnani and Coulson, 1986: 84–5; Williams, 1987 and this volume). For Black women, there is an additional dimension to their relationship with social policy – racism. In the past, and also more recently, there has been a marked reluctance, by the state, the church and medical profession, to allow women control over their own sexuality, through, for example, access to abortion, sterilisation and contraception. Black feminists, however, have criticised white feminist single-issue campaigns, such as abortion on demand, because Black women 'have *always* been given abortions more readily than white women and are indeed often encouraged to have terminations we didn't ask for' (Bryan et al., 1985: 105).

This easier access for Black women – to, for example, abortions – carries with it ideas about Black women as being too sexually active, or as lacking in sexual self-control and as producing too many children, and is tied into racist notions about Black women's sexuality. The influence of racist ideas about Black women's sexuality are so powerful that other forms of sexuality, for instance, lesbianism, are invisible.

The area of education also provides a number of examples of the kinds of assumptions made about women and sexuality within social policy. For example, 'what passes for sex education is, in fact, education about reproduction rather than sex and rarely about sexuality in its broader sense' (Jackson, 1982: 22). The focus of teaching about sexuality tends to be about heterosexuality, marriage, couples, heterosexual sex and reproduction. Homosexuality and lesbianism are rarely dealt with in schools (Trenchard, 1984: 20). If homosexuality is dealt with, it is often pathologised or seen as something from which young people should be protected (City of Leicester Teachers' Association, 1987: 39).

It is thought that the introduction of Section 28 will mean that homosexuality will be dealt with even less favourably than before. Section 28 seeks to prohibit teaching in local authority schools of the 'acceptability of homosexuality as a pretended family relationship' – seeks to reinforce that homosexual parenting is not valid.

Further, young women and girls are often only perceived in terms of their sexuality rather than in terms of their potential or other attributes (Lees, 1986: 15). Similarly, with girl delinquents there is a tendency for the courts also to see them as sexually deviant (Smart and Smart, 1978) and also for girls labelled as sexually promiscuous to be identified as deviant and in need of local authority care (Wolpe, 1987: 38). Wolpe suggests that in 'dominant' ideology there is direct linking of sex with marriage for girls: 'In this way an ideological form of control over girls is established through stipulating that it is only within marriage and for the purpose of having children that women may experience sex' (Wolpe, 1987: 38).

In illustrating the relationship between women, sexuality and social policy I may have given the impression that this relationship is a monolithic one with women passively accepting their position. On the contrary, women, both individually and collectively, have challenged heterosexual ideologies and assumptions about sexuality. For example, as can be seen in campaigns to change the Rape in Marriage law, challenges to Section 28, campaigns for the right to choose whether or not to have children, in fighting for lesbian mothers to get custody of their children and in feminist critiques (particularly from radical feminists) of heterosexuality. I have suggested that social policy incorporates throughout its determination and formulation an image of the 'normal' woman. This image, may not always conform with actual behaviour or practice, yet it presents the majority of women as married mothers in heterosexual relationships when many women are single, are single parents and lesbians; it defines what is normally expected and appropriate female behaviour (Hutter and Williams, 1981: 9). Central to these normative ideas about women's sexuality is the ideology of heterosexuality.

Heterosexuality

Assumed heterosexuality pervades almost every aspect of society, for example, as one lesbian comments, 'Everyone assumes I'm heterosexual because I've been married and have children, they see it as a "natural presumption"' (Taylor, 1986: 30).

Heterosexuality is, 'an institutionalised system (as well as individual attitudes, [practices and relations]) that openly promotes the belief that only heterosexuality and heterosexual family life is "normal" and "natural"' (GLC/GLC Gay Working Party, 1985), and any other practice 'abnormal'. Moreover, the ideology of heterosexuality affects *all* women because it reinforces women's heterosexual sexuality. Feminists have identified the institution of heterosexuality as a system of social control over all women, oppressive to heterosexual women and lesbians alike (Hanmer and Maynard, 1987: 3). It 'lays down the rules and conditions under which all sexualities are valued or devalued in our society, and penalties/benefits are accordingly awarded' (GLC, 1987: 19). Sexuality and heterosexuality, in both popular and also major theories of sexuality, are one and the same; heterosexuality is the only 'natural', 'normal', moral and appropriate expression of male and female sexuality.

Thus heterosexuality acts as a process of social control. Women who have sexual relationships with other women are stigmatised and abused – socially unacceptable. Additionally, women who fail to fit into 'normal' feminine stereotypes may be described as 'unfeminine' or even labelled as lesbians, as in the case of women protesting at Greenham.

The assumption of universal heterosexuality underlies much of social policy and is also central to ideologies of the family and motherhood. A considerable amount of social policy is predicated on the existence of a particular model of the family. The relationship between heterosexuality, the family and motherhood will be considered next.

Familism

The nuclear form of the family with heterosexual parents (comprising one male breadwinner, one dependent wife and children) continues to be perpetuated throughout social policy and social life. Inherent in this particular family model are assumptions about its 'naturalness'. These assumptions are based on a belief in biological determinist ideas which see the sex roles of men and women as fixed. Men are seen as fathers who provide for and who go out to work to support the family; whereas women become mothers and stay at home to care for their families. Hilary Land illustrates this point in her analysis of 'The construction of dependency' (Land, 1989: 152). Men's obligation to take up paid work in order to support their families is evident in social policies, as are women's responsibilities in the home and for the family (see John Moore's speech about 1988 Social Security reforms to the Conservative Political Centre Conference, 26 September 1987: 11, Conservative Party News Service). The implicit assumption is that these roles are natural, a kind of law of nature whereby men are workers and fathers, are 'active', dominant, etc. and women are mothers and stay at home caring for children, the sick and older members of the family.

However, this model of the family has been shown to be a socially constructed rather than universal model (see Edholm, 1982). Notions of this relationship as proper and as the appropriate context for the expression of sexuality abound not just in popular ideology but also in social policy, through, for example, the provision of health care, social services and social security. What is significant about this provision is the way in which appropriate behaviour (such as marriage, motherhood and heterosexual coupling) are rewarded and subsidised relative to behaviour which is labelled as inappropriate or deviant (for example, lesbian and single mothers).

Not only are women's experiences and position structured by the idealised form of the family in society which is endorsed in social policy, but also their sexual behaviour is similarly affected. The nuclear model of the family predominates and as such is accepted as both 'natural' and basic, in the same way that women's role within the family as mother, wife and carer is. This model is reinforced in social policy through a system of 'reward' and 'punishment' as illustrated in the following examples.

Women form the largest proportion of single parents (Millar, 1987: 159). Under the 1988 Social Security Reforms single parents (women) were affected by the abolition of the long-term rate. Long-term claimants not only have greater needs, but constitute 70 per cent of lone parents previously on supplementary benefit (Social Security Consortium, 1987: 11). Additionally, figures from the National Council for One-Parent Families show that in '1986, 55 per cent of single parents were on supplementary benefit, compared to only 7 per cent of two-parent families' (quoted in the *Guardian*, 23 November 1988). These examples show that women whose situation is perceived as inappropriate or not 'normal' are treated less favourably within social policy.

A report on Income Support and 16–17-year-olds from the National Association of Citizen Advice Bureaux (October 1989) shows how young pregnant women are discriminated against under income support regulations which do not allow them to claim support until they are six months pregnant. Compare this to women aged 18 years and over who can claim income support throughout their pregnancy irrespective of whether they can obtain work or not (NACAB, 1989: 9). This reinforces certain ideas about the 'unnaturalness' and immorality of 'teenage pregnancies'.

Additionally, lesbianism is not illegal yet lesbians experience discrimination and abuse within social policy and legal codes. The prime consideration of the courts deliberating child custody cases has been the 'best interests of child'. While various principles have been established about what constitutes this, the most consistent principle in heterosexual custody cases has been that young children should be placed with their mothers. This principle, however, is not one that is often adhered to in lesbian custody cases: 'in the eyes of the courts, a lesbian mother is immediately seen as "exceptional" and the usual assumptions are turned upside down . . . Many lesbian mothers still lose custody of their children solely on the basis of their sexuality' (Rights of Women, Lesbian Custody Leaflet: 1). Social policy also explicitly condemns lesbian couples – as shown earlier in the example of Section 28. The reference to 'pretended family relationship' makes it clear that homosexuals with children are not 'real' families.

Commenting on Section 28, David Wilshire MP, responsible for introducing Section 28 said, 'My actions were motivated wholly by the principle of supporting *normality* . . . Homosexuality is being promoted at the ratepayers expense, *and the traditional family as we know it* is under attack' [my emphasis] (*Guardian*, 12 Dec. 1987).

In highlighting the significance for women's sexuality of representations of the family in social policy I think special care has to be taken to tease out the full implications of this for all women. To identify the family as being responsible for women's oppression and treatment in social policy may be an acceptable analysis for some groups of women but not for others, for example, Black feminists have explained that for them the family is a place of refuge from racism (Williams, 1987 and this volume). Within the ideology of family which is enshrined within the welfare state there is an aspect of affirmation of the role of women as mothers. However, this positive confirmation is not conferred on Black women (Williams, 1987 and this volume); nor is it given to lesbians and single mothers. The concept of motherhood enshrined in social policies is one which is based on and reinforces an 'ideal' of motherhood which is white, heterosexual and 'respectable'. The implications for women of this model of the family and motherhood is that it both defines and controls all women's sexuality. Heterosexuality conveys messages about 'appropriate' motherhood which are reflected in social policy. In particular, what constitutes a 'fit' mother and in what circumstances and under what conditions mothering should take place.

Motherhood

Policies concerning motherhood or reproduction convey implicit messages about biological motherhood as married and heterosexual and of vaginal intercourse as the method of reproduction. This is highlighted by the experiences of women involved in surrogacy, 'virgin births', single women and, particularly, lesbians seeking access to the new reproductive technologies in order to have children.

Parallels can be drawn between ideas about women as mothers and wives in social policy and common-sense views of women's sexuality being about reproduction and motherhood. Ideas about women as mothers and baby makers are central to both social policy and perceptions of women's sexuality. The acceptable context for the expression of female sexuality is procreation and motherhood within marriage (or long-term monogamous heterosexual relationships). An example of this is expressed in a statement from Mrs Thatcher on the 'problem' of 'the young single girls who deliberately become pregnant in order to jump the housing queue and get welfare payments' (*Guardian* 23 November 1988). What Mrs Thatcher appears to be saying is that housing and benefits should only be available to 'respectable' married mothers. Correspondingly, it has also been argued that the provision of adequate income support for young pregnant women would only serve to act as a 'perverse incentive' to them becoming pregnant (see NACAB, 1989: 21). Thus, appropriate sexuality, that is, married motherhood, is rewarded, whilst unacceptable behaviour and sexuality, that is, unmarried motherhood is punished and condemned. McIntyre (1976: 155) observes that pregnancy and childbirth for married women are desirable and 'normal' whilst for single women they are both 'abnormal' and undesirable.

Pregnancy, childbirth and motherhood are also undesirable roles for lesbians. Lesbians are not usually considered suitable parents because of their sexuality. The Department of Health and Social Security (DHSS) 'Guide for Guardian Ad Litem in the Juvenile Court' (1984) advises on when a child might be considered 'exposed to moral danger' for the purposes of the Children and Young Persons Act 1969 (likely to be affected by the Children Act 1991). The section says that it does not aim to stop, punish or disapprove of same-sex parents or their life style. Its purpose is to protect the child from exposure in a lifestyle or behaviour which may harm it. The DHSS (now DSS) acknowledges that some lesbian lifestyles do not impinge on the child's welfare and acknowledges lesbians whose care of their child is 'loving and adequate'.

Two comments can be made about this section. First, it suggests that a lesbian lifestyle *per se* is usually seen as morally threatening to children despite this environment being 'loving and adequate'. Second, certain assumptions are implicit within the statement 'are lesbian or homosexual *but whose lifestyle nevertheless does not impinge on the child's welfare*'. First lesbian and homosexual parents and guardians are mentioned specifically and, therefore, are not perceived as 'normal' parents/guardians. Second, it would seem that there is something 'unnatural' about lesbian and homo-sexual lifestyles, but in this case lesbians and homosexuals are okay because these 'lifestyles' do not impinge on the child. Therefore, presumably, the child is not morally corrupted. This example demonstrates that social policy contains implicit notions of 'fit' and 'unfit' motherhood and that these definitions are influenced by commonsensical ideas about 'appro-priate' and 'normal' sexuality.

Neither, Fiona Williams (1989: 186) argues, have social policies re-inforced Black women's mothering role. Instead immigration and repro-ductive policies have sought to restrict Black motherhood.

Even when women appear to fulfil their role as 'appropriate' mothers they may experience the ideology of Motherhood as contradictory. On the one hand women are placed on pedestals because of their role as mothers, and on the other, women are blamed when they are thought to have failed, because of family poor health (cf. Edwina Currie's comments as Junior Minister for Health about the failure of northern mothers to properly consider their families' health), or for working instead of caring for dependants at home (although some mothers are perceived as 'good' mothers because they have access to nannies, etc. see Hanmer and Statham, 1988: 58). The idea of the 'fit' mother and the mother's responsibility for child care is implicit in health and social work (Hanmer and Statham, 1988: 55–6). Hanmer and Statham argue that there is no corresponding 'fit father' role and that women's fitness as mothers is considered in a variety of situations, for example, where women have committed a criminal offence or in child custody and abuse cases.

This relationship of idealisation and victimisation serves as another means to reinforce and strengthen the ideology itself. The approach moves the focus of blame away from the state and other agencies for malpractice or insufficient provision because mothers can be accused of not taking their responsibilities seriously.

Within the ideology of heterosexuality 'real' women are mothers and dependent on men – they are not lesbians. When lesbians do come into contact with social policy and if their sexuality is acknowledged it is usually treated as deviant and perverse, needing to be controlled and contained. There will, of course, be exceptions to this, where individual lesbians are treated positively, but these are exceptions. Neither in law nor social policies (with the exception of Section 28) are lesbian rights directly or explicitly restricted. It has never been illegal for women to be 'lesbian'. However, women's experience of both the judiciary and social policy is that they are implicitly, if not explicitly, anti-lesbian. In this way, control is exercised over groups of women because of their sexuality. This happens in subtle and informal ways, for instance in women's interactions with agencies such as the personal social services, the DSS, medical professions and the education authorities. All of these groups convey, albeit informally, notions about what is acceptable sexual behaviour for women. This can be seen by the way that lesbians are often discriminated against in housing with joint tenancies and mortgages. Women either requiring or working in council services may fear being 'out' about their sexuality, because of what that might mean at work (they may lose their jobs especially if they work with girls or young women) or because it threatens the custody of their children, or because of the way in which they may be treated by staff providing council services who themselves may be anti-lesbian. A study by Homeless Action of the housing needs and experiences of 28 lesbians in London found that lesbians did experience problems because of their sexuality. Additionally '[w]hen the sample were asked if they thought that other lesbians also experience housing problems because of their sexuality, there was unanimous agreement . . . and all of them knew of cases or incidents that supported this belief' (Anlin, 1989: 6). That homosexuality is assumed unlawful despite the absence of legislation which explicitly states this demonstrates the power of the ideology of heterosexuality. This is both reflected and reinforced, in the main, by the state through social policy.

Conclusion

In summary, social policy, both as a framework of implicit and explicit rationales for action and as a discipline, is socially constructed on the basis of normative rules concerning sexuality. Central to this construction is the ideology of heterosexuality which, as well as feeding into familism and motherhood, also influences gender roles, behaviour and relationships.

This construction of social policy is significant because it functions, first, as a means of regulating sexuality generally in society. Second, it specifically regulates women's lives and particularly their sexuality through the reinforcement within social policy of normative assumptions about sexuality which affect women's roles and behaviour in society. This is achieved through a system of 'reward' and 'punishment', whereby appropriate sexuality, such as married motherhood is rewarded and inappropriate (read also 'unfit') sexuality, as with 'virgin' and lesbian mothers is penalised within social policy.

Although the ideology of heterosexuality pervades much of British society and social policies it does not go unchallenged and cultures of resistance exist. Equally, the interactive nature of the relationship between the ideology of heterosexuality and social policy means that it is often inconsistent and contradictory.

References

Anlin, Sandra (1989) *Out But Not Down! – The Housing Needs of Lesbians*. London: Homeless Action.

Baker-Miller, Jane (1974) *Psychoanalysis and Women*. Harmondsworth: Penguin.

Bhavnani, Kum Kum and Coulson, Margaret (1986) 'Transforming socialist feminism: The challenge of racism', *Feminist Review*, 23: 81–92.

Bryan, Beverley, Dadzie, Stella and Scafe, Suzanne (1985) *The Heart of the Race*. London: Virago.

Bullough, Vern (1987) 'A historical approach', in J. Geer and O'Donohue (eds), *Theories of Human Sexuality*. New York: Plenum Press. pp. 49–62.

Carabine, Jean (1992) 'Women, Sexuality and Social Policy'. Unpublished PhD thesis: University of Sheffield.

City of Leicester Teachers' Association (National Union of Teachers) (1987) *Outlaws in the Classroom: Lesbians and Gays in the School System*. Leicester: City Of Leicester Teachers' Association.

Conservative Party News Service (1987) Conservative Political Centre Conference, 26 September 1987.

Dalley, Gillian (1988) *Ideologies of Caring*. Basingstoke: Macmillan.

Department of Health and Social Security (1984) *Guide to Guardian Ad Litem in the Juvenile Court*. London: HMSO.

Dominelli, Lena (1991) *Women Across Continents*. Hemel Hempstead: Harvester Wheatsheaf.

Driver, Emily (1989) in E. Driver and A. Droisen (eds) *Child Sexual Abuse, Feminist Perspectives*. Basingstoke: Macmillan Educational.

Edholm, Felicity (1982) *Changing Experience of Women*. Milton Keynes: Open University Press.

George, Vic and Wilding, Peter (1985) *Ideology and Social Welfare*. London: Routledge & Kegan Paul.

GLC and GLC Gay Working Party (1987) *Danger! Heterosexism at Work*. London: GLC/London Strategic Policy Unit.

Hanmer, Jalna and Maynard, Mary (1987) 'Violence and gender stratification', in J. Hanmer and M. Maynard (eds), *Women, Violence and Social Control*. Basingstoke: BSA/Macmillan. pp. 1–12.

Hanmer, Jalna and Statham, Daphne (1988) *Women and Social Work: Towards a Woman-centred Practice*. Basingstoke: Macmillan.

Hutter, Bridget and Williams, Gillian (1981) 'Controlling women: the normal and the deviant', in B. Hutter and G. Williams (eds), *Controlling Women, The Normal and The Deviant*. London: Croom Helm in association with Oxford University Women's Study Committee. pp. 9–37.

Jackson, Stevi (1982) 'Constructing female sexuality', in Mary Evans (ed.), *The Woman Question – Readings on the Subordination of Women*. Oxford: Fontana.

Land, Hilary (1989) 'The construction of dependency', in M. Bulmer, J. Lewis and D. Piachaud (eds), *The Goals of Social Policy*. London: Unwin Hyman.

Lees, Sue (1986) *Losing Out – Sexuality and Adolescent Girls*. London: Hutchinson Education.

Local Government Act 1988. London: Home Office.

McIntyre, Sally (1976) 'Who wants babies? The social construction of instincts', in D. Barker and S. Allen (eds), *Sexual Divisions and Society: Process and Change*. London: Tavistock.

McRobbie, Angela (1982) 'The politics of feminist research: between talk and action', *Feminist Review* 12: 46–57.

Manning, Nick (1985) 'Constructing social problems', in *Social Problems and Welfare Ideology*. Aldershot: Gower. pp. 1–28.

Marshall, Kate (1986) *Moral Panics and Victorian Values*. London: Junius.

Millar, J. (1987) 'Lone mothers', in C. Glendenning and J. Millar (eds), *Women and Poverty in Britain*. Brighton: Wheatsheaf Books.

Mishra, Ramesh (1977) 'Marx and welfare', *Sociological Review*, 23(2).

Moss, Rachel (ed.) (1981) *God's Yes to Sexuality*. London: Fount/British Council of Churches.

National Association of Citizen Advice Bureaux (1989) *Income Support and 16–17-Year-Olds*, E/5/89. London.

Parrinder, Geoffrey (1987) 'A theological approach', in J. Geer and O'Donohue (eds), *Theories of Human Sexuality*. New York: Plenum Press. pp. 21–48.

Qureshi, Hazel and Walker, Alan (1989) *The Caring Relationship*. Basingstoke: Macmillan.

Richardson, Diane (1981) 'Theory and practice', in J. Hart and D. Richardson (eds), *The Theory and Practice of Homosexuality*. London: Routledge & Kegan Paul.

Rights of Women Lesbian Custody Group. Lesbian Custody Leaflet.

Rubin, Gayle (1984) 'Thinking sex: notes for a radical theory of the politics of sexuality', in C. Vance (ed.), *Pleasure and Danger. Exploring Female Sexuality*. Boston: Routledge & Kegan Paul. pp. 267–319.

Showstack-Sassoon, Anne (1987) *Women and the State*. London: Century Hutchinson.

Smart, Carol (1981) 'Law and the control of women's sexuality', in B. Hutter and G. Williams (eds), *Controlling Women: The Normal and the Deviant*. London: Croom Helm in association with Oxford University Women's Study Committee. pp. 40–60.

Smart, C. and Smart, B. (eds) (1978) *Women, Sexuality and Social Control*. London: Routledge & Kegan Paul.

Social Security Consortium (1987) *Of Little Benefit – An Update. A Critical Guide to the Social Security Act 1986*. London: Social Security Consortium.

Taylor, L. (1986) *Lesbians and Work*. London: GLC.

Trenchard, Lorraine (ed.) (1984) *Young Lesbians*. London: London Gay Teenage Group.

Viinnikka, Simmy (1989) 'Child sexual abuse and the law', in E. Driver and A. Droisen (eds), *Child Sexual Abuse, Feminist Perspectives*. Basingstoke: Macmillan Educational.

Walker, Alan (1983) 'Social policy, social administration and the social construction of social welfare', in M. Looney, D. Boswell and J. Clarke (eds), *Social Policy and Social Welfare*. Milton Keynes: Open University Press.

Weeks, Jeffrey (1981) *Sex, Politics and Society*. New York: Longman Group.

Weeks, Jeffrey (1985) *Sexuality and its Discontents*. London: Routledge & Kegan Paul.

West, Patrick (1984) 'The family, the welfare state and community care: political rhetoric and public attitudes', *Journal of Social Policy*, 13: 417–86.

Williams, Fiona (1987) 'Racism and the discipline of social policy: A critique of welfare theory', *Critical Social Policy*, Issue 20, Vol 17, No 2, and this volume.

Williams, Fiona (1989) *Social Policy: A Critical Introduction*. Cambridge: Polity.

Wolpe, Ann Marie (1987) 'Sex in schools: back to the future', *Feminist Review* 27: 37–48.

7

Grey Power: Age-based Organisations' Response to Structured Inequalities

Jay Ginn

The ageing of populations in the advanced capitalist countries has not been universally welcomed. On the contrary, the growing elderly population, in combination with a declining workforce, has been portrayed as threatening the viability of welfare states through its consumption of resources. Some commentators predict intergenerational war, on the basis that a growing and politically influential elderly population is enjoying affluence at the expense of young families (Preston, 1984; Longman and Poquet, 1986; Johnson et al., 1989; Button and Rosenbaum, 1990). Assertions about rising pensioner incomes from occupational pensions, for example by the Secretary of State for Social Security (Lilley, 1992), have been used to reinforce Conservative arguments for means-testing the basic state pension and for raising women's state pension age. The motivation behind assertions of elderly affluence is equally clear in the US: the complaint that elderly people were receiving too large a share of federal resources was spearheaded by Americans for Generational Equity (AGE), a pressure group financed by banks, insurance companies, defence contractors and health care corporations whose aim was to promote private insurance at the expense of publicly funded pensions (Quadagno, 1990).

The portrayal of elderly people as relatively affluent and as responsible for a conflict of interests between generations has been termed 'conflictual ageism' (Arber and Ginn, 1991a), as distinct from the 'compassionate ageism' (Binstock, 1984) characterising elderly people as a social problem because of their supposed frailty, poverty and dependence. But both of these ageist attitudes conceptually isolate elderly people from the rest of society. Conflictual ageism has been most virulent in the US, where elderly people have been blamed for the budgetary crisis and for the lack of funds needed for children's welfare. To set the interests of one disadvantaged group against those of another is the classic political device of scape-goating, a divide and rule tactic to divert attention from the structural sources of inequality of power and wealth affecting people of all ages and from the resources absorbed by military (Navarro, 1984; Minkler, 1986).

First published in *Critical Social Policy*, 35, 1993.

Underlying the attack on public pensions is an ideology in which only paid work is valued (whether socially useful or not), an ideology which is both ageist and sexist.

I want first to challenge the myth that elderly people have increasing affluence and political influence in Britain, by reviewing the income of elderly people and the way their income is structured by gender, class and race; second, I focus on the ways in which elderly women suffer from a combination of sexism and ageism, exacerbated for ethnic minority women by racism; and finally I consider how pensioners' organisations in Britain and the US have aligned themselves in relation to issues of class, gender and ethnicity. This latter section is based on a variety of publications by pensioners' campaigning groups in both countries and on personal communications. In spite of its relevance to ageing societies, the subject of elderly people's organisations – or Grey Power – has been little researched.

Influence and Affluence?

The notion that elderly people as a group wield power in developed societies does not stand up to examination. Although grey heads predominate in parliaments, judiciaries and the professions, few of those heads belong to Black or working-class people or to women. It is ironic that although holders of some of the most important positions in society are over 65, the majority of people over this age are defined as socially redundant and excluded from paid employment. The elderly holders of powerful positions are almost entirely upper-middle-class white men, whose power bears no relation to the status or influence of elderly people generally. The extreme powerlessness of most elderly people as individuals is demonstrated in the most horrifying way in attacks on elderly people and in elder abuse by carers. A recent British survey shows that, on a very conservative estimate, 5 per cent of people aged over 60 reported suffering some form of abuse – financial, verbal, physical or sexual – by a relative (Ogg and Bennett, 1992). Earlier research in the US showed that the typical victim was a frail elderly woman, the abuser usually being her son (Lau and Kosberg, 1979). This is not to deny the considerable strain on carers (many of whom are also elderly), which has been well-documented (Brody, 1981; Nissel and Bonnerjea, 1982; Braithwaite, 1990; Wenger, 1990). The stress and financial difficulties in which both carers and care-recipients are trapped are likely to worsen in Britain as community care policies, operative from April 1993, reduce the availability of publicly funded residential and domiciliary care.

It is difficult to estimate the effect on politicians of elderly people's voting potential, but the fact that nearly half of elderly people in Britain voted in the 1992 general election for the only party which did *not* promise to uprate the state pension substantially suggests that there is no simple relationship between election promises and an 'elderly vote'. Whatever the reasons why such a large proportion of elderly people voted Conservative, neither financial self-interest nor concern for well-funded health and welfare services seems to have loomed large. A political movement founded on older people's interests is seen by British commentators as unlikely: 'the scope for this form of political togetherness is limited . . . it is unlikely that grey power has any chance of succeeding in the foreseeable future' (Midwinter, 1992: 23). Even in the US, where ageing group consciousness is more developed than in Britain, observers doubt that elderly people will form a voting bloc: 'there is no evidence to indicate that aging-based interest appeals can swing a bloc of older persons' votes from one party or candidate to another' (Binstock, 1974: 202–3).

'Grey power' in the sense used by conflictual ageists is clearly a myth: elderly people do not form a homogeneous group voting for policies which benefit them at the expense of younger people. However, the phrase has been used by elderly people's organisations to express their collective resistance to ageist stereotypes of dependence and social redundancy and to assert the continuity of human agency into later life. Echoing 'Black Power', the phrase implicitly suggests consciousness of a parallel with the struggles of other groups which are both materially disadvantaged and socially devalued.

In terms of income, elderly people are hardly well-off relative to the national average. In Britain in 1986 elderly people aged 65–74 had a mean disposable income, adjusted for family size, which was 76 per cent of the national average income, while the figure for those aged over 75 was only 67 per cent (Hedstrom and Ringen, 1987). Figures for *average* incomes, however, disguise inequality of incomes and the way this is structured by gender, class and race. For example, in 1985, only a tiny minority of those over 65, less than 5 per cent, were in the top income quintile (top 20 per cent) of the population of Britain (assuming that married women share their husbands' income equally). Elderly individuals with the highest incomes were predominantly healthy middle-class males under age 75 (Falkingham and Victor, 1991). Elderly people are more likely to be poor in Britain than in most other industrialised European countries; only Portugal, Spain, Ireland and Greece have a substantially higher percentage of elderly people below the EU poverty line (Eurostat, 1990). However, in all EU countries working-class people and women are relatively disadvantaged in later life; gender inequality of pension income is least in Scandinavia (Ginn and Arber, 1992). Since women constitute two-thirds of elderly people, it is important to examine their income.

Elderly women's income reflects the low regard in which their unpaid work is held; in spite of Beveridge's rhetoric about 'women's vital work' and the Conservative government's enthusiasm for 'family values', the British pension system, because of the major role played by occupational pensions, penalises those who spend years out of employment to care for others and leaves most elderly women much poorer than men. For example, the median total income of elderly women as individuals (in 1985–6) was less than £40 per week compared with £52 for men (Ginn and

Arber, 1991). Twice as many elderly British women as men received income support (15 per cent), but this underestimates the extent of elderly women's low personal income since married women cannot claim income support in their own right.

Marital status and class affect elderly women's incomes: as might be expected, income is higher for women whose previous occupation was non-manual, and for single women. Those who have ever been married are less likely to have an occupational pension (Ginn and Arber, 1991). The invisibility of married women in some official income statistics masks the extent of gender inequality in occupational pension receipt; during 1992, a number of statements were made by civil servants and politicians to the effect that two-thirds of pensioners retire with an occupational pension (see Appendix). However, while two out of three *men* at state pension age have an occupational pension entitlement, the corresponding proportion for women is less than one in three (Bone et al., 1992) and for those who have an occupational pension, the amounts received by women are much lower than those of men (Ginn and Arber, 1991; Ginn and Arber, 1994). The reason for the discrepancy between the figures quoted by the government and those obtained through OPCS surveys is that the former relate either to men only or to 'pensioner units', in which married women's very low personal income is rendered invisible.

It is difficult to generalise about the situation of ethnic minority elderly people in Britain, due to the diversity of ethnic groups, each with its own cultural norms, migration pattern and experience of colonisation. Among those over state pensionable age the ethnic minority population formed less than 1 per cent in the late 1980s (Arber and Ginn, 1991a). Although this will increase over the next decades, the current small numbers of each ethnic minority in national random sample surveys make analysis of their socio-economic circumstances unreliable. However, data from the US shows that elderly people from ethnic minority groups were on average poorer than whites; one-third of black and one-fifth of Hispanic elderly people lived below the poverty line in the 1980s compared with one-tenth of whites, and women in all three groups were poorer than men (US Bureau of the Census, 1987: Table 18). It is likely that in Britain a similar pattern of racial and gender disadvantage in pension income exists, due to racial discrimination and other obstacles to employment and pension acquisition. For those who migrated to Britain as adults, their shortened pension contribution record will further reduce their state and occupational pensions, while those who entered Britain in later life (such as refugees) lack any pension income.

The prospects for elderly women's income in the next century are no less bleak. Although more women are now employed than before, their occupational and personal pension scheme membership lags behind that of men (Ginn and Arber, 1993), due both to constraints on the type of employment they can undertake if they have domestic commitments and to the persistence of a gender gap in wages for similar work. Whether willingly or not, 'British women take more care of their families than of their pensions' (Joshi, 1987). Women are also subject to age–sex discrimination in returning to employment in their middle years. The traditionally 'feminine' work to which women are usually restricted often requires youthful attractiveness because employers seek a combination of attributes which reflect their own prejudices. In the US, male employers 'prefer the women around them to be young, part of their own aging hang-ups' (Sommers, 1975: 270). A requirement of 'recent experience' is often the ostensible obstacle to older women's re-entry into employment. Even for professional women, a 'glass ceiling' often limits their career in mid-life, whereas middle-class men can expect a career trajectory with ever-increasing salary and responsibility until a well-pensioned retirement. Of all women retiring in Britain after 2023, it is estimated that two out of three will have an income on the margins of poverty (Joshi and Davies, 1992).

Marriage cannot be regarded as a lifelong source of financial support for women; half of elderly women are widows, with only patchy rights to a share in their deceased husbands' occupational pensions. Rising divorce rates pose a further hazard to elderly women's financial security in the future, with one in eight elderly women expected to be divorcees in 2025 (Daneshku, 1992). Divorced women have no access to their ex-husbands' occupational pensions or to their State Earnings Related Pension (SERPS).[1] As a Chairperson of the Women's National Commission warned women; 'Do not mistake a marriage certificate for a pension contract' (*Fawcett News*, 1992).

Increased employment of women, as long as it is low-paid, discontinuous and often part-time, will do little to improve their economic situation in later life because of the close link between pension income and lifetime earnings in the British pension system. The loss of pension rights due to women's roles as wives and mothers needs to be recognised in social security and pensions policy, and new arrangements made which will enable women to obtain an independent and adequate pension income. Reforms within the present pensions system which would go some way towards alleviating women's difficulties in obtaining an adequate pension income include: legislation to ensure splitting of SERPS and occupational pension rights[1] on divorce (Joshi and Davies, 1991); banning the use of sex-based actuarial tables which result in lower annuities for women for the same pension contributions; reducing the effect of family responsibilities on employment by improving the availability of child care and elder care; and reducing the obstacles referred to above for women wishing to return to well-paid full-time employment when domestic commitments diminish. A more radical approach would be to weaken the link between lifetime earnings and income in later life by introducing a Citizen's Pension for each elderly individual, funded from general taxation (Midwinter, 1985; Parker, 1992). However, a Citizen's Pension which was linked to years of residence (as in the Danish model) would discriminate against adult immigrants, reducing their income in later life.

Unfortunately for women, and for all those disadvantaged in the labour market, the Conservative government is bent on reducing state pensions and promoting the private sector. First, the state basic pension is rapidly being eroded related to earnings. Second, means testing is being considered on the (mistaken) grounds that the majority of pensioners will have an occupational pension. Third, after the year 2000, widows will receive only half instead of all their husbands' State Earnings Related Pension (SERPS). Finally, if women's state pension age is raised to 65, as has been proposed by the influential government-appointed Social Security Advisory Committee (1992), women will have to wait an extra five years for state pension.[2] For the majority of women aged 60 to 64, raising the state pension age would not provide an opportunity to earn wages and improve their state and occupational pension entitlements, due to the lack of employment opportunities for older people. In 1992, 23 per cent of women aged between 60 and 64 were employed (Office for National Statistics, 1996), two-thirds part-time (Moore et al., 1994), proportions unlikely to increase given the long-term trend towards earlier exits from the labour market in all developed countries (Laczko and Phillipson, 1991) and the persistently high rate of unemployment. In this context, raising women's state pension age would force the majority into total dependence on husbands or on means-tested benefits until they reach 65. In addition, if the qualifying years for a full state pension for women were made the same as men's (44 years instead of the present 39) it would be even more difficult for women to obtain the full amount. Thus policies introduced and planned by the Conservative government in Britain will substantially worsen women's pension position in the future.

Social Status: The Effects of Age, Gender and Ethnicity

Low income is the most concrete manifestation of the social devaluation of those who do not participate in production. An industrial ideology in which production is given priority over reproduction, the formal economy over the domestic, hardware over humans, leads to ageist prejudice; this in spite of the fact that retirement is socially created (Walker, 1980; Townsend, 1981; Phillipson, 1982). But ageing in industrial societies is more detrimental to women's social status than to men's – a double standard of ageing. Contempt and derision for the elderly female are expressed in the terms 'old woman' or 'silly old moo', as well as in mother-in-law jokes. In nursery rhymes and fairy stories of wicked witches, contempt is mingled with fear and loathing, attitudes most cruelly expressed from the 15th to the 17th centuries in the witchcraze (see Daly, 1979; Hester, 1990). With the entrenchment of patriarchy, elderly women have been largely excluded from their ancient roles of negotiating disputes, facilitating significant events in the life cycle and transmitting culture, especially knowledge of healing (Robbins Dexter, 1990).

Elderly women's low social status derives from a combination of ageism and sexism: industrialism devalues age, patriarchy devalues femaleness. In terms of patriarchal values, older women have outlived their usefulness as sex objects and as childbearers and they are likely to be less amenable to control than a young woman. It is no accident that at *all* ages men marry women younger than themselves, male seniority in this relationship generally ensuring male economic dominance. The contemptuous attitudes, denigration and ridicule of older women can be seen as an alternative means of social control over their behaviour. Whereas older men can counter ageist prejudice through intellectual and occupational achievement and possession of financial resources, these attributes are less valued in older women. Grey hair and wrinkles may convey an air of wisdom and maturity in men, but for older women these signs of ageing are more likely to have negative connotations. All women are to varying degrees excluded from the mainstream of public life, relegated to the backwaters, but older women are also deemed 'past it' in personal terms; because women's value is sexualised, positively in the first half of life, negatively in the second (Itzin, 1990), women are penalised for ageing to a greater extent than men.

For ethnic minority elderly people, the social devaluation associated with ageing is compounded by racism, as summarised in the phrase 'triple jeopardy' (Norman, 1985): first they experience age discrimination in common with other elderly people, but, second, ethnic elders are poorer than average as discussed above. Third, they face greater difficulties than other elderly people in obtaining health care, housing and social services they need (Atkin et al., 1989; Ebrahim et al., 1987; Johnson, 1987; McFarland et al., 1989; Morton, 1993). Ethnic elders suffer from both 'over-intervention' by social services and under-intervention based on the myth that families are always available to help. Lack of information, together with an ethnocentric service provision which is insensitive to their needs, limits take-up of services by ethnic minorities (Fennell et al., 1988). Whether health care and social services should be different in content or delivery for ethnic elders compared with the white indigenous population is a thorny question: clearly services need to cater for any differences in religion, language, dietary preference and behavioural norms. Yet separate provision may operate as a form of apartheid, threatening the ideals of equal citizenship and universalism, and may also be particularly vulnerable to cuts in expenditure. To complicate the matter further, recent research has shown that different ethnic groups have a different perspective, Asian elders preferring special treatment by health and social services, while Afro-Caribbeans are more likely to want integrated services (Askham et al., 1993).

Ethnic elders are likely to feel more socially isolated than other elderly people. The social devaluation associated with ageing in western societies is especially acute for those in whose own culture elderly people are treated with respect, as valued and useful members of the community. Contrary to the belief that ethnic elders are surrounded by an extended family who provide social contact and care when needed, they are usually separated from their family of origin through migration; their British-born descendants cannot necessarily respond to the kin obligations prescribed by the ethnic culture, having often 'moved away' geographically, culturally and linguistically from their elderly relatives. As a result, ethnic elders' own cultural expectations of respect and of close contact with an extended family are violated, exacerbating feelings of loneliness already induced by being a minority in Britain (Fennell et al., 1988). The language barrier is especially acute for elderly women whose cultural norms have restricted their participation in the public sphere and limited their opportunities to learn English. They may be distanced from children and grandchildren by difficulties in communication.

Clubs and centres organised by ethnic voluntary groups go some way to alleviate these multiple disadvantages by providing desired services, facilitating sharing of information, encouraging friendship and articulating the needs of ethnic groups to statutory service providers. Two developments may cause such provision to expand: first, as those who entered Britain in the 1950s age, ethnic minorities will become a growing proportion of the elderly population, and second, community care policies which promote the provision of services by non-statutory bodies could enlarge the scope for centres run by voluntary groups. So far, however, the lack of funds and premises have been major constraints (Norman, 1985), and separate provision carries drawbacks as noted above.

While gender inequality of earnings, employment opportunities and domestic labour among those of working age has had a high profile, both in sociology and in society generally, as a result of the women's liberation movement, the oppression of older women has been less visible (Arber and Ginn, 1991b). This is especially so for ethnic minority older women. The 'burden of caring' borne by daughters looking after elderly parents has received rather more research attention than the feelings of indignity and loss of autonomy in those receiving care (Arber and Ginn, 1992). Elder abuse, and the difficult domestic situations giving rise to it, is only just emerging as a social problem in Britain. These issues affecting older women have neither erupted onto the streets nor been taken up in mainstream sociological literature.

The current changes in welfare policy and the rolling back of the state in both Britain (McCarthy, 1989) and the US (Arendell and Estes, 1991) are likely to compound the disadvantages faced by women, working-class people and ethnic minorities in later life. While state provision of housing, social services and health care has left a great deal to be desired, privatisation of services is unlikely to be an improvement and increased charges will bear hardest on elderly people in these groups because they are more likely to lack their own resources. The effects of the new community care arrangements from April 1993 will be felt mainly by women: 'Any shift from public to private responsibility for community care . . . and any resulting cuts in public expenditure, have severe gender-specific implications

... This pressure on women as carers and as care-recipients has to be resisted' (Bernard and Meade, 1993: 189).

One response to ageist attitudes and to the erosion of publicly funded welfare provision is for elderly people, and particularly older women, to organise themselves and to campaign for improvements. Writers concerned about ageism (for example McEwen, 1990) have argued for ageism awareness campaigns to challenge negative stereotypes, and have presented a comprehensive agenda for change, including legislation against ageist practices. However, combating ageist attitudes and practices will not be easy, as it entails a shift in power relationships. Just as younger women and Black people led the campaigns against sexism and racism, the self-organisation of older people is crucial. I next consider grey power in terms of pensioners' organisations, focusing on the extent to which issues of class, gender and race inequality have emerged in their campaigning.

Grey Campaigning in the US and Britain

In both Britain and the US, different class interests are represented by different 'grey' organisations, but gender issues have received minimal attention within the major British organisations. The campaigning one might expect from older women faced with poverty and social devaluation has so far been muted, perhaps because complaining is part of the derogatory image from which elderly women wish to dissociate themselves; perhaps because a lifetime of 'compulsory altruism' (Land and Rose, 1985) transmutes into habitual resignation; perhaps because activism has been found to depend on high personal esteem (Seeman, 1975) and this is eroded by ageist attitudes (Ragan and Dowd, 1974); perhaps because many of today's elderly women, especially in Britain, were excluded from employment for much of their lives and lack experience of collective action.

USA

In the US, as in Britain, elderly women are poorer than men; 70 per cent of elderly people in poverty are women and Black elderly women are more likely to be poor than white or hispanic. Yet the largest older people's organisation, the American Association of Retired Persons (AARP), founded over 30 years ago by a woman teacher, Ethel Andrus, has done little until recently to highlight gender, class or race inequality. However, in 1984 AARP started a 'Women's Initiative' which focuses on older women's economic and other disadvantages relative to men and seeks remedies through legislation. It has backed several bills to remove inequities in social security, pensions, employment and health care faced by older women and publishes a quarterly newsletter, *Women's Initiative Network* (WIN).

AARP is open to all aged over 50 and claims a membership of 34 million, a quarter of all registered voters in the US. AARP's major achievement has been its campaign against age discrimination culminating in the Age Discrimination in Employment Amendment (ADEA 1967, amended 1978). This makes it unlawful for employers to retire staff compulsorily under age 70, or to discriminate in recruitment, wages or conditions on grounds of age. The class base of AARP can be inferred from its stance on Medicare: instead of joining the campaign for doctors' fees to be limited by law to Medicare-approved levels, AARP encourages its members to join private health insurance schemes.

The Gray Panthers, founded by Maggie Kuhn in 1970, are a smaller organisation with 80,000 members, and they have a very different class and age perspective from AARP. They are not a 'gray lobby' and their newspaper, *Gray Panthers' Network* (GPN), emphasises the need for elderly people to unite with people of all ages to achieve a more equal distribution of power and wealth, a more just and humane society. GPN promotes alliances that cut across generational lines, for example joint activities with child health advocates opposing cuts in federal aid and seeking Medicaid coverage for low-income pregnant women and babies; 'We won't let you pit old against young in the budget because we're in this together' (*GPN*, 1988a: 3). Major demands expressed in GPN conference resolutions include the need for free and comprehensive health care, for housing for the homeless, affordable child care and a war on child poverty. The general thrust is towards increased public spending to meet the needs of *all* those on low incomes, and to release resources currently spent on military research and weapons for this purpose. The Gray Panthers' linking of militarism with cuts in social programmes is expressed by a member who provides a revealing quotation from J.F. Dulles:

> In order to bring a nation to support the burdens of great military establishments, it is necessary to create an emotional state akin to psychology [sic]. There must be the portrayal of external menace . . . a nation-hero, nation-villain ideology and the arousal of the population to a sense of sacrifice. (*GPN*, 1988b: 11)

The greater poverty of older women and of ethnic minorities and the lack of campaigning on this issue is recognised in GPN, although; 'no elder advocacy group has put the older women's issue in the forefront of their concerns' (*GPN*, 1991: 16).

There are signs in the US that older women are beginning to define their own interests and to interpret these to younger women. Betty Friedan, calling for a revolution in thinking about ageing and the role of elderly people, observes that the concerns of the elderly are closely related to women's issues (Friedan, 1993). The Older Women's League (OWL), an offshoot of the National Organisation of Women (NOW), was the first organisation formed solely to take up older women's issues.

OWL, founded in 1980 by two older women, Tish Sommers and Laurie Shields, has 20,000 members organised into over 100 chapters. Its aims include achieving economic and social equity for older women, improving their image and status, and providing mutual support for its members. Its methods centre on legislative reform and include giving Congressional Testimony, developing Model State Bills and producing reports highlighting issues such as job discrimination, low retirement income, the needs of elderly caregivers and the shortcomings of the US health care system. OWL has exposed the flaws in the legislation against age discrimination in employment (ADEA), which is of limited value for women because it does not cover sex. That is, it does not specify that employers must be willing to hire older people of *both* sexes. Similarly, the 1964 Civil Rights Act (Title VII) outlaws sex discrimination but does not cover age. By ensuring that both older men and young women are hired, 'many employers can actively (although not openly) pursue a policy of discrimination against older women, yet escape the sting of the law' (Older Women's League, 1982: 12).

A notable success was achieved following OWL members' campaigning against the use of sex-based actuarial tables in private pension plans. Until recently, the same amount of money accumulated at retirement bought a smaller annuity for a woman than a man because of women's greater life expectancy. As NOW pointed out to the Equal Employment Opportunities Commission (EEOC) in 1972, whites have a life expectancy seven years longer than Blacks, but have not suffered such actuarial reduction (Scott-Heide, 1984). Finally in 1983 a Supreme Court decision (under the 1964 Civil Rights Act) required sex-neutrality in employer-sponsored pension schemes, a major achievement for older women's campaigning. Such a change has not yet been made in Britain.

Several member organisations of the elderly cater for ethnic minorities: the National Caucus and Centre of Black Aged, founded in 1970 and publishing a newsletter, Golden Page, the National Hispanic Council on Ageing, founded in 1980, with a newsletter entitled *Noticias*, and the National Indian Council for Aging, founded in 1976, whose newsletter is *Elder Voices*.

Britain

It is not clear yet whether in Britain similar levels of activity by older women will be achieved as in the US, but there has been a recent upsurge in membership of some older people's organisations. Organisations for older people in Britain vary in their history, age structure and membership, and in their perspective and policy goals. Most have not so far developed policies which directly address women's disadvantages in financial resources in later life.

The Association for Retired Persons over 50 (ARP) is the British equivalent of the AARP and was founded in 1988. It has grown rapidly and in 1991 claimed approximately 125,000 members. It represents the perspective of younger middle-class retired people, many of whom have or expect to have good earnings-related pensions. The main aims of ARP are to change attitudes to age, to end age discrimination in employment (including compulsory retirement), and to equalise the ages at which men and women become eligible for pensions and associated benefits. ARP dissociates itself from the demand for a basic state pension linked to average national earnings which is made by other pensioners' organisations. It also shows little concern at the likely adverse effects for older women if the state pension age is equalised at 65. There is no specific policy on women's pensions, as it is assumed that either their employment or their husbands' will ensure an adequate income for all but a minority. ARP looks forward to closer integration with the European Union in pension policy, and favours a two-tier model of pension provision similar to that in West Germany (as it was), with earnings-related pensions for employed people and means-tested public assistance for those lacking an adequate insurance record. The way such a policy perpetuates class, gender and race inequalities into later life is not considered a problem by ARP, which takes a similarly anti-collectivist position on the provision of health care; instead of campaigning to defend and improve the NHS, ARP offers its members an arrangement for a discount on private health care. Its literature inviting membership is based mainly on a range of discounted services such as this and on social networks of those over 50.

One of the oldest pensioner pressure groups is the National Federation of Retirement Pensions Associations (NFRPA), with its magazine *Pensioners' Voice*. It was founded in 1939 as a militant grassroots campaigning organisation, independent of any political party, and has about 600 branches. Critical of the level of state pensions proposed by Beveridge at the time, the NFRPA has continued to campaign for an adequate basic income for all elderly people, although its magazine does not explicitly recognise the pension disadvantage of women and ethnic minorities. Composed mainly of older elderly people and failing to attract the recently retired, NFRPA has experienced a drop in membership from a quarter of a million in the 1970s to 25,000 in the early 1990s, and has recently, with some reservations, affiliated to the National Pensioners Convention.

The only pensioners' organisation to operate as an aspiring parliamentary party is the Pensioners Protection Party (PPP), formed in 1989, and with an individual membership of 3,000 in 1991. Candidates planned to stand in the 1992 general election and in local elections to publicise the needs of elderly people, and eventually to gain a voice in Parliament. Major goals of the PPP in 1991 were: a basic pension of £110 per week for all elderly people as of right, to eliminate the need for means-tested benefits; the restoration of SERPS to its original formula, which they believe would meet the pension needs of women; re-establishing the NHS as a caring service, rather than a cost-conscious one; and ending the privatisation of local services. The PPP claim that all the existing political parties ignore pensioners, treating them as 'second class citizens, who are powerless and unable to improve our situation' (PPP leaflet, undated, published in Torquay). The fact that this organisation failed to make any impact on the

1992 general election and has subsequently disappeared seems to bear out the view of Midwinter and others that elderly people would not vote as an age-interest group.

Another recently formed group, the Pensioners' Rights Campaign (PRC), was started in 1989 to campaign for a Pensioners' Charter including a better state pension, a retirement age of 60 for both men and women, and a full state pension for women irrespective of their employment record or marital status. It is the only pensioners' organisation to acknowledge, in its demands, the impact of women's domestic roles on their pension income and the need for an independent income for all elderly women. However, it is relatively small, with about 30,000 members in 1993. The PRC recently affiliated to the British Pensioners and Trade Unions Action Association (BPTUAA), and its gender-awareness may influence the larger body.

The BPTUAA was founded in 1972 to organise retired trade unionists and their partners into a campaigning body, although it is open to all pensioners. It is one of the larger organisations, claiming over 100,000 members in 400 branches. It aims to mobilise trade unions in support of pensioners' interests, and has 400 trades councils and 32 national trade unions affiliated. The national paper *British Pensioner* and North-west region paper *Grey Power* indicate the concerns of members and the policies advocated. These display an awareness of class interests, and are strongly collectivist, centred on defending the universalist benefits of the welfare state. The BPTUAA produced the British Pensioners' Charter, which broadly reflects the aims of the Declaration of Intent of the National Pensioners Convention. The Charter served as a focus for pensioners' campaigning in 1992, and gained the support of trade unions for its petition, presented to the government, with some 200,000 signatures, in August 1992. Its two major demands are a universal basic state retirement pension of at least one-third of national average earnings for each pensioner, and free health and community care when needed. Although the particular problems of women in obtaining adequate pensions are not mentioned, the demand for a minimum state pension for each *individual* is of great significance for women, since it implicitly acknowledges their need for an income amount which does not depend on marital status, and their right to a pension as citizens, whether their work has been paid or unpaid. Means-tested benefits are abhorred as undermining dignity and independence, and the possibility that the government has plans to means-test the basic state pension has generated renewed campaigning on this issue.

Until recently, BPTUAA showed little evidence of concern with ethnic minority elders. However, a recent issue of *British Pensioner* carried an article on 'Ethnic elderly in Britain' in which Bill Morris (General Secretary of the TGWU) pointed out their problems of access to appropriate services and of state pensions 'frozen' at a fixed level on return to their country of origin. Morris also draws attention to unity of interest between workers and pensioners, urging;

the plight of ethnic minority elders needs to be brought to the surface and taken on board . . . The working population have a duty to address their needs and indeed it is in our interests to do so . . . Whatever we do today will affect us tomorrow as we become the next generation of elderly people. (Morris, 1993: 5)

The National Pensioners Convention (NPC), formed in 1979 following a TUC initiative and reconstituted at the 1992 Birmingham Congress, has co-ordinated the policies and actions of a wide variety of pensioners' organis-ations (BPTUAA, trade union Retired Members' Associations, NFRPA, county-based Pensioners' Associations, Pensioners' Liaison Forums). Charities such as Age Concern and Help the Aged, with their rather different perspective, also maintain links with the NPC. Some organisations are affiliated directly to the NPC, others through the BPTUAA, as shown in Figure 7.1. The NPC unites approximately 1,500,000 pensioner members in the affiliated organisations, and the only major organisation outside the NPC is the ARP. The demands of the Pensioners' Movement (that is, NPC affiliates) are expressed in a 'Declaration of Intent', which differs from the British Pensioners' Charter in specifying a pension of half national average earnings for a couple. Thus the movement as a whole has not yet taken on board the demands of the PRC and BPTUAA charters, which would improve married women's positions.

The success of the NPC as an umbrella group in drawing most British pensioners' organisations together should enhance their ability to influence government policy by presenting a united voice, and several recent initiatives developing links within the EU should also help to raise the profile of British pensioners' demands. These initiatives have been oriented towards the European Year of Older People in 1993, an EU project which draws attention to the common interests of older people with younger in its subtitle 'and Solidarity between Generations'. The European Platform of Seniors' Organisations (EPSO) sought the opinions of elderly people all over Europe in order to present their views to the leading EU bodies. Significantly, their 1992 conference was entitled 'Europe for all Ages', again stressing the wish to avoid isolating elderly people politically from younger people. A European Pensioners Parliament was also organised in 1992 by the socialist group of British MEPs. It brought together 518 pensioner delegates from 12 countries. Both of these events, in comparing the situation of elderly people across the EU, highlighted the extent to which British pensioners lag behind their counterparts in other countries in terms of pension income. A European Pensioners' Charter resulted from the parliament, although British pensioners, remembering the fate of the Social Charter, are not holding their breath awaiting its adoption by the British government. Also in 1992, retired trade unionists from EU countries formed the Federation of European Retired Persons (known as FERPA) pledged to promote the EU's Year of Older People through rallies and demonstrations in each country.

In spite of (or perhaps because of) their class consciousness, most British pensioners' organisations give no prominence to the structuring of income equality by gender and race. 'Their charters demand improvements that will

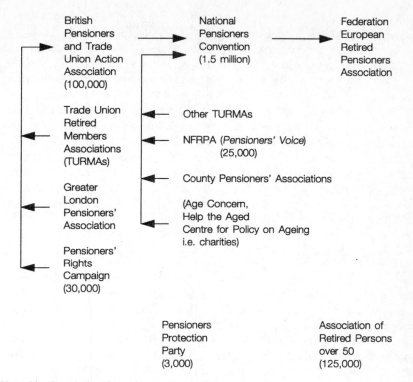

Note: Numbers in brackets show approximate membership.

Figure 7.1   *Main Pensioners' Organisations, Britain 1992: affiliation structure*

affect all old people but that ignore differences arising from race or gender' (Bernard and Meade, 1993: 183). Thus the concentration of poverty among elderly women due to the linkage between pension rights and lifetime earnings receives negligible attention in the journals sampled (*Pensioners' Voice*, *British Pensioner*, *Grey Power*, *Greater London Pensioner*). There is no recognition of the personal poverty of married women dependent on their husbands, nor of the financial problems faced by women who are widowed or divorced. The apparent lack of concern about the way pension arrangements affect women is surprising, given that the majority of the affiliated membership are women and that women are well-represented in the organisational structures. Since the policies adopted by NPC affiliates (unlike those of the ARP), are universalist and egalitarian in their demand for an improved basic pension, they would in fact benefit women more than men if implemented; but they would not affect gender inequality in SERPS or in occupational pensions.

The special difficulties faced by Black and ethnic minority elderly people have not so far been addressed in the Declaration of Intent or the Charter.

The Standing Conference of Ethnic Minority Senior Citizens (SCEMSC) represents 59,000 ethnic minority elderly people, including Afro-Caribbean and African (134 groups), Asian (82), SE Asian (19), Mediterranean (14) and Latin American (3) and is therefore in an excellent position to voice their concerns within the wider pensioners movement. Unfortunately, SCEMSC has no links with the NPC, receives no information about pensioners' campaigns and its officers feel that ethnic minority elders' needs are not understood or represented by the white organisations. Locally, pensioners' organisations are more responsive to ethnic minorities. For example the *Hackney Pensioners' Press* has published a series entitled 'Across Seven Seas and Thirteen Rivers' in which a number of ethnic minority groups describe their experiences of living in Britain and in which clubs for ethnic elders are promoted. In March 1992, the Greater London Pensioners' Association held a conference for Black and ethnic minority pensioners to express their views on the British Pensioners' Charter. This was followed up with a further conference in March 1993.

A clue to the minimal attention to gender and race in the British pensioners' movement may be found in the strong links maintained with trade unions, whose structures, procedures and culture have formed a model for the NPC. Although such links are likely to foster intergenerational solidarity, counter ageist attitudes and bring a wealth of campaigning experience to the pensioners' movement, there may be a price. As women, ethnic minorities and disabled people know to their cost, trade unions have been slow to recognise and respond to their needs, on the grounds that singling out disadvantaged groups could be divisive. The main pensioners' organisations reflect the gender imbalance of power found in other political structures; although women contribute a great deal to the running of the organisations, the campaigning priorities are determined mainly by white men, neglecting issues of particular importance to women or to ethnic minorities. The invisibility of older women's issues in the pensioner movement may be a reflection of this historical weakness of British working-class organisations. This explanation, however, begs the question as to why elderly women themselves have not been more successful in raising gender issues within pensioners' organisations. It is possible that, as in other organisations, women have only been able to achieve a leading position if they deny or minimise the existence of gender disadvantage and tacitly accept men's agendas and methods.

Gender is not entirely neglected, however, since in addition to the PRC charter (see above) certain local groups have highlighted the needs of older women. For example, the Pensioners' Forums in Lewisham and Hounslow are assisted by Local Authority Units concerned with equality, and have developed projects and policies for older women. The Lewisham Forum is taking part in the European Older Women's Project, a three-year venture jointly funded by the London Borough of Lewisham, the City of Perugia in Italy and the EC. Through exchange visits, groups of older women in Lewisham, Perugia and the Netherlands are learning about women's position in other cultures. At least one charity has chosen to focus on older women: Help the Aged's 'In Praise of Older Women' campaign, from October 1992 until International Women's Day 1993. Another initiative highlighting older women was the recent London conference on International Women's Day (1993) on the theme 'Fifty Plus and Female'. The emphasis in these projects appears to be more on sharing experiences, combating ageism and celebrating older women's capacities than on challenging the patriarchal structures, such as pension systems, which disadvantage women. A recent report of the Women's National Commission (WNC, 1992) highlights older women's many disadvantages relative to older men and recommends several reforms of the pension system; these include banning the use of sex-based tables in calculation of private pension benefits, basing SERPS on the best 20 years' earnings, and extending Home Responsibilities Protection to part-time employees. A broad agenda for older women's needs in Europe is found in the statement of rights for older women adopted by the 1988 International Congress of the European Federation for the Welfare of the Elderly (Bernard and Meade, 1993).

The only member organisations which cater specifically for older women are the Older Women's Project of Pensioners' Link and the Older Feminists' Network (OFN), both based in London and both formed to give a voice to older women. The Older Women's Project (OWP), formed in 1985, has a newsletter reaching about 600 older women and it runs training courses, campaigns and conferences, including, in 1991, a Black and Minority Ethnic Older Women's conference which enabled them to identify campaigning priorities. OWP is funded (originally by the GLC, later by the Greater London Grants Unit and a charity) and staffed. The OFN, in contrast, is entirely run by its members, having no funding. Formed in 1982 to redress the lack of attention by the Women's Liberation Movement to older women, this small organisation (with about 200 subscribers) provides contact for a nationwide membership through a collectively produced regular newsletter, organises London workshops and contributes to the National Association of Women's Organisations and to both pensioners' and feminist campaigns. But so far the OFN, unlike the Older Women's League (OWL) in the US, has not played a leading role in campaigning on issues which are central to older women's welfare.

In view of the importance of the state pension to women's incomes in later life, one might expect an upsurge of protest, lobbying and campaigning by women against raising women's age of eligibility to 65 and robbing every woman who has a full National Insurance contribution record of a total of over £14,000 of state pension (at 1992/3 rates). Yet the arguments against this change and in favour of an overhaul of the pension system to make it fairer to women have been marshalled most effectively by the Equal Opportunities Commission (1992). The task of providing leaflets and mobilising public opinion has been undertaken by the 'State Pension at 60 Alliance', an *ad hoc* group of (non-pensioner) women trade unionists, rather than by pensioners' organisations or the older women's networks.

This may be partly due to the fact that a raised pensionable age is unlikely to affect women currently over 55. Yet this is an issue of principle, and one on which older women, aware of the many inequalities affecting women as they age, might be expected to campaign. It seems that older women in Britain have a long way to go to match the level of activity of their counterparts in the OWL in the US and that it may be more fruitful to work with equality-oriented and feminist organisations than within pensioner structures. The fact that the campaign against raising the state pension age is led by women active in the trade union movement suggests that such experience is the key to self-organisation of older women in the future. If this is so, then the development of 'black sections' in the labour movement is all the more welcome as providing experience of self-organisation for ethnic minorities as they age.

Conclusions

Although the economic problems of Western societies are formidable, and exacerbated by the ageing of populations, their origin does not lie in elderly people using their electoral strength or organisational power to gain a privileged standard of living; on the contrary, most elderly people are less well-off than the rest of the population. The roots of conflictual ageism are to be found not in concern for younger generations but in an ideological preference for privatisation of pensions and in the interests of the financial institutions. Ageism neglects the intergenerational bonds formed within classes and the continuity of structured inequality over the life course as exemplified by elderly women's relative poverty. However, the myth of elderly affluence, bolstered by use of misleading figures on occupational pension receipt, may help to legitimate cuts in public provision for elderly people if left unchallenged.

So far the direct influence of pensioners' organisations on government policy has been rather limited, although greater in the US than in Britain. The mushrooming of British 'Grey Power' in terms of organisational membership in the 1980s indicates elderly people's desire to continue to participate in society and to age with dignity and independence in the face of ageist stereotypes and, for most, low incomes.

In both Britain and the US, organisations of elderly people are sharply divided by class. Both the AARP and ARP cater mainly for a middle-class membership, assuming that their needs can be met in the private market, while the Gray Panthers and National Pensioners' Convention affiliates represent the interests of less advantaged pensioners in defending collectivist benefits. The more egalitarian groupings, far from being in conflict with younger people, have stressed their solidarity with those of all ages who are poor and powerless. Their defence of public welfare has not been confined to pensions, but has included benefits and services for younger people. However, there are differences in approach between organisations in the two countries: whereas the Gray Panthers identify with and campaign with low income-groups of all ages and ethnic origins, the British NPC is heavily influenced in its structure and style by trade union traditions.

None of the major organisations of elderly people in either country shows more than a passing recognition of gender inequality of income among the elderly, and its origin in pension systems which relate pension income to lifetime earnings. The reasons for the neglect of older women's issues are not obvious; women participate in the organisations at all levels, but gender inequality has not emerged in the campaigning. Lobbying on gender issues has come mainly from organisations concerned with women's equality, OWL in the US and EOC in Britain.

The radical improvements in women's pensions needed to achieve gender equality of income in later life are unlikely to be won unless older women themselves are able to voice their needs to their organisations and to the wider society. Although older women's groups have not adopted the imaginative direct action techniques used by the Raging Grannies of Canada (whose campaigns have been concerned mainly with the environment and with peace) there are signs of an increasing awareness among older women of the importance of their contribution to society and of their right to a better deal in later life. Successive cohorts of women, influenced by second-wave feminism and with longer education, careers and experience of collective action behind them, are likely to have higher expectations and to organise more effectively.

Appendix

Statements made in the context of discussion of the adequacy of the state pension or of raising women's state pension age:

1   Social Security Advisory Committee Report, sent to Secretary of State in July 1992:

    'Now almost two thirds of those who retire can do so with an occupational pension.'

2   Letter from DSS to British Pensioners and Trade Union Association, 5 September 1992:

    '57 per cent of all pensioners and 69 per cent of recently retired pensioners had occupational pensions in 1988.'

3   Peter Lilley's speech to the International Conference on Social Security 50 years after Beveridge, 27 September 1992:

    'nearly 70 per cent of those now retiring in the UK will have supplemented their income in this way'.

Acknowledgements

I am grateful to all those who gave me information about older people's organisations, especially Astra Blaug, Eli Sanchez, Elizabeth Sclater and

Jack Thain, and to those who commented on an earlier version of the paper, especially Sara Arber, Kathy Meade and Zelda Curtis. For access to the General Household Survey data I am indebted to the ESRC Data Archive, University of Essex, and to the Manchester Computing Centre. I am grateful to the Office of Population Censuses and Surveys for permission to use the GHS data. The OPCS bear no responsibility for the analysis of the data. The paper is based on research projects funded by the Economic and Social Research Council (Grant Nos. R000233240 and R000231458).

Notes

1. The Pensions Act (1995) will in future allow splitting of occupational pension entitlements at divorce.
2. The Pensions Act (1995) has raised the state pension age for women born after April 1950, phasing in the change from 2010 to 2020 (Ginn and Arber, 1995).

References

Arber, S. and Ginn, J. (1991a) *Gender and Later Life: A Sociological Analysis of Resources and Constraints.* London: Sage.
Arber, S. and Ginn, J. (1991b) 'The invisibility of age: gender and class in later life', *Sociological Review*, 39(2): 260–91.
Arber, S. and Ginn, J. (1992) 'In sickness and in health: care-giving, gender and the independence of elderly people', in C. Marsh and S. Arber (eds), *Families and Households: Divisions and Change.* London: Macmillan.
Arendell, T. and Estes, C. (1991) 'Older women in the post-Reagan era', in M. Minkler and C.L. Estes (eds), *Critical Perspectives on Aging: The Political and Moral Economy of Growing Old.* New York: Baywood Publishing Company. pp. 209–26.
Askham, J., Henshaw, L. and Tarpey, M. (1993) 'Policies and perceptions of identity: service needs of elderly people from black and minority ethnic backgrounds', in S. Arber and M. Evandrou (eds), *Ageing, Independence and the Life Course.* London: Jessica Kingsley.
Atkin, K., Cameron, E., Badger, F. and Evers, H. (1989) '"Asian Elders" knowledge and future use of community social and health services', *New Community*, 15(3): 439–45.
Bernard, M. and Meade, K. (1993) *Women Come of Age: Perspectives on the Lives of Older Women.* London: Edward Arnold.
Binstock, R. (1974) 'Ageing and the future of American politics', in F. Eisele (ed.), *Political Consequences of Aging.* Annals of the American Academy of Political and Social Science. pp. 199–212.
Binstock, R. (1984) 'Reframing the agenda of policies on aging', in M. Minkler and C. Estes (eds), *Readings in the Political Economy of Aging.* Farmingdale, NY: Baywood. pp. 157–67.
Bone, M., Gregory, J., Gill, B. and Lader, D. (1992) *Retirement and Retirement Plans. A survey carried out by OPCS on behalf of the Department of Social Security.* London: HMSO.
Braithwaite, V. (1990) *Bound to Care.* Sydney: Allen & Unwin.
Brody, E. (1981) '"Women in the Middle" and family help to older people', *The Gerontologist*, 21(5): 471–9.
Button, J. and Rosenbaum, W. (1990) 'Gray power, gray peril, or gray myth? The political impact of the aging in local sunbelt politics', *Social Science Quarterly*, 71(1): 25–38.
Daly, M. (1979) *Gyn/Ecology.* London: Women's Press.
Daneshku, S. (1992) 'Pensions may be split in Divorces', *Financial Times*, 29/30 August: iv.
Ebrahim, S., Smith, C. and Giggs, J. (1987) 'Elderly immigrants: a disadvantaged group', *Age and Ageing*, 16: 249–55.
Equal Opportunities Commission (EOC) (1992) *A Question of Fairness.* Response by the Equal

Opportunities Commission to the Department of Social Security's Discussion Paper, Options for Equality in State Pension Age, Manchester: EOC.

Eurostat (1990) *Poverty in Figures. Europe in the Early 1980s*. Luxembourg: Office for Official Publications of the European Communities.

Falkingham, J. and Victor, C. (1991) *The Myth of the Woopie? Incomes, the Elderly, and Targeting Welfare*. Welfare State Programme Paper No 55, London: Suntory Toyota International Centre for Economics and Related Disciplines.

Fawcett News (1992) 'Older women are challenging the myths and looking for change', *Fawcett News*, November, London: The Fawcett Society.

Fennell, G., Phillipson, C. and Evers, C. (1988) *The Sociology of Old Age*. Open University Press: Milton Keynes.

Friedan, B. (1993) *The Fountain of Age*. New York: Simon & Schuster.

Ginn, J. and Arber, S. (1991) 'Gender, class and income inequalities in later life', *British Journal of Sociology*, 42(3): 369–96.

Ginn, J. and Arber, S. (1992) 'Towards women's independence: pension systems in three contrasting European welfare states', *European Journal of Social Policy*, 2(4): 255–77.

Ginn, J. and Arber, S. (1993) 'Pension penalties: the gendered division of occupational welfare', *Work Employment and Society*, 7(1): 43–66.

Ginn, J. and Arber, S. (1994) 'Heading for hardship: how the British pension system has failed women', in S. Baldwin and J. Falkingham (eds), *Social Security and Social Change: New Challenges to the Beveridge Model of Social Security*. Hemel Hempstead: Harvester Wheatsheaf.

Ginn, J. and Arber, S. (1995) 'Moving the goal posts: the impact on British women of raising their state pension age to 65', in J. Baldock and M. May (eds), *Social Policy Review*, 7. London: Social Policy Association. pp. 186–212.

Gray Panthers' Network, Washington, DC: GPN; Bergman, G. (1991) quoting Gonyea, Vol 20, No 2. p16. Amidei, N. (1988a) Vol 17, No 5, p3. Cowen, A. (1988b) Vol 17, No 5, p11.

Hedstrom, P. and Ringen, S. (1987) *Age and Income in Contemporary Society*. Stockholm: Swedish Institute for Social Research.

Hester, M. (1990) 'The dynamics of male domination using the witch craze in 16th and 17th century England as a case study', *Women's Studies International Forum*, 13 (1/2): 9–19.

Itzin, C. (1990) 'Age and sexual divisions: a study of opportunity and identity in women', University of Kent, PhD thesis.

Johnson, M. (1987) 'Towards racial equality in health and welfare: what progress?' *New Community*, 15 (1/2): 128–35.

Johnson, P., Conrad, C. and Thomson, D. (1989) *Workers versus Pensioners: Intergenerational Conflict in an Ageing World*. Manchester: Manchester University Press.

Joshi, H. (1987) 'The cost of caring', in C. Glendinning and J. Millar (eds), *Women and Poverty in Britain*. Brighton: Wheatsheaf. pp. 112–33.

Joshi, H. and Davies, H. (1991) *The Pension Consequences of Divorce*, Discussion Paper No. 550, London: Centre for Economic Policy Research.

Joshi, H. and Davies, B. (1992) *Women and Personal Pensions*. London: EOC/HMSO.

Laczko, F. and Phillipson, C. (1991) *Changing Work and Retirement*. Milton Keynes: Open University Press.

Land, H. and Rose, H. (1985) 'Compulsory altruism for some or an altruistic society for all?' in P. Bean, J. Ferris and D. Whynes (eds), *In Defence of Welfare*. London: Tavistock.

Lau, E. and Kosberg, J. (1979) 'Abuse of the elderly by informal care-givers', *Aging*, 2 (Sept./Oct.): 10–15.

Lilley, P. (1992) 'Address to the International Conference on Social Security 50 Years after Beveridge', York University, September.

Longman, P. and Poquet, G. (1986) 'The Age War', *The Futurist*, Jan.–Feb.

McCarthy, M. (ed.) (1989) *The New Politics of Welfare: An Agenda for the 1990s?* London: Macmillan.

McEwen, E. (ed.) (1990) *Age: The Unrecognised Discrimination*. London: Age Concern England.

McFarland, E., Dalton, M. and Walsh, D. (1989) 'Ethnic minority needs and service delivery: the barriers to access in a Glasgow inner-city area', *New Community*, 15(3): 405–15.

Midwinter, E. (1985) *The Wage of Retirement: The Case for a New Pension Policy*. London: Centre for Policy on Ageing.

Midwinter, E. (1992) *Citizenship: From Ageism to Participation, Carnegie Inquiry into the Third Age*, Research Paper No. 8, Carnegie United Kingdom Trust, Dunfermline.

Minkler, M. (1986) '"Generational equity" and the new victim blaming: an emerging public policy issue', *International Journal of Health Services*, 16(4): 539–51.

Moore, J., Tilson, B. and Whitting, G. (1994) *An International Overview of Employment Practices Towards Older Workers*, p. 88, Table D. London: Employment Department.

Morris, B. (1993) 'Ethnic elderly in Britain', *British Pensioner*, 8, Erith: British Pensioners and Trade Union Action Association.

Morton, J. (ed.) (1993) *Recent Research on Services for Black and Minority Ethnic Elderly People*. Report of Proceedings of the Ageing Update Conference held in London, July 1992. London: Age Concern Institute of Gerontology.

Navarro, V. (1984) 'The political economy of government cuts for the elderly', in M. Minkler and C. Estes (eds), *Readings in the Political Economy of Ageing*. Farmingdale, NY: Baywood. pp. 37–46.

Nissel, N. and Bonnerjea, L. (1982) *Family Care for the Elderly: Who Pays?* London: Policy Studies Institute.

Norman, A. (1985) *Triple Jeopardy: Growing Old in a Second Homeland*. London: Centre for Policy on Ageing.

Office for National Statistics (1996) *Labour Market Trends*, Table 3, p. 213, May. London: ONS.

Ogg, J. and Bennett, G. (1992) 'Elder abuse in Britain', *British Medical Journal*, 305 (24 Oct.): 998–9.

Older Women's League (1982) *Gray Paper No. 8: Not Even for Dogcatcher*. Washington, DC: Older Women's League.

Parker, H. (1992) *Citizen's Income and Women*. Basic Income Discussion Paper No. 2, London: Citizen's Income (formerly Basic Income Research Group).

Phillipson, C. (1982) *Capitalism and the Construction of Old Age*. London: Macmillan.

Preston, S. (1984) 'Children and the elderly in the US', *Scientific American*, 25(6): 44–9.

Quadagno, J. (1990) 'Generational equity and the politics of the welfare state', *International Journal of Health Services*, 20(4): pp. 631–49.

Ragan, P. and Dowd, J. (1974) 'The emerging political consciousness of the aged: a generational interpretation', *Journal of Social Issues*, 30: 137–58.

Robbins Dexter, M. (1990) *Whence the Goddesses*. Oxford: Pergamon Press.

Scott-Heide, W. (1984) 'Now for the feminist menopause that refreshes', in G. Lesnoff-Caravaglia (ed.), *The World of the Older Woman*. New York: Human Sciences Press. pp. 162–74.

Seeman, M. (1975) 'Alienation studies', *Annual Review of Sociology*, 1. Palo Alto, CA: Annual Reviews.

Social Security Advisory Committee (1992) *Options for Equality in State Pension Age: A Case for Equalising at 65*. London: HMSO.

Sommers, T. (1975) 'Social security: a woman's viewpoint', *Industrial Gerontologist*, 2(4): pp. 266–79.

Townsend, P. (1981) 'The structured dependency of the elderly: a creation of social policy in the twentieth century', *Ageing and Society*, 1(1): pp. 5–28.

US Bureau of the Census (1987) *Money Income and Poverty Status of Families and Persons in the United States: 1986 Census Population Reports*, series P60, No 1157, Washington, DC: US Bureau of the Census.

Walker, A. (1980) 'The social creation of poverty and dependency in old age', *Journal of Social Policy*, 9(1): pp. 49–75.

Wenger, G. (1990) 'Elderly carers: the need for appropriate intervention', *Ageing and Society*, 10(2): pp. 197–219.

Women's National Commission (1992) *Older Women, Myths and Strategies*. London: HMSO.

PART II

CITIZENSHIP, NEEDS AND PARTICIPATION

Introduction

David Taylor

Themes in Part II

The issue of social exclusion discussed by contributors to Part I raises the question: *on what basis may individuals be included in welfare?* This in turn begs the further questions: *what is the nature of inclusion?*; *what are appropriate strategies of participation?*; and *on what basis can entitlement and participation be guaranteed?* These questions are addressed in different ways by the contributors to Part II. However, a number of dilemmas arise, related to tensions between what we might loosely call 'modernist' and 'postmodernist' perspectives (for useful discussions of postmodernism and social policy see, Burrows and Loader, 1994; Hewitt, 1994; Taylor-Gooby, 1994; Williams, 1992). At their most general these are tensions between *universal* and *particularist (or selectivist)* approaches, both to the analysis of social policy and to forms of provision. They frequently emerge as debates between *universalistic rights-based arguments in defence of state welfare,* and *particularistic needs-based arguments associated with the self-advocacy of 'new social movements'*. One of the implicit themes of Part II is the problem of finding some common ground between what appear to be opposing principles.

The first way these issues are explored is through a critical examination of the essentially universalistic notion of *citizenship*. The central question is: does the concept of citizenship have the potential to be *inclusive* rather than *exclusive*? As a *legal* and *discursive* status can citizenship guarantee entitlement based on universal social rights or is there the danger of marginalising the needs of particular groups, or of articulating a view of the citizen which excludes particular identities? Contributors to Part II draw attention to the way citizenship has been constructed as essentially male and white, and consider possible approaches to a more inclusive definition.

A second issue in Part II is the question of *empowerment* and *participation*. Participation implies active involvement in the social sphere and this can be seen either as a strategy for the achievement of particular welfare goals or as an end in itself. Put another way, is participation simply a means to the end of meeting need, or should needs be met in order to enable participation as an essential characteristic of human subjectivity (see Twine, 1994, Doyal and Gough, 1991, for the latter position)? A further, and more practical issue arises concerning the nature of participation. Much contemporary political debate has employed a view of participation as *choice within a mixed economy of welfare*. This passive view of *participation as consumerism* is in sharp contrast to participation as *collective self-advocacy* discussed by some of the contributors here.

Considering collective self-advocacy by user-groups raises a third thematic point: what is the relationship between advocating particular needs and defending universal rights to welfare? This question is often addressed to the so-called 'new social movements' or in this case 'new social welfare movements'. Can such movements sustain a lasting politics of welfare which outlive particular issues or transcend particular viewpoints?

Lastly, the opposition between *universalist* and *particularist* standpoints is problematised by a number of contributors. Are the two necessarily in opposition; are there degrees of both; and is there the possibility of combining a politics of welfare and a philosophical justification of social provision which allows for *equality* and *difference*?

Articles in Part II

'Citizenship and social power', by the present author (first published in 1989), argues that citizenship rights operate within the context of power. In particular, power relations of class, 'race' and gender underlie the 'false universalism' of state welfare and the 'consumerist democracy' of the market and have marginalised, 'those excluded from the "collective" nature of state welfare provision, on the one hand, and those unable to compete as market consumers on the other' (p. 156). Historically, citizenship is seen as exclusive of those not deemed appropriate to bear the rights and duties of community membership. This 'community' is usually the nation-state and its legitimating ideology nationalism. The rights of the 'included', therefore have to be set against those outside the nation and citizenship seen in a world context, where the 'international division of labour and the processes of exclusion of "racialised" groups and migrant labour' (p. 163) are addressed. The article touches on the need to integrate appeals to universal notions of rights with a 'dynamic concept of need' (p. 164) and looks critically at those 'new social movements' whose conception of political struggle is limited to the sphere of 'civil society'. A confrontation with organised power is seen as inevitable if genuine challenges to the social relations of power are mounted in the name of an inclusionary social citizenship.

The critical investigation of citizenship is taken further by Ruth Lister in 'Citizenship engendered' (first published in 1991). The author criticises 'gender-blind' conceptions of citizenship which, because women are no longer excluded from formal civil and political rights of citizenship . . . [have] . . . no perception that our relationship to citizenship and the public sphere, in which it is conventionally sited, may be different from that of men. Nor that, as currently understood, the very notion might be problematic for women. (p. 168)

She also recognises the mediation of citizenship by 'other factors such as "race", class, poverty, disability, sexual orientation and age' (p. 169) and acknowledges debates about diversity and difference. Her starting point, however, is 'the public–private divide and the power relations that both underpin and are sustained by it' (p. 169).

Drawing on Nancy Fraser's work Lister argues that 'treating everything outside the domestic sphere as "the public" conflates at least three analytically distinct things: the state, the official economy of paid employment and arenas of political discourse' (p. 169). She goes on to show how women are disadvantaged in all three spheres and how each is related to the other. Women's lack of time (the presumption of the caring role and paid work) and of money (poorer conditions in the labour market and dependency in the benefit system) mean that women are less able to participate in what Fraser calls the 'strong publics'. These are the political arenas associated with decision-making, as opposed to the 'weak publics' associated with opinion-forming occupied by the new social movements, in which women are well represented. Yet, she argues, it is 'hard to imagine any positive changes in women's private and political life, if they are not encouraged to enter the public sphere and fight for a more democratic citizenship' (p. 172). If women are to enter into full citizenship, she concludes,

this would mean a transformation of the sexual division of labour (paid and unpaid) and of time; in the organisation of paid work and politics. It would mean extending and strengthening social rights of citizenship so as to recognise the value of unpaid caring work without trapping women further into it. (p. 173)

Participation in the public sphere is the central focus of Suzy Croft and Peter Beresford's contribution, 'The politics of participation' (first published in 1992). The authors identify four developments which have increased concern with notions of empowerment and participation: the emergence of new social welfare movements which express 'their concern with a different politics: a participatory politics' (p. 178); the rekindling of interest in human need – especially the work of Doyal and Gough and its concern with social participation, by which 'they mean the quantity and quality of social interactions' (p. 178); the re-emergence of the idea of citizenship – particularly the concern with social exclusion; and, postmodernism, where the 'recognition of diversity . . . offers us a way of going beyond the universalism versus selectivity debate in social policy and of taking account of people's different needs as well as their universal rights' (p. 181).

While these developments have led to a renewed interest in participation, there is some confusion as to its precise meaning. Participation is linked, they argue, to the concept of *user-involvement* associated with the 'shift away from *service-* or *provider-led* public provision to more *user-centred* services' (p. 184). There are two competing approaches to user-involvement: the 'consumerist and the democratic approaches' (p. 186). The former is more usually associated with service providers and the latter with service users and their organisations. There is more to genuine participation, however, than simply advocating greater user-involvement. Some forms of involvement may not challenge existing power relations, and indeed, organisations may co-opt users to give the impression of participation. 'Participatory initiatives can be a route to redistributing power, changing relationships and creating opportunities for influence. Equally they can double as a means of keeping power from people and giving a false impression of its transfer' (p. 191). The key to 'resolving the paradox of participation', as they call it, is being clear about the objectives of participation – do they genuinely reflect the needs of users? – and of making sure users are able to participate. In order to achieve this both *access* and *support* are necessary.

They conclude by arguing that

> participation in social policy need not and probably should not only be conceived in narrow terms, for example, as the province solely of the subjects of marginalising policies and services. Instead it is linked with much broader issues. Indeed we would argue that participatory social policy can offer a route to a more participatory politics. (p. 195)

Relating the particular needs of social movements to a wider perspective is the central concern of Martin Hewitt's contribution, 'Social movements and social need: problems with postmodern political theory' (first published in 1993). Do the goals of social movements, he asks, 'have a bearing on the predicament society faces? Put another way, how might it be said that a movement with its own particular concerns comes to reflect a more universal viewpoint?' (p. 199).

He addresses this question through a consideration of postmodernism. Postmodern theorists he argues, 'are strongly wedded to a particularist view of the goals and needs of social movements' (p. 200), yet it is possible to detect another less explicit thread in postmodern thought 'which suggests that social movements are seeking to found new arrangements governed by a different order of *universal* values and needs' (p. 201, emphasis added). At the level of theory this is present in 'the inescapable need to employ universalist concepts in thinking through new problems' (p. 203), especially where 'universal recognition permits *identity and difference to co-exist* – a position currently explored in feminist political theory . . . and in Habermas' theory of communicative action' (p. 207). In the latter, Habermas sees social movements as engaged in a search for 'cultural identity' and a 'range of specific cultural objectives about the quality of life' (p. 207) which transcend *particular* welfare measures. 'In this way [Habermas] stresses the particularist concerns of social movements with equality, self-realisation, participation and human rights' (ibid.), *combined with a universal* concern to recover the communicative foundations of social life. As Hewitt points out,

Habermas is more circumspect about what he calls 'defensive' social movements than the 'universal' movements such as feminism (though the universalism of feminism is something challenged by many of the writers here – see Part I in particular). Nevertheless, Hewitt sees a means of combining particularism and universalism in Habermas' work:

> he [Habermas] appears to suggest that even 'defensive' movements concerned with problems of local identity seek to overcome their specific . . . horizons of personal and collective fulfilment. Thus a defence of specific identities and needs provides the grounds for raising more universalistic concerns. (p. 209)

One way in which universalist and particularist approaches can be combined is in Doyal and Gough's work on need. Hewitt uses their work to show how, 'culturally specific needs can be articulated in the language of universal needs' (p. 210). They combine an argument for the universal human needs of physical survival and personal autonomy with a recognition that the way these needs are met will be culturally specific:

> while their discussion conceives needs in universal terms, they recognise that in identifying actual conditions of needing and the satisfiers required, intermediate needs must be interpreted in culturally relative terms . . . However, for Doyal and Gough the process of meeting needs is emancipatory and rational, and so cannot be resolved in terms of cultural relativism alone. (ibid.)

Hewitt concludes by noting that recent empirical studies of public perceptions of poverty have found a close correlation between subjective views of the 'poverty line' and objective measures used in social science research. 'Recent developments in social policy studies of need provide empirical support for the existence of a universal dimension of need beyond the contextualisations of relative definitions of needs' (p. 217).

The exploration of *universalist* and *particularist* principles in welfare is the focus of the final contribution by Paul Spicker, 'Understanding particularism' (first published in 1994). Universalist principles are usually employed to defend an institutional model of welfare, especially where benefits are available to all, and particularist principles are traditionally associated with residual or 'targeted' models of welfare based on needs. There is another, 'thinner' sense of universalism, however, which Spicker says could be applied to both institutional and residual models – one in which, put simply, 'the same rules are applied to everyone' (p. 220). The most common form of contemporary particularist arguments is 'communitarianism'. 'Communitarians argue that the values and norms on which a social critique can be founded must be drawn from specific social contexts' (p. 221). The debate between universalists and communitarians cuts across 'left' and 'right' and Spicker's aim is 'to try to reconcile [communitarianism and particularism] with the universal values on which socialism depends' (p. 221).

In his critical examination of particularism, Spicker highlights its inherently discriminatory nature, but points out, 'discrimination is not necessarily random, irrational or indefensible; it is based on criteria like kinship, friendship, community and nationality. The kinds of responsibilities which people recognise to each other are not universal; they depend on existing ties' (p. 222). The effect of communitarian discrimination is to exclude outsiders, but this exclusion may be grounded in morally acceptable imperatives like 'mutual support, community, personal relationships and loyalty' (p. 227).

> Particularist doctrines suggest that, in the way in which people relate to us, they are not equivalent; we have special responsibilities to some people which we do not have to others. The effect of the universalist argument might be to impose duties on everybody, but these duties will not be as strong or as demanding as those which are specific to other people. (pp. 227–8)

However, unless based upon some limited universal criteria, communitarian positions may become exclusive and discriminatory (in the sense of prejudice) and may 'encourage separatism and racism' (p. 226). The kind of universalism which Spicker is referring to can again be found in the work of Doyal and Gough and their conception of universal human needs. It may also be found in notions of universal human rights. Spicker calls approaches which combine these elements 'moderate particularism'. Particular claims may be understood within specific contexts, but they must still be weighed against certain universal criteria:

> Increasing people's freedom, and reducing their disadvantage, are general principles, even if they can only be understood in a social context; they apply to everyone. If principles like 'community' and 'solidarity' are advocated as a means of empowerment and removal of disadvantage, there does not have to be any inconsistency. But this means that they must be treated as secondary rather than primary values; universal claims like freedom and equality have priority. (p. 231)

Reflecting on empowerment, Spicker points out that those who are 'empowered' to participate, may end up protecting their own position, as through participation:

> People are being empowered to do the kinds of things which other people do; and the kinds of things which other people do are often discriminatory. The real dilemma for communitarian socialism rests not, then, in the need to reconcile universalism with particularism in theory, but in the problem of respecting universal values in practice. (p. 232)

It is clear, then, that the themes in Part II are all closely interrelated. Strategies to make welfare socially inclusive raise questions about the nature of participation; participation and empowerment raise questions about the relationship between particular and universal needs and interests; the question of interests relates to the potential or otherwise of social welfare movements to generate generalisable welfare goals. These questions, have themselves, to be understood in the context of issues raised in Part I about the role of social relations as they underpin the entire project of social welfare. They are central for those concerned with the non-discriminatory forms of welfare.

References

Burrows, R. and Loader, B. (eds) (1994) *Towards a Post-Fordist Welfare State?* London: Routledge.

Doyal, L. and Gough, I. (1991) *A Theory of Human Need.* London: Macmillan.

Hewitt, M. (1994) 'Social policy and the question of postmodernism', in N. Manning and R. Page (eds), *Social Policy Review 6.* Canterbury: Social Policy Association.

Taylor-Gooby, P. (1994) 'Postmodernism and social policy: a great leap backwards?' *Journal of Social Policy,* 23(3): 385–404.

Twine, F. (1994) *Citizenship and Social Rights.* London: Sage.

Williams, F. (1992) 'Somewhere over the rainbow: universality and diversity in social policy', in N. Manning and R. Page (eds), *Social Policy Review 4.* Canterbury: Social Policy Association.

8

Citizenship and Social Power

David Taylor

The concept of 'citizenship' is enjoying something of a renaissance amongst political philosophers and welfare theorists. Market liberals, welfare pluralists, social democrats and neo-Marxists have all laid their claims, and campaigns such as Charter 88, in England, have based their call for a 'Bill of Rights' and for democratic reforms on a reassertion of citizens' rights against the usurpation of power by an increasingly authoritarian state. Authors such as Melucci (1989), Keane (1988a, 1988b), Habermas (1989), Cohen and Arato (1984) have become increasingly interested in the idea of 'public spaces' within civil society as locations for the 'democratisation of everyday life' (Melucci, 1989). The idea of individuals forming themselves into voluntary public associations in a space between the state and the market and organising in non-traditional political forms to realise their interests, guaranteed by the 'rule of law' is seen as a basis for promoting active citizenship. In this context, writers like Melucci (1989), Touraine (1985) and others look to the practices of the 'New Social Movements' (NSMs) for progressive models of 'anti-political politics'.

Some authors (most notably Keane, 1988a, 1988b) have faith in the 'best elements' of the liberal tradition to provide us with a foundation for a theory of citizenship, while others are happy to rework Herbert Marshall's (1950) classic views on welfare. A different approach is suggested here, however. If the concept of citizenship is to be of any use to progressive politics in Britain, it must be taken out of its liberal history and inserted into a very different set of theorisations and political practices. Indeed, the liberal tradition of citizenship, resting on an abstract notion of rights and an appeal to *universalism* has ignored the particular reality of power. In this context, social relations of power are seen as taking historically varying forms, but most notably those associated with class gender and 'race'. These historically specific power relations have undermined attempts to realise the liberal ideal of citizenship through either the false collectivism of state welfare or the consumerist 'democracy' of the market. Both these ways of attempting to meet citizenship rights have led to the marginalisation of those excluded from the 'collective' nature of state welfare provision on the one hand, and of those unable to compete as market consumers on the

First published in *Critical Social Policy*, 26, 1989.

other. Abstract conceptions of rights and entitlements attached to citizenship, then, must come to terms with the underlying structural power relations which underscore practices of *both* state and market mechanisms.

In addition, the political history of citizenship rights is inextricably linked to the history of Western European nationalism, which in turn must be situated in its world historical context. This history is one in which the consolidation of national states to which citizens belong and against which they have claims has to be understood in terms of an international division of labour, a particular world distribution of resources and the super-exploitation of human labour and the environment by the capitalist core. Citizenship (in Western Europe) becomes not only a process of the struggle for rights and entitlements in Western European nation states but also a struggle to reject claims of entitlement by those initially residing outside the core, and, subsequently, of migrant and immigrant labour. The 'liberal' history of citizenship, then, must be viewed in the context of a set of *inclusionary* and *exclusionary* practices, aimed at consolidating a particular set of social relations and of rights and entitlements. A reappropriation of citizenship must not simply be tied to an abstract set of rights guaranteed by the 'rule of law', but address the deeper bases of social power. This does not, I believe, entail an abandonment of the idea of social claims against the state, in fact just the opposite. It demands a reconceptualisation of citizenship based on the notion of need. A claim to entitlement abstracted into the form of rights can, however, be anchored in the concept of need. In this respect recent claims, such as those by Harris (1987) that it is not possible to identify needs objectively, and more general claims that rights form the only universalisable basis for welfare, are not accepted here. Doyal and Gough (1984, 1989) have attempted a definition of need which may address some of the problems raised by liberal theorists, and others (most notably Gould, 1988) have implicitly argued for a universal basis of need in terms of potentiality – the need of each individual for access to the conditions and resources necessary for their own self-development. Whereas Harris (1987), for example, rejecting the universalising prospects for a concept of need and acknowledging the limited impact of rights collapses his argument into a call for 'communitarianism' (the idea that rights flow from membership of a community), it is argued here that membership of a community may in fact be seen as a basis for exclusion from rights.

It is possible, however, to conceive of need in a dynamic sense the content of which is not fixed, but consists of a set of conditions which can be expressed in terms of rights – where these refer to the conditions necessary for the fulfilment of differential need.

The State Versus the Market: A False Dichotomy

The idea of a space between the state and the market, somewhere in 'civil society' where citizens can make democratic initiatives is put forward most forcefully by Keane (1988a, 1988b). In this territory, occupied politically by the NSMs, it may be possible to construct new political forms by 'making state policy more accountable to civil society and by democratically expanding and reordering non-state activities within civil society itself' (Keane, 1988a: 3). This conceptualisation depends upon the retention of the distinction between civil society and the state and the idea of an area outside the state/market division in which public spaces can be 'freed up'.

There seems to me to be a fundamental difficulty with this 'civil society socialism' (Hoffman, 1988) due, in large part, to its essentialist conception of democracy and rights. First, the state/market couplet leads us into an intellectual cul-de-sac where collectivism and individualism, authoritarianism and freedom, etc. come to be depicted as discrete alternatives within capitalist social formations. This analytic distinction between the state and the market, has a limited descriptive use at the level of organisational principle, but turns out to be of less use when confronting underlying power relations which underscore both state and market mechanisms. At one level, it can be argued that both are underscored by the structural divisions of class, gender and 'race' which take different forms through state and market mechanisms – both organising social power in different ways. The history of state intervention in the provision of welfare in Britain, however, shows not the clash of opposites, but the interweaving of different mechanisms which often work in a complementary fashion. Indeed, the current experiences of restructuring in contemporary Britain are increasingly revealed, as the rhetoric slips away, not as a direct choice between the state and the market in welfare provision, but of a new set of arrangements: internal or state regulated markets. Recent developments in Britain, for example the Education Act, 1988, the NHS Review (1988), the Housing Act 1988, reveal a direction in which both state provision and competitive consumerism play an interlinked role. (For a discussion of the implications of the NHS Review in this respect, see Petchey, 1989.) In fact the historically complementary relationship between the state and the market as different organisational forms of power is shown in the way in which these apparently opposing principles have been unable to act as real counterbalancing tendencies upon the operation of each other. The market has not been a democratising force against the bureaucratic collectivism of state control, and neither has collective welfare provision overcome the known problem of inequality and marginalisation associated with the market. Admittedly, there may be openings for the left to rethink new forms of welfare provision in the interstices of these mechanisms, but there is a danger of disappearing down a chasm into a notion of civil society (or community) which itself fails to acknowledge power at the base.

The state and the market, then, are more usefully thought of as different organisational forms within the totality of social relations, which institutionalise social power. This enables us to understand why Marshall's idea of welfare citizenship (1950) has foundered on the rocks of a fragmented collectivism. The hoped-for integration effect of the welfare state found in both Fabianism and the more functionalist brands of Marxism (see Williams, 1987 for a critique) has rightly been criticised by feminist and anti-racist writers (Pascall, 1986; Dadzie et al., 1986) for ignoring both the patriarchal and racist structures of state welfare which separate and disunify 'universal' interests, and for its Eurocentric and nationalist understanding of citizenship – a classic example is the way in which positive entitlements to pension rights during the Liberal reform period were tied to the exclusion of 'aliens' from rights and based on the advancement of certain sections of labour at the cost of the super-exploitation of the colonies.

The idea then, of freeing up a space somewhere between the state and the market, operates mainly on the ideological terrain. Indeed, according to Melucci (1988, 1989) the actors in this space – the NSMs – operate largely on symbolic grounds, challenging the 'codes' of contemporary discourse. However, these NSMs often have class, gender or 'racial' positions which fragment their apparent unity or have histories of their own (in this respect the reference to the Black liberation struggle as an NSM is revealing) which situate them in very specific power relations. If there is a 'prefigurative' (Deacon, 1983) potential in some of the forms of political organisation adopted by NSMs, careful attention must be paid to whether they challenge not only the symbolic codes of contemporary discourse, but the underlying structures of power organised through both the state and the market. Do they confront the false consumerist democracy of the market and do they challenge the structures of the state? When they do, for example in the case of Black urban protests in Britain in the early 1980s, they find this 'public space' or 'community' suddenly 'swamped' by the repressive structures of state power. Unless a set of citizenship rights won from the state embraces the 'racialisation' of citizenship, it may come up against some very difficult decisions, given its liberal basis, about alternative claims to rights.

Civil Society Versus the State

Second, the civil society/state distinction also proves problematic. The whole notion of civil society as a separate sphere, beyond the state, in which citizenship claims might emerge, overlooks a number of important issues. Again, whether this analytic distinction bears any relationship to the lived reality of social relations seems doubtful. Almost all contemporary political philosophers seem at pains to point to the extensive intervention and regulation of 'private' life via the apparatuses of the state, and indeed, the vast spread of state agencies and apparatuses is one of the dominant characteristics of late capitalist societies. How far there is life, 'beyond the gaze of the state' in western capitalist societies is not at all clear. Where there is a formal absence of regulation and control expressed in law and formal social policy, there is often the informal (semi-formal?) regulation through the back door. An obvious example is the way in which welfare agencies are often used to police the implementation of immigration policies, through the requirement of citizenship proof. Civil society in which 'communities' exist is structured through the power relations which underlie both the state and the market.

The way in which community is often seen as an undifferentiated collectivity has been pointed out by feminist writers in particular. Their arguments about the gendered nature of community (Finch, 1984; Croft, 1986 and others) show us that the spaces of civil society are themselves riven by power relations. The patriarchal assumptions behind such notions as 'informal caring networks', for example, have been roundly exposed. The unproblematic assimilation of the nature of community as a basis for citizenship is clearly demonstrated in Harris' recent arguments (1987: 145):

> The core of the citizenship theory of the welfare state is community membership. Community membership is the good to be promoted by welfare institutions in a market economy – from our membership of our community flow the welfare rights we can assert and the duties we owe to contribute to the support of our fellows.

Membership of the assumed community of 'informal caring networks' may serve, not only to reinforce certain gender role expectations, but to disenfranchise those carers. Precisely because they are informal, caring networks bring with them no formal basis for democratic control and accountability. There is no community basis, within such networks, for the assertion of citizenship rights or of democratic control.

At a deeper level, a number of writers (Pateman, 1988a, 1988b; Benhabib and Cornell, 1986; Benton, 1988) have mounted a serious critique of the concept of civil society as it has emerged in liberal philosophy. They point to the way in which the 'civic public' of Locke, Rousseau and utilitarianism, is a gendered realm, identified with reason and public virtue. This classic Enlightenment view of reason is tied, according to Young (1986), to a notion of objectivity, of being detached in order to be 'public spirited'. This notion emerged in Western Europe along with the separation of the public and the private and the distinction between reason and desire in Enlightenment philosophy. These two spheres come to be identified increasingly with the male and the female respectively, as women are charged with the moral and emotional side of private life, and increasingly associated with desire, emotionality and irrationality, and a closeness to nature, unlike 'cultured' men. This becomes, quite explicitly in the case of Rousseau, a reason for the exclusion of women from civil society (Young, 1986). Carol Pateman has shown (1988a, 1988b) how the ideal of citizenship as it develops in this tradition, involves the notion of 'fraternity' – an equality of brotherhood, that is, the modern patriarchy of equal men, as opposed to the traditional patriarchy of rule of the father – in which the public is based on what she calls 'the fraternal social contract' (1988b), and agreement amongst equals about the exclusion of women from the realm of public life.

If we accept this interpretation of citizenship then as Sarah Benton argues (1988: 19) the civil liberties we scrutinize today should not just be those of the Great Tradition, of freedom of speech and movement and assembly and against the state's invasion of privacy. There are 'privacies' the state must invade if women are to be full citizens. For they cannot begin to enjoy the classic liberties while their lives are curtained within the veiled area of private life, cut off from the state's protectorate by the protectorate of men.

The intervention of the state into the 'private' realm is, of course, more problematic than Benton perhaps implies. We know how the state is involved in the regulation of the 'private' space of the family through a whole range of welfare and social measures which attempt to reinforce female dependency and gender roles. We know also how the state tries to regulate Black family life and attempts to restrict Black women's fertility and keep Black family members apart. All of this, of course, is circumscribed by nationality, immigration and welfare legislation anchored in chauvinistic, Eurocentric and racist practices which shape conceptions of citizenship.

Attempts, then, to extend the realities of citizenship in civil society must not just seek an extension of rights from the state, but must challenge the patriarchal and racist structures of state power and engage in a wider practice tied to the emancipatory struggles of those opposing such powers. Young (1986: 76) offers a view of the political process in a reconstituted 'public space':

> the Enlightenment ideal of the civic public where citizens meet in terms of equality and mutual respect is too rounded and tame an ideal of public. The ideal of equal citizenship attains unity because it excludes bodily and affective particularity, as well as the concrete histories of individuals that make groups unable to understand one another. Emancipatory politics should foster a conception of public which in principle excludes no persons, aspects of persons' lives, or topic of discussion and which encourages aesthetic as well as discursive expression. In such a public, consensus and sharing may not always be the goal, *but the recognition and appreciation of differences, in the context of confrontation with power.*

Young cites the 1984 Jesse Jackson campaign and the idea of a rainbow coalition (as opposed to the idea of a popular front) as an example of this type of politics.

Citizenship, Nationalism and Welfare

Writers from most perspectives on citizenship, whether pro-market (cf Judge, 1987) or collectivist in orientation (Plant et al., 1980) stress the *integrative* aspect of citizenship, especially as it is tied to welfare (Marshall, 1950). Welfare rights are often identified as a compensation for inequalities, and a means to equal treatment. In this context the claims of citizenship in terms of a codified access to welfare through rights is increasingly argued as a counterbalance to the privatisation and marketisation of welfare in Britain. In this sense, there is a strong, anti-authoritarian element that can be used as a campaigning plank in liberal and democratic arguments about welfare provision.

However, we must be very cautions about the concept of integration, whether taken from the 'social administration' tradition or from the more functionalist inspired Marxisms of the recent years (see Williams, 1987 and this volume). It is not difficult to see the practical ways in which welfare mechanisms have failed to 'integrate' many sections of a differentiated 'collectivity' both formally and informally. The formal denial of welfare rights to women and to racialised groups both in the welfare legislation from the period of the 'Great Liberal Reforms', through Beveridge to present-day legislation, is well documented (Cohen, 1985 and this volume; Dadzie et al., 1986) and the unofficial racism and sexism associated with the workings of welfare institutions is increasingly being exposed. But these criticisms should not be seen as referring to some aberration in practice of a collectivist principle. The abstract conception of integration, theorised as it is from a notion of systemic needs and riven with tautological assumptions (see Lee and Raban, 1988), has to be set in a wider context.

Citizenship, as a legal entitlement to rights and subjection to law, carries with it, not just the formal membership of a nation state, but a whole set of socio-economic and ideological practices associated with nationalism. These amount to mechanisms of *exclusion* and *inclusion* of particular groups and categories of individual. These have included, most notably, those without property, women, racialised groups and the differently abled, children and lesbians and gay men.

Citizenship, then, is related to the socio-economic and ideological construction of nation, nationality and of 'culture' (Gilroy, 1987; Cohen, 1985 and this volume). Its task at the political level has been to construct a social formation, within which claims to rights can be judged according to the rule of law. Arguments around citizenship thus tend to be around an appeal to legal rights. This, however, abstracts these rights from their historical context and out of their international context in a world division of labour.

An instructive example of the exclusionary nature of citizenship is the case of the British Nationality Act, 1982. This piece of legislation, which merely extends and codifies trends set in motion in earlier legislation, has been described as 'constitutionalising racism' (Dixon, 1981). This Act established three categories of citizenship: British Citizen, Citizen of the British Dependent Territories and British Overseas Citizen, with different entitlements to abode and to rights. The last category carries with it no right of abode and is a completely worthless citizenship – for example it cannot be passed on to the 'citizen's' children. A major intention of the legislation is to exclude particular groups (mainly Black groups) from right to reside and thus to make claims against the state.

Alongside this must be placed the Immigration Act 1988, which, codifying the existing racist and sexist content of previous immigration legislation, extends the infamous 'no recourse to public funds' clause.

Whereas the wives of British and Commonwealth men who settled in Britain on or before 1 January 1973 could be brought into the country by their husbands under the previous Immigration Act of 1971, it now has to be demonstrated that if they do come they can be supported themselves and will have 'no recourse to public funds'. This is not defined in the Act, but is interpreted to include public housing and the NHS, for example. Where a husband is already, himself, receiving 'public funds' such as in council housing, then right to entry is likely to be refused altogether. (For a discussion of the effects of immigration policy on Asian women, see Brah, 1987.)

These exclusionary practices are not arbitrary or accidental – nor are they the result merely of extreme 'New Right' thinking. The basis for these exclusionary practices can be found in the immigration legislation of Labour governments in the 1960s and the Liberal legislation in the pre-First World War era (for example, the Aliens Act of 1905). They were intimately bound up with the processes of British nationalism. The 'integrative' advantages of welfare policies for some sections has been inextricably linked to the denial of citizenship for others and the super-exploitation of the underdeveloped nations. It is indeed very difficult to see the concept of citizenship outside its international context. Advances in the capitalist core have rarely led to advances for the periphery. In this context, then, arguments for citizenship must address the international division of labour and the processes of exclusion of 'racialised' groups and of migrant labour. Failure to do this allows the formation of another set of interests – 'the national interest' above and beyond the abstract rights of individuals. This is then invoked to exclude those who do not find their lived experience of citizenship validated by the rule of law from challenging the power relations upon which rights are based. A concept of citizenship, if it is to be genuinely liberatory, must be internationalist and anti-nationalist. This may entail a radical rethinking of traditional forms of entitlement which have given rights to a particular set of citizens at the expense of others.

Citizenship and Need

Citizenship rights and entitlements must be tied to a fulfilment of need. Need in this respect can be seen as dynamic and differentiated, as against the universal and abstract basis of rights. The meeting of need, implies not just a set of rights but the power to achieve needs, in terms of access to resources. Needs can only be satisfied in an active process of human development, both individually and socially. The concept of citizenship tied to the idea of the right to satisfy need becomes dynamic, political and comes into a confrontation with power. This means challenging the nationalistic and exclusionary practices associated with state power and the marginalisation effects of the market. As Hoffman (1988: 201) has recently argued, 'without confronting the question of state power, the participatory democrat cannot meet the challenge posed by the rhetorical libertarianism of the New Right'. This is going to bring those engaged in radical arguments about citizenship and needs into confrontation with the repressive apparatuses of the state. A political movement which fails to address this may find itself tolerated within the sphere of civil society, but unable to deliver anything beyond that already encompassed in present legislative programmes.

A dynamic concept of need, as an openly political issue, can address the fact that the formal equality of rights still remains situated within different power relations. It is possible to identify a universal set of *principles* which guarantee common human needs (Doyal and Gough, 1989), and Gould (1988) in an interesting discussion of freedom and democracy, defines freedom in a similar way as need is approached here. Freedom is defined in a 'positive' way as access to the social conditions necessary for individual development. This is premised on a notion of equality in terms of each individual's entitlement to the conditions necessary for human self-development (Gould, 1988: 60). Alongside a concern with positive freedom, goes the concern with negative freedom, of the right not to be denied access to these conditions by others. This immediately raises the question of confrontation with those who have the power to deny access to resources. This means extending rights beyond the political sphere to the socio-economic sphere:

> The principle of equal rights is familiar in traditional liberal democratic theory, but there it appears as a principle of political equality, that is equality in voting and in civil liberties and rights. Here, however, the principle of equal rights applies not only to such political contexts but to social and economic ones as well. (1988: 60–61)

The well-known limitations of traditional welfare citizenship theories associated with Marshall's work (1950), which fail to extend the argument for rights into the economic sphere, into production as well as consumption, can be challenged using this approach. Rights can only be meaningful if they raise the possibility of access to and control over the resources necessary to realise the human need for self-development. Thus the passive tradition of redistribution of resources through welfare, which as Le Grand (1982) and other theorists have demonstrated is a false one is substituted by a politics which tackles issues of democratic control of production processes. This, however, must be situated in the context of an expanded view of production which is tied not only to property relations but recognises the gendered and racialised basis of power in capitalist social formations.

From this perspective, arguments for welfare citizenship and for the extension of democratic rights, are extended beyond formal legal entitlements and the rule of law, to include political practices of a collective nature which challenge the structures of power inherent within both the state and market mechanisms. The difference between this and an 'NSM' approach is that here it is argued that movements which fail to tackle the structures of power, codified and organised through both the state and the market, will have only transitory effects and will remain issue based. When the issue fades from public discourse there is no guarantee that gains won will be maintained.

An argument against the above position is the question of how do we arrive, through a democratic decision-making process, at a calculation of need in a society divided by power? This philosophical argument fails to observe that in the most advanced countries the most basic of human needs for the conditions of self-development are not met for large numbers of people, and that, in a world context, the most basic needs are constantly undermined and refused for the people of large parts of the globe. Doyal and Gough's taxonomy of 'individual needs' (1984: 10) includes, 'survival/ health, autonomy/learning' which should be optimised through the universal need of human liberation. These needs can hardly be said to have been met in Britain for those denied access to housing, the right to education or the rights and entitlements of citizenship through nationality legislation. In a world context, it means an awareness of and a political alliance with those movements challenging the over-provision of 'wants' for a small number in the West on the basis of the super-exploitation of the underdeveloped world. In this sense, arguments or rights which encapsulate access to the resources to meet needs must be sensitive to the world distribution of resources, both human and natural and realise that a liberatory politics cannot be simply nationalistic.

Need, in this respect, can be judged differentially in the context of an acknowledgement of power associated with existing exclusions from rights and practices necessary to have access to resources, both within and between nations. Acknowledging the right of marginalised or excluded groups to demand their own forms of collective action to achieve their needs is one step. This means that the universalistic rule of law criteria for forms of political organisation have to be very carefully thought out. What would be the attitude, for example, of a citizenship state to the autonomous organisation and demands of republics, ethnic minorities or of racialised groups who express their demands in non-traditional forms of political organisation and protest? Citizenship theory has to be able to allow those autonomous movements, not just the 'public spaces' of civil society, but the right to challenge the state and market structures of power.

Conclusion

The concept of citizenship has a radical purchase in opposing the authoritarian denial of civil rights and liberties. In the context of a restructuring of welfare its appeal is clear: a reassertion of claims against the state and as a demand for just and equal treatment and demands for welfare rights. Directed towards an appeal to the 'rule of law', however, its political effect is likely to be limited to an intellectual campaign. The abstract liberal tradition of rights must come to terms with feminist and anti-racist critiques which demonstrate the failure of citizenship rights vested in liberal democratic institutions to meet the needs of women and racialised groups and the socially and economically marginalised. This is because the liberal traditions of citizenship are tied inextricably to a set of exclusionary practices associated with nationalism.

A radical movement inspired by the idea of citizenship must challenge its Eurocentric focus, tied to the development of the capitalist core at the expense of the periphery, and thus see citizenship in an international context and acknowledge the super-exploitation of the world division of labour. The movements of those fighting the exclusionary practices associated with citizenship rights both within and outside the core must be part of the struggle to realise a transformed notion of citizenship. Without this acknowledgement rights campaigns run the risk of maintaining a narrow and inward-looking focus. It is by no means the case that 'the creation (or strengthening) of democracy in countries such as Britain, Poland, Yugoslavia and the Bundesrepublic would sensitize more European citizens and governments to the need for radically different policies towards Africa, Asia and Latin America' (Keane, 1988a: xi). The rights basis of citizenship, which must of necessity fix and abstract human actions into a set of legislative entitlements, should be tied to a dynamic concept of needs, as a set of conditions necessary for the individual and social fulfilment of human development. In a society fractured by divisions of class, gender and 'race', and characterised by the marginalisation of social groups, through, age, disability, sexual orientation, etc., such a movement will be confronted with relations of power crystallised through both state and market mechanisms. New forms of politics which acknowledge the different situation of groups within power structures and which allow diversity in terms of political organisation may become the basis for an assertion of citizenship based on need. A simple New Social Movements approach, with its stress on autonomy and self-determination, may 'take us to the heart of the participatory-democratic credo' (Hoffman, 1988: 195) but 'a rhetorical demolition of hierarchies is one thing: getting rid of the state . . . is quite another' (ibid.).

References

Benhabib, S. and Cornell, D. (eds) (1986) *Feminism as Critique*. Cambridge: Polity.

Benton, S. (1988) 'Citizen Cain's silenced sisters', *New Statesman Society*, 2 December.

Brah, A. (1987) 'Women of South Asian origin in Britain: issues and concerns', *South Asia Research*, 7(1).

Cohen, J.L. and Arato, A. (1984) 'Social movements, civil society and the problem of sovereignty', *Praxis International*, 4.

Cohen, P. and Bains, H. (1988) *Multi-racist Britain*. London: Macmillan.

Cohen, S. (1985) 'Anti-semitism, immigration controls and the welfare state', *Critical Social Policy*, 13, and this volume.

Croft, S. (1986) 'Women, caring and the recasting of need', *Critical Social Policy*, 16.

Dadzie, S., Bryan, B. and Scafe, S. (1986) *The Heart of the Race*. London: Virago.

Deacon, B. (1983) *Social Policy and Socialism*. London: Pluto.

Dixon, D. (1981) 'Constitutionalising racism: The British Nationality Act', *Critical Social Policy*, 1(2).

Doyal, L. and Gough, I. (1984) 'A theory of human needs', *Critical Social Policy*. 10: 6–38.

Doyal, L. and Gough, I. (1989) *A Theory of Human Need*. London: Macmillan.

Finch, J. (1984) 'Community care: developing non-sexist alternatives', *Critical Social Policy*, 9.

Gilroy, P. (1987) *There Ain't No Black in the Union Jack*. London: Hutchinson.

Gould, C. (1988) *Rethinking Democracy*. Cambridge: Cambridge University Press.

Habermas, J. (1989) *The Transformation of the Public Sphere*. London: Polity.

Harris, D. (1987) *Justifying the Welfare State*. Oxford: Blackwell.

Hoffman, J. (1988) *State, Power and Democracy*. Brighton: Harvester Wheatsheaf.

Judge, K. (1987) 'The welfare state in transition', in R. Friedman, N. Gilbert and M. Sherer (eds), *Modern Welfare States*. Brighton: Harvester Wheatsheaf.

Keane, J. (1988a) *Democracy and Civil Society*. London: Verso.

Keane, J. (ed.) (1988b) *Civil Society and the State*. London: Verso.

Lee, P. and Raban, C. (1988) *Welfare Theory and Social Policy*. London: Sage.

Le Grand, J. (1982) *The Strategy of Equality*. London: Allen & Unwin.

Marshall, T.H. (1950) *Citizenship and Social Class*. Cambridge: Cambridge University Press.

Melucci, A. (1988) 'Social movements and the democratisation of everyday life', in J. Keane (ed.), *Civil Society and the State*. London: Verso.

Melucci, A. (1989) *Nomads of the Present*. London: Hutchinson.

Pascall, G. (1986) *Social Policy – A Feminist Analysis*. London: Tavistock.

Pateman, C. (1988a) *The Sexual Contract*. Cambridge: Cambridge University Press.

Pateman, C. (1988b) 'The fraternal social contract', in J. Keane (ed.), *Civil Society and the State*. London: Verso.

Petchey, R. (1989) 'The politics of destabilisation', *Critical Social Policy*, 25.

Plant, R. et al. (1980) *Political Philosophy and Social Welfare*. London: Routledge & Kegan Paul.

Touraine, A. (1985) 'An introduction to the study of social movements', *Social Research*, 52.

Williams, F. (1987) 'Racism and the discipline of social policy', *Critical Social Policy*, 20, and this volume.

Young, I. (1986) 'Impartiality and the civic public', in S. Benhabib and D. Cornell (eds), *Feminism as Critique*. Cambridge: Polity.

9

Citizenship Engendered

Ruth Lister

The literature on citizenship is burgeoning. The *Critical Social Policy* Special Issue (No. 26) addressed critically a number of elements in the revived citizenship debate but did not focus explicitly on gender. Arguably, though, some of the most challenging perspectives on the citizenship debate involve its meaning for women.

In a review of Geoff Andrews' edited book *Citizenship*, David Marquand complained that, at times, citizenship

> is mercilessly whipped for stumbling under burdens that were never within its capacity in the first place. A characteristic example from this book is a brilliant essay by Sarah Benton, savaging the whole notion of citizenship on the grounds that it has nothing to say about the private sphere where women are most oppressed. Even if she were right, it does not follow that women should be indifferent to the citizenship ideal. They inhabit the public sphere as well as the private, after all; and even a quarter loaf is surely better than no bread. (Marquand, 1991)

In other words, we should be content with the crumbs that the men are prepared to throw our way. I quote this passage because it is illuminating and in many ways typical of writings on citizenship by a certain strand of male political and social scientists who, in their gender-blind conceptualisation of citizenship would have us believe that it is also a gender-neutral conceptualisation – which it most certainly is not.

That it is not is hardly surprising given that the classical notion of citizenship was predicated on women's exclusion. Yet, because women are no longer excluded from formal civil and political rights of citizenship, there is little or no perception that our relationship to citizenship and the public sphere, in which it is conventionally sited, may be different to that of men. Nor that, as currently understood, the very notion might be problematic for women.

Marquand's statement also supplies a clue as to the main source of this myopia. Elsewhere, he has written that 'citizenship is nothing, if it is not

Paper presented at the *Critical Social Policy* Conference, 'Citizenship and Welfare' in London, March 1991, and subsequently published in *Critical Social Policy*, 32, 1991.

public' (Marquand, 1989). The implications for citizenship of what goes on in the so-called private sphere are therefore treated as irrelevant; 'a burden' that it is unrealistic to expect citizenship to bear. We might, however, ask how it is possible to consider the meaning of citizenship for over half the adult population *without* taking on board the burdens *they* bear because of the obligations women are deemed to have in the private sphere. Are these obligations really nothing to do with citizenship?

Of course, such myopia can be very convenient, as it enables the public–private divide, upon which the power of male citizens rests, to disappear out of the focus of what constitutes political and social theory and instead become a boundary around it. Thus, the first point to be made is that any consideration of citizenship from a gendered perspective has to bring into focus the public–private divide and the power relations that both underpin and are sustained by it.

In talking about gender and citizenship, I am conscious that there is a danger of treating women and men as two monolithic groups. Yet the relationship of each to citizenship will be mediated by other factors such as 'race', class, poverty, disability, sexual orientation and age. Ultimately, therefore, the development of a gendered conception of citizenship has to be part of a broader project which gives space to diversity and difference. Stuart Hall and David Held have asked whether there is 'now an irreconcilable tension between the thrust to equality and universality entailed in the very notion of the "citizen" and the variety of particular and specific needs, of diverse sites and practices which constitute the modern political subject?' (Hall and Held, 1989: 16–23). I am not going to try to answer that question here but it does pose a challenge to those of us who are attempting to rescue the citizenship ideal from its more traditional limited and limiting formulations. My focus, instead, is the political and social rights of citizenship and political, social and economic conditions which shape women's ability to exercise those rights.

My starting point is the public–private divide which is implicit in the notion of citizenship. As many feminist writers have pointed out, the two are not totally separate spheres and the dividing line between them cannot be taken as given. Where it is drawn is a political act. It is culture-specific (Yuval-Davies, 1991). The line can also be drawn in different places for particular groups such as disabled people and poor families whose rights to privacy are not always acknowledged.

There are, furthermore, different meanings of the public and the private. In this context, we are talking about what Carol Pateman calls the patriarchal separation between the domestic and the rest (Pateman, 1989).

Nancy Fraser, though, has argued that treating everything outside the domestic sphere as 'the public' conflates 'at least three analytically distinct things: the state, the official economy of paid employment and arenas of political discourse' (Fraser, 1990). I found this a helpful distinction and will use it as a framework for this paper.

The 'Official Economy of Paid Employment'

Writers such as Carol Pateman have noted that employment has replaced military service as 'the key to citizenship' (Pateman, 1989: 186). Women and men have a very different relationship to paid employment, with implications for their role as citizens vis-à-vis both the state and the polity.

Part of the difference lies in the perception of the differential meaning of the wage for women and men. The ideology of the family wage and of women's economic dependency on men still runs deep, despite women's increased labour market participation and the growth in the number of female-headed households. It shapes women's opportunities in the official economy of paid employment, even if there is no male breadwinner in sight. Thus, for example, Afro-Caribbean women heads of household are not necessarily immune from the impact of the ideology.

At the same time, women and men enter the labour market under very different conditions. By and large, not only do men enter it unencumbered by responsibility for the physical care of children or adults, but they are also serviced domestically. They are thereby freed to be full-time wage-earning citizens and, if they so choose, active political citizens.

Most women, on the other hand, at some stage(s) of their lives are either excluded from the official economy of paid employment altogether by the care of young children or of adults, or they stagger under what Kollontai dubbed the 'triple burden' of child care, domestic labour and paid work. To this can be added a fourth demand of adult care.

Some women with money can ease the burden, sometimes by buying the services of women without money. It is, however, still the woman's responsibility and money. For the poorest women, including many lone mothers, the burden can be especially acute as they have no money to substitute for time.

The public spheres of the economy and the state have not seen it as their responsibility to ease the burden on women with domestic responsibilities, in this country at least (Moss, 1988/9). This contrasts with some other European countries, especially in Scandinavia.

Some employers are beginning to make adjustments because of demographic trends but the current recession suggests that some of these might be short-lived and the main beneficiaries tend to be middle-class rather than working-class women.

The state's attitude, at least under the present government, was summed up by John Patten when Minister with responsibility for women. He told the *Guardian*: 'I don't think the state should step in to help the working mother unless her life has collapsed' (Patten, 1989).

The sexual division of labour which governs women and men's relationship to paid and unpaid work also has important implications for their respective positions as citizens in the other two public spheres of the state and what Fraser called the 'arenas of public discourse'.

The State

It is through the state that social rights of citizenship are determined and allocated. These social rights are, for the most part, closely tied to position in the labour market. Thus, one's position as economic citizen in one dimension of the public sphere affects one's position as social citizen in another.

As Arnlaug Leira has argued in the Norwegian context, a dual concept of citizenship is at work: 'one associated with citizen as wage-earner, the other with citizen the carer, the former attracting the more generous and institutionalised benefits' (Leira, 1989: 33–4).

Thus, for example, in Britain, the non-contributory social security benefits, introduced to help fill some of the gaps left by the contributory principle, are deliberately maintained at a lower level than the contributory benefits available to those who satisfy the contribution conditions. These conditions reflect essentially male employment patterns (Land, 1988).

The Beveridge Plan was quite explicit about married women's claim to social citizenship attaching to their maternal role, and an imperialistic one at that (Williams, 1989). However, this claim gave them only indirect rights of social citizenship, through their husbands and children, thereby underpinning their economic dependency within the family. Rights that come second-hand in this way, mediated via men, are not genuine rights of social citizenship. They leave many women in poverty, often hidden within the family.

Lone mothers, other than widows, were excluded from the Beveridge social insurance scheme altogether. They have had to rely on the inferior rights of means-tested assistance, again spelling poverty.

We are now seeing an attempt to replace even those rights by renewed economic dependency on the fathers of their children, not just to meet the needs of their children but also their own needs. This is an aspect of current policy on maintenance which has gone virtually unremarked.

Although women played an important role in early campaigns around the welfare state in this country, ultimately they lacked the political power to shape it according to their needs. The same has been said of the more advanced, 'woman-friendly' welfare states of Scandinavia where women have still 'been the object of welfare policy and not its creators' (Hernes, 1987: 86). The lesson drawn by Scandinavian feminist theorists is that 'it is necessary that women participate in the determination of what their social needs and political interests actually are' (Borchorst and Siim, 1987: 154).

This brings us to the third dimension of the public sphere – 'the arenas of political discourse' in which the political element of citizenship is played out.

The 'Arenas of Political Discourse'

Fraser divides these arenas into 'strong' and 'weak' publics according to whether or not they encompass decision-making as well as opinion-forming.

Women are particularly under-represented in the strong publics. Many lack the two resources which facilitate involvement in formal political processes – time and money. The sexual politics of time are key in making full political citizenship a reality for more women, with implications for the organisation of both political and domestic life (Lister, 1990).

Women are better represented in the weak publics, especially community based groups and the new social movements. On the whole, these weak publics represent a more accessible, fulfilling and enjoyable form of politics. Thus, to an extent, it's not just that women are excluded from formal politics, but that many of us also choose to stay outside.

At one level, this could be considered a very rational decision. However, if women do not engage directly with the strong publics where political (even if not economic) power resides, we will continue to live in man-shaped institutions under man-made laws and policies. As Birte Siim has observed 'it is hard to imagine any positive changes in women's private and political life, if they are not encouraged to enter the public sphere and fight for a more democratic citizenship, where women would be social and political agents' (Siim, 1988: 166).

Conclusion

I want to conclude with some questions which are, in a sense, different formulations of the old question of equality versus difference. The first, however, is whether a universal concept, originally predicated on the exclusion of all women and still de facto excluding many women, is of any value to women? If it can be freed of its previous associations and limitations, is it a concept or ideal that could be used as the basis for women's struggle for political, social and economic power and also that of other groups such as the Black and other ethnic minority communities and disabled people?

If it is believed that citizenship does have a potential value, this raises a question which can take a number of different forms. Its essence is whether the aim is a genuinely gender-neutral form of citizenship based on women as equals of men in the public sphere or a gender-differentiated form of citizenship which recognises difference and values women's responsibilities in the private sphere.

In the political arena, is the objective to challenge the conditions, including the sexual division of labour, which curtail women's rights as citizens or to develop concepts and practices of citizenship which take into account the sexual division of labour and value women's caring role within it?

In the social arena, is the aim to change the nature of social citizenship rights so that earning is no longer privileged over caring in the allocation of those rights or is it to improve women's access to the labour market so that they can compete on equal terms with men and can gain the same employment-linked social citizenship rights?

Jane Lewis has examined this last question in the context of Sweden where she suggests that there has been an attempt to resolve the dilemma by 'the grafting of the right to make a claim on the basis of difference onto a policy based on equal treatment'. Thus, for example, 'Swedish mothers have first had to become workers in order to qualify for the parental leave scheme at a favourable level of benefit but, paradoxically, having taken a job they could then exert a claim to be mothers and to stay at home for what has proved to be a steadily lengthening period' (Lewis, 1990).

While it raises fundamental questions, the equality versus difference debate can lead us into a cul-de-sac and a degree of pragmatism is perhaps necessary if we are not to get stuck in it.

If women are to enter into full citizenship, it is going to require radical changes in both the private sphere and each of the public spheres I have discussed as well as a challenge to the rigid separation between the two spheres. In the words of Carol Pateman, 'liberal principles cannot simply be universalised to extend to women in the public sphere without raising an acute problem about the patriarchal structure of private life . . . the spheres are integrally related and women's full membership in public life is impossible without changes in the domestic sphere' (Pateman, 1989: 129).

This would mean a transformation of the sexual division of labour (paid and unpaid) and of time; in the organisation of paid work and of politics. It would mean extending and strengthening social rights of citizenship so as to recognise the value of unpaid caring work without trapping women further into it.

Ultimately the question of citizenship cannot be divorced from that of power. As Dave Taylor has argued, 'a reappropriation of citizenship must not simply be tied to an abstract set of rights guaranteed by the "rule of law" but address the deeper bases of social power.' (Taylor, 1989 and this volume).

One of these bases is the power of men over women in the private and public spheres and in establishing the boundaries between the two and therefore controlling the meaning of citizenship. That power will have to be challenged if the left's attempt to fashion a new concept of citizenship is to serve women's ends and not just end up as yet another seemingly gender-neutral figleaf for bolstering male power and privilege.

References

Borchorst, A. and Siim, B. (1987) 'Women and the advanced welfare state: a new kind of patriarchal power?' in A. Showstack-Sassoon (ed.), *Women and the State*. London: Hutchinson.

Fraser, N. (1990) 'Rethinking the public sphere: a contribution to the critique of actually existing democracy'. Madrid: World Sociological Conference.

Hall, S. and Held, D. (1989) 'Left and rights', *Marxism Today*, June.

Hernes, H. (1987) 'Women and the welfare state: the transition from private to public dependence', in A. Showstack-Sassoon (ed.), *Women and the State*. London: Hutchinson.

Land, H. (1988) 'Women, money and independence', *Poverty* 70. London: Child Poverty Action Group.

Leira, A. (1989) *Models of Motherhood*. Oslo: Institutt for Samfunns Forskning.

Lewis, J. (1990) 'Equality, difference and state welfare: the case of labour market and family policies in Sweden', Unpublished.

Lister, R. (1990) 'Women, economic dependency and citizenship', *Journal of Social Policy*, 19(4): 445–67.

Marquand, D. (1989) 'Subversive language of citizenship', *Guardian*, 2 January.

Marquand, D. (1991) 'Deaf to duty's call', *New Statesman and Society*, 25 January.

Moss, P. (1988/9) 'The indirect costs of parenthood: a neglected issue in social policy', *Critical Social Policy*, 24: 20–37.

Pateman, C. (1989) *The Disorder of Women*. Cambridge: Polity/Basil Blackwell.

Patten, J. (1989) *Guardian*, 2 January.

Siim, B. (1988) 'Towards a feminist rethinking of the welfare state', in K.B. Jones and A.G. Jonasdottir (eds), *The Political Interests of Gender*. London: Sage.

Taylor, D. (1989) 'Citizenship and social power', *Critical Social Policy* 26: 19–31, and this volume.

Yuval-Davies, N. (1991) 'The citizenship debate: ethnic processes, women and the state', BSA Sexual Divisions Study Group and PSA Women and Politics Group Conference on Women and Citizenship, 16 February, London.

Williams, F. (1989) *Social Policy: A Critical Introduction*. Cambridge: Polity/Basil Blackwell.

10

The Politics of Participation

Suzy Croft and Peter Beresford

'Participation' is one of those contentious words like 'community' and
'care' which can seem to mean everything and nothing. There is little
agreement about its definition. Even its terminology constantly changes, for
example, from 'participation' and 'empowerment', to 'self-advocacy' and
'involvement'. 'Participation' generates enthusiasm and hostility in equal
proportion. For some it is bankrupt; for others it offers hope. Interest in
participation appears to be episodic. Currently we are going through
another period when it seems to be heightened. According to our views on
the subject, this may be a problem or an opportunity. What it certainly
seems to demand is a closer look at participation. It is an enormous idea,
but one which frequently seems to be treated in the most superficial and
depoliticised way,

Now, at a time of major political, economic and social changes, when
ideas of involvement constantly crop up in social policy discussions, it is
particularly opportune to try and make sense of participation's strengths
and weaknesses and to ask some basic questions about it, for example: why
has it had such a chequered career? Can it be helpful? What would be
needed for it to have meaning? What implications does it have for social
policy and politics more generally? This discussion is offered very much as
an initial attempt to explore some of these questions. Hopefully it will
generate further debate which will take forward our understanding of
'participation'. First we need to put participation in some context.

The Current Context of Participation

The collapse of political regimes in Eastern Europe has been equated in the
West with the failure of the left. It is offered as evidence to show that what
the architects and supporters of communism and socialism envisaged as an
empowering alternative can now be called into question on two key counts.
These are, first, its apparent unpopularity, rejected by the people as over-
powering and undemocratic, and, second, its economic incompetence,
unable to maximise production, distribution or consumption.

First published in *Critical Social Policy*, 35, 1992.

The 'collapse of communism' has not only strengthened the political, economic and military power of western market democracies, most dramatically by reducing the number of superpowers from two to one. It has also confirmed their own and perhaps other people's view of their credibility and effectiveness.

But fundamental problems associated with western market economies, which first gave impetus to the emergence of the political left, remain unresolved. These include gross inequalities, the concentration of political and economic power, and the failure to reconcile profit and the accumulation of capital with the meeting of need and guaranteeing of people's rights. The market success and rising poverty and material inequality that were synonymous with Britain in the 1980s are symbolic of this unresolved issue (Oppenheim, 1990).

Yet paradoxically the market is now being offered as the solution to the shortcomings of state and collective action. We are not only witnessing this in the West's interventions in the social and economic institutions of Eastern Europe, it is also happening much closer to home in social policy. It is embodied in the changing economy of welfare, the purchaser–provider split and the new welfare consumerism. With one bound, the market is transformed into a remedy for the shortcomings of state policies and services to meet need, although the inspiration of such policies was the market's own failure to meet such need in the first place.

So, if left alternatives are now held up as defective with increasing confidence, the market's own weaknesses remain unresolved. But the two politics have other important characteristics in common. Both are economics-led. The strength of western democracies is seen to rest on the market. The Eastern European socialist republics were based on state ownership of the means of production. One was led by state command economy; the other by capital accumulation of the market. As more information emerges from Eastern Europe a clearer picture is also emerging of the shortcomings of both on environmental issues and in meeting social need. Finally, both have been associated with a politics that is narrowly based.

But there is also growing interest in and search for a different politics. Its focus is more civil and social then economic. It is reflected in a number of developments and discussions. A key feature which links them is a common concern with people's *increased involvement* and *participation*. It is this we particularly want to explore. We shall focus on four of these developments. They are: the emergence of new social movements; the rekindling of interest in human need; the re-emergence of the idea of citizenship; and post-modernism. While it might be suggested that some of these developments are narrowly based, others draw on wide involvement. Some are international, others are more local. There are also overlaps between them. We don't include them on the basis of any particular allegiance of our own, but rather because all of them appear influential. Let's look at them in more detail.

New Social Movements

The 1970s saw the emergence of many new movements. These included the gay and lesbian, Black, women's, disability and environmental movements. Oliver (1990: 113) offers a helpful description of them:

> These movements have been seen as constituting the social basis for new forms of transformative political change. These social movements are 'new' in the sense that they are not grounded in traditional forms of political participation through the party system or single-issue pressure group activity targeted at political decision-makers.
>
> Instead they are culturally innovative in that they are part of the underlying struggle for genuine participatory democracy, social equality and justice, which have arisen out of 'the crisis in industrial culture'. These new social movements are consciously engaged in critical evaluation of capitalist society and in the creation of alternative models of social organisation at local, national and international levels, as well as trying to reconstruct the world ideologically and to create alternative forms of service provision.

One criticism made of the new social movements is that they have resulted in an over-rapid retreat from class analysis and politics and the possibilities these offer of united action (Meiksens-Wood, 1986). Another concern has been that their focus on different identities may result in conflict and fragmentation rather than unity and concerted action. At the same time, there is now growing recognition of the overlapping identities that new social movements reflect: disabled women are women too; gay people may also be Black people.

Oliver identifies four characteristics associated with the new social movements. These are:

1   They tend to be located at the periphery of the traditional political system and sometimes are deliberately marginalised.
2   They offer a critical evaluation of society as part of 'a conflict between a declining but still vigorous form of domination and newly emergent forms of opposition' (Boggs, 1986: 4).
3   They are concerned with the quality of people's life as well as narrowly materialist needs.
4   They tend to focus on issues that cross national boundaries and thus they become internationalist (Oliver, 1990: 118–23).

Some analysts are beginning to make links between new social movements and the organisations developed by people who use traditional welfare services to take collective action to secure their rights and needs; for example, disability organisations, organisations of people with mental distress and of people who are HIV positive. These have been described as 'new social welfare movements' (Williams, 1992: 16) although this conceives of their members in terms of services which their struggles are often concerned with challenging.

These groups are increasingly seeing themselves as new social movements, identifying themselves with other new social movements and pointing to their shared characteristics and goals. They share a number of key qualities with them. They experience institutionalised social oppression; recognise and value their own particular history and culture; frame their activities in political terms; 'come out' about themselves and assert their identity instead of trying to keep 'in the closet'; take a pride in who they are. They also highlight the concern of new social movements with participation and empowerment. People are concerned with speaking and acting *for themselves*. It is a primary concern. It extends beyond the involvement of their constituency, to the active involvement of as many members of it as possible. It is an explicit expression of their concern with a different politics; a participatory politics.

Human Need

The debate about human need has been a curious one. It is an idea which continues to inform the practice and analysis of social policy and which is still regularly used in much political discourse. Yet as Doyal and Gough argue, it is 'regularly rejected in the domain of theory': 'Economists, sociologists, philosophers, liberals, libertarians, Marxists, socialists, feminists, anti-racists, and other social critics have increasingly regarded human need as a subjective and culturally relative concept' (Doyal and Gough, 1991: 1). Doyal and Gough have sought to rescue human need from the resulting confusion they see 'for providers of welfare and for those who are committed to the political struggle for the increased provision of welfare'. In a germinal article in 1984, they argued: 'It is time either to defend and refine the concept of human needs or to banish it entirely from our vocabulary' (1984: 6).

Doyal and Gough have condemned the ways in which the idea of need has been abused by professionals, experts and politicians foisting their own demands and perceptions upon people. In the theory of human needs they have developed, they identify *objective* and *universal* needs as well as a range of intermediate needs to which everyone must have access for these to be met. The objective and universal needs they identify are physical health and individual autonomy, because they are essential preconditions for *participation in social life*. They place an emphasis on the social character of human action. By social participation they mean the quantity and quality of social interactions. Doyal also argues more specifically for the involvement of welfare service users alongside providers if these services are to 'optimise need satisfaction' (1992: 285).

Some may question whether such a theory will win the political argument as its authors believe. Others have pointed to the importance of people's own broader involvement in the development of such ideas (Croft and Beresford, 1989). What is clear though is that ideas of involvement and participation have now become central to the discussion of human need.

Citizenship

The late 1980s saw a reawakening of interest in the idea of citizenship. Just as it emerged as a key concept at the time of the creation of the welfare state (Marshall, 1950), so it again became one when we seemed to be moving into a post-welfare state age.

The debate about citizenship has come from many quarters. Citizenship entails both rights and responsibilities. While the political left and centre have emphasised the social *rights* and *entitlements* of citizenship, extending to pressure for a British Bill of Rights, from the mid-1980s, there has been an emphasis among sections of the political right on its social *responsibilities* and *obligations*. As Lister (1990: 7) says: 'The language of obligation is replacing that of rights. These two words "welfare" and "rights" are being uncoupled as attempts are made to reduce expectations of what the State will provide and thereby dependency on the "benefits culture".'

But in this discussion, the rights and responsibilities of citizenship sometimes seem to be confused. For example, if the American writer Lawrence Mead (1986: 229) sees the obligation of employment as 'as much a badge of citizenship as rights', for many disabled people and single parents, it is a *right* which they are denied through discrimination, lack of access and lack of child care.

The citizenship debate is complex and wide ranging and has not always been politically connected. One expression it has taken has been the growing number of 'citizens' charters' produced by local authorities and political parties. In 1986, seeking something more than a straightforward consumerist approach to public services, Clarke and Stewart identified a new approach with what they called a public service orientation where: 'The emphasis is both on the *customer* for whom the service is provided and on the *citizen* to whom the authority is accountable' (1986)

In his analysis of the citizens' charters produced by the three major political parties, Taylor (1992) points the way in which the citizen is confused with the consumer. So far, citizens' charters have been more concerned with consumers' than citizens' rights; with quality assurance, customer care and the rights of redress and exit (see also Walker, 1992). They have also ignored citizenship's history. Taylor has argued that to be of use 'the concept of citizenship must be taken out of its liberal history and rethought' (1989: 19, and this volume).

The citizen idea can be used both to exclude and to involve. As Taylor puts it, it 'has long been used to marginalise, and is bound up with the republican tradition of male politics organised around an exclusive national culture' (1992: 87).

But the new debates about citizenship are concerned with people's *inclusion* rather than exclusion. As Andrews (1991: 14) observes:

> It has often been argued that a concept which has historically been under-written by a patriarchal, eurocentric and heterosexual consensus, did not admit those whose 'private' identities were different. Cultural and gender difference challenges

the historical idea of the citizen. However, there are indications that citizenship can remain an emancipatory ideal without entering a new theoretical jungle. New arguments are being produced which are redefining the rights, responsibilities and status of citizens, in the light of difference.

Taylor (1992: 92–3) argues that:

> The debate of citizenship . . . automatically raises the question of nationality and immigration, poverty and resources, marginalisation from the public sphere through discrimination based on age, disability, sexuality, 'race' and gender. It also raises the question of the private and the public. Is citizenship constructed simply through the public world of consumerism or equally through the social relations of reproduction and the family? And lastly, it raises the nature of the power of the citizen. Is the content of citizenship something to be handed down in a charter or something that should be built on the self-advocacy of citizens?

The idea of citizenship is now being used as a way of highlighting people's exclusions and of giving force to arguments and campaigns for their *involvement*. Lister (1991, and this volume), for example, challenges 'gender-blind' conceptualisations of citizenship to press for the full and equal citizenship of women. Earlier (Lister, 1990), she examined the ways in which poverty excludes people from the full rights of citizenship, undermining their ability to fulfil either their private or social obligations. This offers a way of reconceiving poverty as well as an argument for poor people's full inclusion and involvement in society.

Postmodernism

Postmodernism is both a set of developments and changes identified as taking place in society and a particular analysis and discussion which is part of this. Both are concerned with major shifts from *standardisation, uniformity* and *universalism* to *fragmentation, diversity* and *difference*. At the economic level, this is characterised by a trend towards differentiation in both production and consumption: from the mass production line to semi-autonomous workgroups; from standardised to diverse products aimed at diverse groups of consumers and by a move from a production to consumption-led economy. The workforce is now more clearly demarcated as a skilled and relatively well rewarded 'core' of largely white male workers and a 'periphery' of low-paid, less secure and often Black and women workers. At the social and cultural level, there is a greater acknowledgement of heterogeneity and diversity. This is reflected at the political level by the breakdown of traditional class politics and the emergence of a 'politics of identity based on ethnicity, gender and/or sexuality' (Williams, 1992: 16)

While this debate has not always been concerned with issues of power and inequality, postmodernism offers a framework for focusing our attention on them. In her exploration of the links between postmodernism and social policy, for example, Fiona Williams (1992: 9) argues that diversity: 'is part and parcel of a complexity of power and inequality. We need to reconnect diversity and difference to the struggles from which they emerge, the conditions in which they exist and the social relations they reflect and challenge.' Recognition of diversity also offers us a way of going beyond the universalism versus selectivity debate in social policy and of taking account of people's different needs as well as their universal rights. Fiona Williams writes:

> by supplanting the notion of 'selectivity' with the notion of 'diversity' it's possible to move the debate on to new ground which admits the possibility of people articulating their own needs. It also points to what I think is a fundamental issue for social policy – not the counterposing of diversity to universality, but the need to resolve the tensions between universal principles and policies, on the one hand, and the recognition of diversity, on the other. (1992: 10)

This it does by recognising the importance of people's own involvement in the process.

Linking with the History of Participation

This idea and objective of participation, then, is central to these debates and developments. It is also of more general importance in modern political and social policy discourses. But participation is not an issue that is always well understood. Frequently it is taken for granted, as if the desire for or commitment to participation is sufficient to ensure it will happen. There is a tendency for such ideas to be used lightly and rhetorically in abstract discussion. There is also a risk that insufficient attention may be paid to the issue of participation in debates which are themselves relatively narrowly based and whose authors are unfamiliar with the practice of participation, whereas people who are directly concerned with their own exclusion on a day-to-day basis, like those involved in the women's, Black and disability movements, are only too conscious of the politics of participation.

Because of this it is important that any concern with participation is clearly *connected* with existing knowledge and experience. It is essential to put participation in its historical and political context. Otherwise its ambiguities and contradictions are likely to remain unexplored and unresolved. Ultimately, discussions of participation which are not grounded in an understanding of its practice and politics are likely to be superficial and unhelpful.

In its broadest sense the idea of participation is part of the wider discussion about democracy that extends over nearly 3,000 years. More specifically, it is linked with efforts to move from representative to participatory democracy and with arrangements to enable people's direct involvement in political, administrative and other processes which affect them. The modern history of such thinking and developments around participation extends over at least 30 years. We can identify three overlapping developments during this period which are central to it. These are: public participation in land-use planning; community development; and user-involvement. A critical examination of all three is likely to be helpful in developing our understanding of ideas of involvement and participation. Let's look at each of them in turn.

Public Participation in Land-Use Planning

The movement for public participation in land-use planning gained momentum in the late 1960s and early 1970s, not least because of the deluge of bad planning with large-scale urban redevelopment and central government's desire to free itself of the burden of innumerable appeals. Its two landmarks were the 1969 Skeffington Report, *People and Planning* and the Town and Country Planning Acts of 1968 and 1971. Provisions for public participation were introduced into both the main provinces of planning: development planning and general planning control. The notion of public participation embodied in the two Planning Acts was essentially one of public consultation and appeal. In the case of local plans, objections would be heard by public local inquiry.

This development in land-use planning marked the first large-scale government intervention in 'participation'. It introduced the term 'public participation' into the political vernacular. It anticipated provisions for consultation in community care planning contained in the National Health Service and Community Care Act by 20 years and through it many community organisations became involved in planning issues.

However, it had several important shortcomings. It rested on a model of planning as a technical exercise, as if land-use decisions were made on a neutral basis, unaffected by political or commercial considerations. It emphasised planning as a *professional* activity. Some planners have continued to suggest that the professional planner and planning hold the answer to many of society's problems and that planning has a key role to play in regenerating inner city areas, despite the increasing weakness of the planning process (Bruton and Glasson, 1984). While pressure from community organisations led to some changes, public participation in planning was based on a narrow notion of 'planning issues' and did not pay sufficient attention to issues of social need so that judgements did not distinguish, for example, between the provision of low-cost housing for local people and expensive housing which would exclude them. The picture emerging from research was that the public participation which followed from this process was limited and biased (Sheffield University, 1974–1978; Beresford and Croft, 1985).

Finally the process of planning and participation was not related to the wider political process. For example, in 1981 in his report on the public local inquiry into objections and representations concerning the Wandsworth Borough Plan, the inspector stated that his recommendations might 'give rise to a need to make more drastic revision of the plan than might normally be expected'. He severely criticised major parts of the plan saying the Conservative council had turned it into political dogma. The leader of the council wrote to the Under Secretary of State at the Department of the

Environment and the inspector was himself subsequently admonished by the junior minister who stated:

> the inspector made an error of judgement . . . He went outside the proper bounds of his function in his expression of criticism of some council policies, such as those on housing, and in particular, the sale of council houses . . . I need hardly add that these policies accord with those advocated by the government. (Beresford and Croft, 1985: iii)

However they clearly did not accord with the views of local people expressed in public participation. When Michael Heseltine, the then Secretary of State for the Environment, visited North Battersea after the inspector reported, and local people questioned him in the street, reminding him what his inspector had said about the Borough Plan and unmet local housing need, he replied, 'He has his opinion and I've got mine' (Beresford and Croft, 1985: iii).

Community Development

The state-sponsored community work which expanded in Britain and the United States during the 1960s had its origins in community development approaches used by the West in the developing world, first to integrate colonial territories and subsequently to support western political and economic objectives there (Chambers, 1983; Marsden and Oakley, 1982; Mayo, 1975).

The emphasis of community work and community development is on collective rather than individual action. Its focus has been both the workplace and the neighbourhood. It has been concerned with the economic infrastructure, for example, housing and employment; with supporting people's personal growth and development, and with work performed by women in the community – often unpaid – for example, in playschemes, nurseries and carers' groups. Community development is an activity which may be undertaken by unpaid community activists, specialised community workers or other professionals adopting this approach. The objectives of community development range from encouraging self-help and mutual aid to politicisation and pressure group activity; from collaboration to confrontation. Commentators identify a wide variety of models. There is no consensus. Twelvetrees (1982) identified three overlapping approaches:

1 community development: creating and servicing community organisations, bringing people together to identify their needs and work on them;
2 political action: a class-based approach, organising and linking working class organisations and campaigns;
3 social planning: promoting joint action between voluntary and community organisations and the local state to change and improve services.

In the 1970s and 1980s community work came in for criticism from feminists and Black people for its male dominance and failure to address racism

(Mayo, 1977; Ohri and Manning, 1982). Women and Black people initiated their own forms of community development, leading Dominelli (1990) to add two new models of community work to her typology: feminist community action and community action from a Black perspective.

While there are different models of community work and community development, they share two common concerns; bringing about change and involving people in the process. This is where the first of three important tensions emerges which affect traditional community development. These are between: change and involvement; the rhetorical and real scale of involvement; enabling and organising. Let's begin with the first of these. It is often difficult to reconcile change and involvement. The time and resources it takes in community development to involve people effectively often sit uncomfortably with pressures to undertake initiatives and achieve results. When one has to be sacrificed it's usually people's participation.

While the rhetoric of community development is of large-scale involvement – 'tenants got together' or 'local people produced their own community plan' – the reality is more often one of limited numbers or small groups. Broad based involvement may not even be a primary issue on the hard pressed community worker's agenda. But since community work is 'concerned principally to promote collective action on issues or in areas selected by the participants' (Twelvetrees, 1982: 5), narrowly based involvement clearly may pose problems.

The final tension is between support and direction. The role of organiser sits uncomfortably with that of facilitator. Yet community development embraces both (for books which reflect these different approaches, see Ward, 1984; Freire, 1972). While a supportive approach seems consistent with enabling and extending people's involvement, an organising one suggests a more one-sided relationship, with leaders and followers. This may be a way of creating more 'community' or 'user leaders', but whether that is the same thing as increasing people's participation remains open to question.

User-involvement

The 1980s witnessed a new focus for participation and new terminology. There has been pressure for a shift away from *service-* or *provider-led* public provision to more *user-centred* services. This has been particularly apparent in the context of welfare services. The demands have been for different, better and more responsive services. A unifying idea underpinning this development has been that of *user-involvement*. A growing view is that the switch to more user-centred services is likely to be achieved by making possible the increased involvement of service users.

Interest in more user-centred services can be traced to a number of broader developments. They come from many quarters. Most can be traced to disenchantment with the British post-war welfare state. They include:

1 The rise of the political right and the election of Conservative governments from 1979, with their concern with the cost of public services,

dislike of a 'nanny' welfare state which was perceived as creating and perpetuating dependency, their objections to government intervention and preference for a greater role for the private market.

2 More general public disquiet about the poor quality, paternalism and lack of responsiveness of welfare and other public services.

3 The emergence of a wide range of organisations and movements of people using such welfare services – from young people in care to people with mental distress – who were frequently not happy with the services they received and wanted something different.

4 The struggle for equal opportunities highlighting the frequent failure of welfare services to ensure equal access, opportunities and appropriate provision for women, Black people and members of other minority groups (Williams, 1989).

5 Progressive professionals and other service workers who wanted to work in different, more egalitarian ways, concerned about the oppressive nature and lack of accountability that frequently characterised their services and agencies (London Edinburgh Weekend Return Group, 1979).

6 The appearance of new kinds of support services. By showing that things really could be different, they emphasised the deficiencies of the old. Women's, Black and gay organisations, for example, set up lesbian lines, rape crisis centres, women's and Black women's refuges, advocacy schemes and buddy schemes. These established different relationships between service users and providers, met needs that had previously been ignored and were often run in more collaborative ways.

7 The emergence of new philosophies which gave greater force and focus to ideas of involvement. The theory of 'normalisation' or 'social role valorisation' as it has also come to be called, with its emphasis on social integration and a valued life for people, offered a coherent value base and a participatory framework for services, first for people with learning disabilities and then for other groups, although it has come in for criticism for its acceptance of dominant values and ideas of normality in society (O'Brien and Tyne, 1981).

8 The development by disabled people of a new politics of disability based on a critique of existing services, a redefinition of the problem and an attempt to create an alternative service structure controlled by disabled people. This followed from a social model of disability which emphasises that people's disability is caused by social factors, including the discrimination and oppression they face in society and not by their individual impairments. What disables people is their inability to function in an able-body oriented world which denies or does not take account of their rights and needs (Oliver, 1990).

The interest in involvement that increased concern for more user-led or user-centred services has heralded has not meant that there has been any consensus in the conception or definition of 'involvement'. It is easy to see why, given the very varied origins of this interest. Two main approaches to user-involvement are increasingly identified; the 'consumerist' and the 'democratic' approaches (Beresford, 1988; Pfeffer and Coote, 1991; Walker, 1991). While there are some overlaps between the two, they reflect different philosophies and objectives. The first has been associated with the politics of the New Right and the second with the emergence of rights, disabled people's self-advocacy and service users.

Both these approaches may have their merits, but they should not be confused. They are very different. The emergence of consumerist thinking on health and welfare services has coincided with the expansion of commercial provision and political pressure for a changed economy of welfare. Service users or clients are now conceived of as consumers. Now the discussion of participation is overlaid with the language of consumerism and the concerns of the market (Ward, 1990). Consumerism starts with the idea of buying the goods and services we want instead of making collective provision for them. Two competing meanings underpin the idea of consumerism; first, giving priority to the wants and needs of the 'consumer' and, second, framing people as 'consumers' and commodifying their needs; that is converting these needs into markets to be met by the creation of goods and services.

In the debate about user-involvement, while the consumerist approach has tended to come from service providers and to address the concerns and needs of services, for example, improving management to achieve greater economy, efficiency and effectiveness, the democratic approach has largely been developed by service users and their organisations. What distinguishes these organisations from traditional pressure groups is that they seek to *speak for themselves* instead of other groups speaking on their behalf. Here the primary concern has been with empowerment, the redistribution of power and people gaining more say and control over their lives (Campbell, 1990). The democratic approach is not service centred. It is about much more than having a voice in services, however important that may be. It is concerned with how we are treated and regarded more generally; with the achievement of people's civil rights and equality of opportunity. This is reflected in the three current priorities of the disability movement; for anti-discriminatory legislation, a Freedom of Information Act and the funding and resourcing of organisations of disabled people. The politics of liberation don't necessarily sit comfortably with the politics of the supermarket.

The Marginalisation of Participation

Participation would appear to be an important idea which demands our attention. As we have seen, it is central to a number of key debates and developments. It is the primary objective of large-scale state-supported initiatives for public participation in planning, community development and user-involvement. Yet its achievements seem to be limited and it is surrounded by suspicion. Why is this? Why does participation seem to be marginalised? First, let's look at some of the expressions of this marginality.

However important we may think participation is, its development has been slow and uncertain. A bibliography of public participation in Britain published in 1979 included nearly 1,400 entries (Barker, 1979). The number has greatly increased since (see, for example, Harding and Upton, 1991). Yet during this period only two books analysing and exploring the idea of participation have been published in Britain (Hallet, 1987; Richardson, 1983). Both the debate and developments around participation have been hesitant and unprogressive. There is now an enormous body of knowledge and experience, but often this is inaccessible or unavailable and this has made progress difficult. There have been practical problems in the way of recording participation's history. People involved in innovatory schemes often don't have the time or confidence to write about them. Those on the receiving end are even less likely to have the opportunity. Community and user groups have not often had the chance to develop and monitor their own initiatives.

There have been few systematic studies of participatory initiatives. There has been little cross-learning between different policy areas. For example, community social work initiatives which were intended to involve local people were slow to draw on the lessons learned by community work and community workers. Hoggett and Hambleton (1987) commented on the failure of decentralisation debates of the 1980s to draw on earlier practical and theoretical work on public involvement. If ever the cliche 'reinventing the wheel' epitomised an area of human activity, it is in the case of participation. The predominant pattern of participation's history is one of cyclical development which rarely seems to build on, or go much further than what has gone before.

The debate about participation has rarely taken the lead in challenging the exclusions faced by women, Black people and other groups. Unless specific initiatives are taken to ensure the involvement of such groups, they are likely to be left out, and frequently such steps have not been taken. Typically participatory schemes have mirrored rather than challenged broader oppressions and discriminations. The average participant of traditional public participation in planning exercises has been typified as a middle-class, middle-aged, able-bodied white man. Such participation is likely to have the damaging effect of reinforcing such biases. Pressure for change has come primarily from *outside* participatory debates and structures, from feminist, Black and disabled people's organisations. Distinctions have not been properly drawn between the public and private spheres of participation and adequate consideration given to the ways in which women are restricted to the private sphere.

The limited success of initiatives to involve people has not been confined to those emerging from the political right or centre. It has also been true of two major developments from the left in the early 1980s concerned with increasing public involvement; the popular planning initiative of the

Greater London Council and the decentralisation schemes developed by left Labour local authorities. Hoggett and Hambleton noted that 'whereas rapid advances have been made in terms of organisational decentralisation, progress towards greater local democracy has been faltering indeed' (1987: 3). They were not alone in this view (see Beresford and Croft, 1986; Khan, 1989). In her first-hand account of 'popular planning not in progress', Mantle described some of the tensions that existed in the GLC's policy. She wrote:

> In terms of funding this meant that although I had learnt the procedures and didn't like them, I didn't make the step of proposing an alternative, more accessible system. Challenging the grant getting system would also mean that you wouldn't get the money so easily, if at all, and this clashed with my wish to see things set up which were needed . . . I regularly felt frustrated with workers whom I regarded as never getting past the initial discussion stage on anything. I felt that the urgent need for these proposals overrode what might be gained if all the emphasis was put on getting active community support for the proposal by getting others involved in the tedious task of getting funding. (1985)

But it's not just the hesitancy of discussions and developments concerned with participation that suggest its marginalisation. It is also its *ambiguity*. One of the student slogans of the 1960s headlined this: 'I participate. You participate. *They profit.*'

Discussions of participation have frequently ignored or underplayed structural issues – the role of the state and market – and been confined within services or 'communities' (Gibson, 1979). When we look at the substantive purposes that participatory arrangements may actually serve, we discover that they are not always consistent with people's effective involvement and increased say. Instead a range of other functions are identified. These include:

1 *Delay*: action is made to wait on people's involvement. The need to consult, to set up 'self-advocacy' groups, is used as a reason for procrastination.
2 *Incorporation/co-option*: people are drawn into participatory arrangements which limit and divert their effective action.
3 *Legitimation*: people's ineffectual involvement is used to give the appearance of their agreement and consent to predetermined decisions and plans. Participation serves as a public relations and window-dressing exercise.
4 *Tokenism*: encouraging the minority involvement of members of oppressed groups, unrelated to the representative structures established by their organisations.

Arnstein (1969) included eight rungs in her influential ladder of citizen-participation. These were:

8 Citizen control
7 Delegated power   }   Degrees of citizen power
6 Partnership

5 Placation }
4 Consultation } Degrees of tokenism
3 Informing }

2 Therapy } Non-participation
1 Manipulation }

Most of the current initiatives concerned with user-involvement fall into the last two categories (Croft and Beresford, 1990). Dowson describes the ways in which service providers keep 'self-advocacy' safe so that it becomes a means of controlling people with learning disabilities instead of them being able to take control (Dowson, 1990).

Participation schemes have also tended to focus on groups facing particular disadvantage and marginalisation. For example, the focus of community work has traditionally been council tenants on deprived estates in poverty stricken inner and outer city areas. Currently the idea of user-involvement is directed at users of disempowering and devalued health and welfare services, for example, people with learning difficulties, people with mental distress and disabled people.

Now there are powerful reasons why people and groups experiencing particular powerlessness and exclusion should be the special subject of participatory initiatives and special efforts should be made to challenge and overcome the discrimination and oppressions they experience. But a question that remains is whether such a focus serves other functions, intentionally or otherwise. For example, it mirrors the areas where the state can most readily intervene and shape the nature of participatory initiatives and includes many of the groups who are most susceptible to state intervention. This focus also means that we don't have to look more closely at the nature of our overall political structures. After all these groups face special, additional difficulties and problems. For some analysts it can be a short and convenient step from this to seeing the cause of the difficulties and non-participation of such groups in their own particular characteristics and inadequacies. At base this approach allows us to maintain our assumptions that existing institutions and structures *are* democratic. Everything may not be perfect, but we have our elected representatives, political parties and interest groups. There are chains of accountability and formal procedures for complaint and redress.

Against this though we can set the fact that by many criteria people's objective and perceived involvement is highly qualified. It is important not to ignore or underplay the oppressions faced by some groups, differences in power between people, and the different material and other resources available to them to become involved. But at the same time, *most* of us face considerable constraints. The demand for more say is widespread. Even people who can exert a negative influence over others less powerful than themselves may feel they have little control over the world in which they live. Indeed the two may be connected.

One large-scale local study of public participation in planning, for example, found that the view that the council took little notice of local people extended to *all* social groups and was not confined to council tenants or the worst off (Beresford and Croft, 1985: 10). Another expression of such broader disempowerment and exclusion is the emergence of the new social movements of women, Black people, gay men and lesbians which we have already discussed.

The limited nature of most people's political and civic involvement is well documented (Croft and Beresford, 1989: 6–7). The fact that citizenship seems to be an idea few people give much thought to, appears to reflect people's more general lack of involvement in the political process and public affairs (Richardson, 1990). Official reports highlight this. One, for example, drew attention to the serious under-representation of women in Parliament, in public bodies, in recognition in the honours system, on Boards and Trade Unions' Executives (*Hansard*). Another government report showed that in 1985 less than 20 per cent of councillors were women. Home owners, professionals and managers are also greatly over-represented among councillors. Only 5 per cent of councillors worked or used to work in semi-skilled or unskilled manual occupations, as compared with 25 per cent of the general population (The Local Government Councillor, 1986).

Participation, then, is an idea whose development is restricted, whose role is ambiguous and whose focus has been limited. Are these arguments for ignoring or rejecting it? They may be, but a number of other arguments are also offered for paying it serious attention and trying to *increase* people's involvement and participation. They are both practical and philosophical: participation works and it is right. It makes for more efficient and cost-effective services; ensures accountability; reflects the democratic ethos of our society; encourages people's independence and self-determination; is consistent with people's human and civil rights. Thus a set of strong economic, moral, political and psychological arguments are advanced for people's participation. Equally important, people *want* to be more involved. What research there is indicates that most people want more say and involvement. Three-quarters of a random sample of comprehensive school students said they wanted more say (Beresford and Croft, 1981: 19). Two-thirds of the people interviewed in the study of public participation in planning referred to earlier, expressed a desire to have more say in decisions affecting them (Beresford and Croft, 1985: 73). Two-thirds of a random sample of people interviewed in one neighbourhood as part of a study of local social services, felt that service users, workers and other local people should have more say in them (Beresford and Croft, 1986: 228). The desire of people for more involvement is also reflected in the large and growing numbers of community, disability, users, and rights organisations which are pressing for more say and involvement over issues and decisions affecting people's lives and neighbourhood and in the organisations and institutions which affect them (see, for example, Lister and Beresford, 1991; Thompson, 1991).

How do we resolve the contradiction between the possibilities and the frequent reality of participation? The answer seems to be in untangling its ambiguities. At the heart of these lies the issue of *power*.

Participation and Power

Generally people want to get involved to exert an influence and to be able to make change. Some of the features that are associated with people's desire for more involvement are: influencing decisions and outcomes; changing the distribution of power; ensuring equal access to marginalised and oppressed groups and constituencies; providing for broad based involvement, moving beyond the creation of new leaderships. That is why terms like 'having a say' and 'empowerment' have become synonymous with involvement in people's minds. But as we have seen they are not necessarily synonymous with the *practice* of participation.

Let's look more closely at power. The model proposed by Lukes may be helpful here. For Lukes power involves conflict of interest, though conflict may also be pursued by power and influence – falling short of the exercise of power. He assumes at least two parties in conflict and that power is exercised when one of them (call them A) gets the other (B) to act in a way which is against B's interests as perceived by B. The two parties need not be individuals. Groups and institutions also exercise power between each other.

Lukes is also concerned with the hidden dimensions of power. Hidden power is exercised, he says, when conflict of interest has been excluded from public debate and decision-making. As a result, though others appear to acquiesce in what happens, in reality their viewpoint has been prevented from being raised. The absence of overt conflict means only that they have been 'denied entry into the political process'. Lukes also proposed a third dimension of power, 'The complex and subtle ways in which the inactivity of leaders and the sheer weight of institutions – political, industrial and educational', serves to keep people out of the process and 'from even trying to get into it' (Lukes, 1974: 24, 38)

Enabling people's participation represents a challenge to all this. It's an enormous challenge and one that is often very unpalatable to powerholders. But involvement and empowerment don't only mean power being taken from one and going to another. They don't necessarily mean losing power. They are not part of a zero-sum game, so that if I have more, then you must have less. Instead involvement can be concerned with changing the nature of the relationship between participants. Nonetheless, the idea of people's involvement is still frequently seen as threatening by organisations, institutions and their personnel. A way in which they can resolve this tension is by *manipulating the ambiguity* of participation. Participatory initiatives can be a route to redistributing power, changing relationships and creating opportunities for influence. Equally, they can double as a means of keeping power from people and giving a false impression of its transfer. They can be put to two conflicting purposes, according to whether their initiators want to hold on to or share power.

Resolving the Paradox of Participation

Recognising the two faces of participation helps us to understand why it is so often treated as a rhetorical flourish rather than a serious policy and why it has become so devalued. But there may be a problem in then just dismissing the idea of participation out of hand. As we have seen, many people seem to want to be more involved. If their aspiration remains unsupported then it is likely that they will continue to be excluded and existing dominations perpetuated. We may find ourselves colluding in this process unintentionally.

The answer may lie not in rejecting participation but first in being clear about its nature and objectives; where control lies and what opportunities it may offer. Then people can make rational decisions about whether to get involved. We also need to draw a crucial distinction. Participation does not only mean participatory initiatives set up by state or service providers. It is also about people struggling to gain more say and involvement for themselves and working to enable the broader involvement of their peers in their own organisations. This mirrors the distinction emerging between 'democratic' and 'consumerist' approaches to 'user-involvement'. As people involved in community, rights, disability and user groups quickly learn from experience, power is generally not something that is handed over or can be given. It has to be taken.

We should therefore distinguish between state or service provider-led schemes and initiatives for involvement, and our own initiatives and organisations to achieve it. Increasingly organisations of disabled people and other groups are only getting involved in initiatives over which they have control.

As Richard Wood, Director of the British Council of Organisations of Disabled People has said:

> It's a growing concern. Our participation is expected to be free . . . Money must be found for disabled people to develop their expertise. We're getting a bit fed up with being asked to participate in events which are meant to be about user-involvement where on the day the professionals who are involved in organising these things and talking about user-involvement show very little evidence of being committed to it. They're just picking our brains. We've decided we've got to put what ever resources we've got into disabled people's organisations . . . If you want us to participate, you go and find more money and we can get some development workers. (quoted in Beresford and Croft, 1991: 71–2)

This opens the way to a twin-track policy of checking out the aims and objectives of provider-led initiatives, to be able to make a judgement about our response to them and working for broad based and anti-discriminatory involvement in our own initiatives.

As well as being clear about the nature and limits of participatory initiatives we also need to understand how to support people's involvement effectively. Two components seem to be essential here, if people are to have a realistic chance of exerting an influence and all groups are to have equal access to involvement. These are *access* and *support*. Both are necessary. Experience suggests that without support, only the most confident, well-resourced and advantaged people and groups are likely to become involved. This explains the biased response that participatory initiatives have typically generated. Without access, efforts to become involved are likely to be arduous and ineffectual.

Access includes equal access to the political structure at both local and central government levels and to other organisations and institutions which affect people's lives. In the more specific context of services it includes physical accessibility; the provision of services which are appropriate for and match the particular needs of different groups, and access points providing continuing opportunities for participation within both administrative and political structures, including membership of sub-committees, planning groups, working parties and so on.

The need for *support* arises not because people lack the competence to participate in society, but because people's participation is undermined by, or not part of, the dominant culture or tradition. Gaventa used Lukes' model of power to explain why poor Appalachian farmers appeared to accept domination and oppression by large corporations. The formal rights and channels open to them remained unused. Gaventa argued that focusing on people's apparent choices, we ignore the possible use of power to stifle and exclude conflict, 'blaming the victim for [his/her] non-participation' (Gaventa, 1980). People may not know what's possible or how to get involved; may not like to ask for too much or be reluctant to complain. There are four essential elements to support. These are:

1   *personal development*: to increase people's expectations, assertiveness, self-confidence and self-esteem;
2   *skill development*: to build the skills they need to participate and to develop their own alternative approaches to involvement;
3   *practical support*: to be able to take part, including access to information, child care, transport, meeting places, advocacy, etc.;
4   *support for people to get together and work in groups*: including administrative expenses, payment for workers, training and development costs.

A number of routes to achieving people's greater participation at both micro and macro level are already apparent. These include:

1   people working for it in their organisations and social movements;
2   gaining support for the enterprise from allies in public services and state institutions (for example, as Chamberlin, 1988, has observed, the support of radical mental health workers has been one of the features

which has characterised the growth of the mental health system survivors' movement in Britain);

3 clarifying the issue of participation in order to develop effective strategies to pursue it;

4 learning systematically from existing experience.

Participation and Social Policy

Another route lies in a changed role for social policy. Before we turn to this, let's look first at the roles the welfare state has traditionally been seen as serving. These have been typified as: palliating and compensating for the inequalities of the market; and acting as a form of state control. Functions ascribed to the welfare state have ranged from ensuring cohesion, managing conflict and appeasing the public. More recently it has been criticised for perpetuating traditional dominances and mirroring oppressions on the basis of age, race, sexuality, disability and gender. Williams suggests that we see the notions of family, nation and work as three central and inter-connected themes in the development of welfare, within the context of the shifting relations of patriarchy, capitalism and imperialism and argues that: 'welfare policies have both appealed to and reinforced (and occasionally challenged) particular ideas of what constitutes family life, national unity and "British culture"' (1992: 12).

The idea first propounded by Marshall (1950) and more recently restated by Dahrendorf (1989) of the welfare state providing a floor safeguarding people's rights by ensuring their social citizenship is now widely seen to have failed. Le Grand has also suggested that the 'strategy of equality' has been unsuccessful, arguing that: 'In all relevant areas, there persist substantial inequalities in public expenditure, in use, in opportunity, in access and in outcomes' (1982: 3–4).

What has unified social policy of the political left and right and also been a common characteristic of the British welfare state under governments of contrasting political colours has been the *very limited* involvement of its users and other citizens in shaping and controlling it. In this it has reflected the political systems of the left and right to which we referred at the beginning of this discussion. The regulation of the market has been replaced by state paternalism.

Partly because of the groundswell of dissatisfaction with such paternalism, there is currently a great debate about participation in social policy. But it has predominantly been framed in narrow terms of consumerism and 'user-involvement'. In the discussions of disability and user movements and among supportive workers, though, something different is emerging. Just as people are seeking a third way in politics, so these discussions suggest a third option for social policy, beyond both the old paternalism and the new consumerism. *People's participation* is the cornerstone of this third approach to social policy, just as it is of the new politics. Some of the features associated with such social policy include:

1   citizens having an effective say and involvement in the development and
    management of social policy;
2   user-led services and alternatives;
3   people being accessed to the mainstream instead of being segregated in
    separate provision;
4   equal access for groups facing discrimination, and services and pro-
    vision consistent with and supportive of people's cultural and other
    differences;
5   policy and provision which are consistent with and safeguard people's
    civil rights;
6   support for people to secure their own rights and involvement.

This list reflects the struggles of disability and other movements of people
who use welfare services to gain access to the mainstream; a say in support
services and the achievement of their civil rights.

It also makes clear that participation in social policy need not and
probably should not only be conceived in narrow terms, for example, as the
province solely of the subjects of marginalising policies and services.
Instead it is linked with much broader issues. Indeed, we would argue that
participatory social policy can offer a route to a more participatory politics.
It can make this possible not only by providing a series of settings and
opportunities for people's participation, but also by *enabling* and *supporting*
their participation. This is implicit in the characteristics we have identified,
but it also becomes explicit if we consider any particular policy from this
perspective. Take education, for instance. This could enhance people's
capacity to participate, by ensuring their involvement through:

1   *a participatory process of learning*: based on shared learning which
    supports our self-confidence, increases our assertiveness and encourages
    us to challenge and question;
2   *learning how to participate*: both by gaining skills and having a say in
    our own education and the services and policies associated with it;
3   *learning about participation*: finding out about the rights and responsi-
    bilities of our citizenship.

Conclusion

In outlining these ideas, we do not underestimate the structural constraints
restricting people's involvement or the obstacles that are likely to be in the
way of increasing it. We, alongside many other people, have long experienced these in our own efforts to gain more say. Instead we are arguing the
importance of *clarifying* and *highlighting* the issue of participation. Earlier
we identified this as one of the strategies for increasing people's
participation. Much work has already been done on supporting people's
greater say and involvement in education, health care, social services and
other social policies. But often this has not been pulled together as a basis

for action or theory building. We are arguing for participation to be taken seriously in social policy. Then social policy may escape from its prescriptive past and come to have an empowering role in people's lives and in public politics.

Acknowledgement

We would like to thank Alan Stanton for all his help and support.

References

Andrews, G. (ed.) (1991) *Citizenship*. London: Lawrence & Wishart.
Arnstein, S. (1969) 'A ladder of citizen participation', *Journal of the American Institute of Planners*, 35(4): 216–24.
Barker, A. (1979) *Public Participation in Britain: A Classified Bibliography*. London: Bedford Square Press.
Beresford, P. (1988) 'Consumer views: data collection or democracy?' in I. White, M. Devenney, R. Bhaduri, P. Beresford, J. Barnes and A. Jones (eds), *Hearing the Voice of the Consumer*. London: Policy Studies Institute.
Beresford, P. and Croft, S. (1981) '"It's not much of a prospect": first findings from a study of young people, participation and powerlessness', *Community Care*, 10 September: 18–20.
Beresford, P. and Croft, S. (1985) *A Say in the Future: Planning, Participation and Meeting Social Need*, 2nd edn. London: Battersea Community Action.
Beresford, P. and Croft, S. (1986) *Whose Welfare? Private Care or Public Services?* Brighton: Lewis Cohen Urban Studies Centre.
Beresford, P. and Croft, S. (1991) 'User views', *Changes*, 9(1): 71–2.
Boggs, C. (1986) *Social Movements and Political Power*. Philadelphia: Temple University Press.
Bruton, M. and Glasson, J. (1984) 'Planning planning', *Times Higher Education Supplement*, 9 March.
Campbell, P. (1990) 'Self-advocacy: working together for change', presentation to MIND Conference, Survivors Speak Out, 10 Oct.
Chamberlin, J. (1988) *On Our Own: Patient-controlled Alternatives to the Mental Health System*. London: MIND.
Chambers, R. (1983) *Rural Development: Putting the Last First*. London: Longman.
Clarke, M. and Stewart, J. (1986) *The Public Service Orientation: Issues and Dilemmas to be Faced*. INLOGOV Working Paper 4, Luton: Local Government Training Board.
Croft, S. and Beresford, P. (1989) 'User-involvement, citizenship and social policy', *Critical Social Policy*, 26: 5–18.
Croft, S. and Beresford, P. (1990) *From Paternalism to Participation: Involving People in Social Services*. London: Open Services Project/Joseph Rowntree Foundation.
Dahrendorf, R. (1989) Paper presented to the Commission on Citizenship Seminar, Commission on Citizenship, April.
Dominelli, L. (1990) *Women and Community Action*. Birmingham: Venture Press.
Dowson, S. (1990) *Keeping it Safe: Self-advocacy by People with Learning Difficulties and the Professional Response*. London: Values Into Action.
Doyal, L. (1992) 'Human need and the moral right to optimal community care', in J. Bournat, C. Pereira, D. Pilgrim and F. Williams (eds), *Community Care: A Course Reader*. Basingstoke: Macmillan. pp. 276–86.
Doyal, L. and Gough, I. (1984) 'A theory of human needs', *Critical Social Policy*, 10: 6–38.
Doyal, L. and Gough, I. (1991) *A Theory of Human Needs*. London: Macmillan.

Freire, P. (1972) *Pedagogy of the Oppressed*. Harmondsworth: Penguin.

Gaventa, J. (1980) *Power and Powerlessness: Quiescence and Rebellion in an Appalachian Valley*. Oxford: Clarendon.

Gibson, T. (1979) *People Power: Community and Work Groups in Action*. Harmondsworth: Pelican.

Hallet, C. (1987) *Critical Issues in Participation*. Newcastle: Association of Community Workers.

Harding, T. and Upton, A. (1991) *User Involvement in Social Services: An Annotated Bibliography*, Briefing Paper No. 5. London: National Institute for Social Work.

Hoggett, P. and Hambleton, R. (eds) (1987) *Decentralisation and Democracy: Localising Public Services*, Occasional Paper 28, School of Advanced Urban Studies, University of Bristol.

Khan, U.A. (1989) 'Neighbourhood forums and the New Left: representation beyond tokenism?' Paper presented to the Annual Conference of the Political Studies Association, April.

Le Grand, J. (1982) *The Strategy of Equality: Redistribution and the Social Services*. London: Allen & Unwin.

Lister, R. (1990) *The Exclusive Society: Citizenship and the Poor*. London: Child Poverty Action Group.

Lister, R. (1991) 'Citizenship engendered', *Critical Social Policy*, 32: 65–71, and this volume.

Lister, R. and Beresford, P. (1991) *Working Together Against Poverty: Involving Poor People in Action against Poverty*. Open Services Project and Dept of Applied Social Studies, University of Bradford.

Local Government Councillor, The (1986) Committee of Enquiry into the Conduct of Local Authority Business Records, Vol. 11. London: HMSO.

London Edinburgh Weekend Return Group (1979) *In and Against the State*. London: Pluto.

Lukes, S. (1974) *Power: A Radical View*. Basingstoke: Macmillan.

Mantle, A. (1985) *Popular Planning not in Practice: Confessions of a Community Worker*. London: Greenwich Employment Unit.

Marsden, D. and Oakley, P. (1982) 'Radical community development in the Third World', in G. Craig, N. Derricourt and M. Loney (eds), *Community Work and the State: Towards a Radical Practice*. London: Routledge & Kegan Paul.

Marshall, T.H. (1950) *Citizenship and Social Class*. Cambridge: Cambridge University Press.

Mayo, M. (1975) 'Community development: a radical alternative', in R. Bailey and R. Brake (eds), *Radical Social Work*. London: Routledge & Kegan Paul.

Mayo, M. (1977) *Women in the Community*. London: Routledge & Kegan Paul

Mead, L. (1986) *Beyond Entitlement: The Social Obligations of Citizenship*. New York: The Free Press.

Meiksens-Wood, E. (1986) *The Retreat From Class: A New True Socialism*. London: Verso.

O'Brien, J. and Lyle, C. (1987) *Framework for Accomplishment: A Workshop for People Developing Better Services*. Georgia, USA: Responsive Systems Associates.

O'Brien, J. and Tyne, A. (1981) *The Principles of Normalisation – A Foundation for Effective Services*. London: Values into Action.

Ohri, A. and Manning, B. (1982) *Community Work and Racism*. London: Routledge & Kegan Paul.

Oliver, M. (1990) *The Politics of Disablement*. Basingstoke: Macmillan.

Oppenheim, C. (1990) *Poverty: The Facts*. London: Child Poverty Action Group.

People and Planning (1969) Report of the Committee on Public Participation. In *Planning*, (The Skeffington Report), Department of the Environment, Scottish Development Department, Welsh Office, HMSO.

Pfeffer, N. and Coote, A. (1991) *Is Quality Good for You? A Critical Review of Quality Assurance in Welfare Services*. Social Policy Paper No. 5. London: Institute for Public Policy Research.

Richardson, A. (1983) Participation: Concepts in Social Policy, One. London: Routledge & Kegan Paul

Richardson, A. (1990) *Talking About Commitment*. London: The Prince's Trust.

Sheffield University (1974–78) 'The linked research project into public participation, interim research papers 1–13', Department of Extra-mural Studies.

Taylor, D. (1989) 'Citizenship and social power', *Critical Social Policy*, 26: 19–31, and this volume.

Taylor, D. (1992) 'A big idea for the nineties: the rise of the citizens' charters', *Critical Social Policy*, 33: 87–94.

Thompson, C. (ed.) (1991) *Changing the Balance: Power and People Who Use Services*. Community Care Project, London: National Council for Voluntary Organisations.

Twelvetrees, A. (1982) *Community Work*. Basingstoke: Macmillan.

Walker, A. (1991) 'Towards greater user involvement in the social services', in T. Arie (ed.), *Recent Advances in Psychogeriatrics 2*. Churchill Livingstone.

Walker, D. (1992) *Citizens and Local Democracy: Charting a New Relationship*. Luton: The Local Government Management Board.

Ward, C. (1990) 'Product-minded', *New Statesman and Society*. 12 Oct.: 31.

Ward, S. (1984) *Organising Things: A Guide to Successful Political Action*. London: Pluto Press.

Williams, F. (1989) *Social Policy: A Critical Introduction*. Cambridge: Polity Press.

Williams, F. (1992) 'Somewhere over the rainbow: universality and diversity in social policy', in N. Manning and R. Page (eds), *Social Policy Review, 1991–92*. Canterbury: Social Policy Association.

11

Social Movements and Social Need: Problems with Postmodern Political Theory

Martin Hewitt

A central issue about social movements is whether their vision is one that proves relevant to society at large. That is, do their goals have a bearing on the predicament society faces? Put another way, how might it be said that a movement with its own particular concerns comes to reflect a more universal viewpoint?

These kinds of questions have, not surprisingly, two sides. First, there is the *empirical* question under what circumstances one could claim that a specific group's needs are similar to society's social needs. Second, there is the *conceptual* question about whether needs can be understood as common to both members of a group and members of society at large. This chapter is concerned with the second question. But later I will endeavour to illustrate this point with reference to empirical research into poverty.

The question about the universalisability of human interests and needs has of course exercised the minds of political theorists since antiquity. In modern times, theorists have been occupied with various approaches to this problem: for example Marx's notion of a class-in-itself becoming a class-for-itself as the proletariat assumes its role as the universal class of history (1975: 192); Lukacs' notion of subjective class consciousness overcoming false consciousness and becoming objective knowledge in the formation of a universal understanding of the social totality (1971: 50); the problematic universalism in Sartre's notion of the 'fused group', struggling against the 'practico-inert' and emerging from the 'seriality' of individuals and groups, to take command of its own praxis, only to dissolve back again into seriality (1976: Book II, Ch. 1); and, coming from a Durkheimian direction, Runciman's concept of reference group behaviour as a basis whereby social identities are extended or restricted and a sense of social injustice intensified or abated (1966: Ch. 2).

However, the moral and political outlook of the late twentieth century – embracing pluralism and diversity – appears less sympathetic to the theoretical traditions of modernity which have addressed central political

First published in *Critical Social Policy*, 37, 1993.

questions within a universal framework employing terms like 'society' and 'totality' and similar holistic concepts. Indeed against this drift of thought, new social movements have come to express a new postmodern politics (see Gibbins, 1989: 1–2), and theorists of new social movements to be seen as theorists of postmodern politics (cf. Eyerman and Jamison, 1991: 147).

The issue of universal interest is better understood by narrowing the focus onto a core concept, that is need, and considering whether the needs which motivate social movements are the same as those with which individuals generally identify? Social movement theorists refer to the role of need in discussing the politics of social movements (for example, Habermas, 1987: 394; Touraine, 1981: 2; Melucci, 1985: 790; Eyerman and Jamison, 1991: 6), and the importance of the welfare state as the core institution of late capitalism responsible for identifying, shaping and satisfying needs (for example Eyerman and Jamison, 1991: 153; Habermas, 1987: 347). However, with few exceptions they tend not to consider the wider theoretical implications posed by the concept; whether, for example, needs which are common to all humankind can provide a basis on which universal interests are determined.

It might seem that the question becomes clearer if there is general agreement over which needs are common to all (see Mack and Lansley, 1985: 46–8). On this basis, social movements would be acceptable if they sought conditions that satisfy universal needs. By contrast, social movements pursuing more specific needs would not be society's collective concern. However, *pace* consensus theorists, the point about social movements is that they claim to possess insights into need that the rest of us lack. Pre-defined needs, however widely supported, are unlikely to appeal to social movements whose *raison d'être* lies in highlighting new needs and uncovering government's failure to provide for them. Alternatively, a theory identifying universal need in terms of social practice and communication – of the kind advanced by Habermas and more recently by Doyal and Gough (1991) – might help to create a political climate more open to some of the claims of social movements. The issue turns on how 'settled' debates on consensus are, varying between those treating consensus as a more or less organic reflection of society at large – for example by using sampling techniques (see Veit-Wilson 1987; Walker, 1987) – and those such as social movements researchers who study the formative, differential and transitory nature of the social attitudes of specific movements.

However, postmodernist theorists are strongly wedded to a particularist view of the goals and needs of social movements. New needs are seen as arising at a particular time and place. Needs serve to redraw the boundaries of community around individuals and groups sharing the same identity, to disrupt a prevailing consensus blind to those needs, and so to challenge state ideologies of need. The issues posed within postmodernist theory are of interest to the study of social policy and need. Fiona Williams has recently suggested several such lines of study, of which one involves exploring:

> The ways in which needs for universal welfare provision may be resolved with the need to meet diversity and difference, both at the level of policy planning and at the level of collective action around welfare demands and at the level of individual and collective empowerment to articulate needs. (1992: 210)

Yet, notwithstanding the claims of postmodernist theory, it is possible to detect another less distinct thread running through some influential post-modernist theorists – for example Touraine and Melucci – which suggests that social movements are seeking to found new arrangements governed by a different order of universal values and needs. I want to use this chapter to tease out this thread and thematise it in relation to universalist theories of need. I will first argue that the anti-universalism of postmodern theorists of social movements is sustained problematically alongside something akin to a universal dialectic of recognition which they attribute to the politics of social movements. For this reason it is premature to abandon universalist arguments. Second, I hope to provide some insights into social movements by exploring accounts of needs which argue that humankind is charac-terised by universal needs despite the diverse cultural forms under which they appear, as has been argued in the recent work of Doyal and Gough and the more long-standing work of Townsend.

The Specificity of Social Movement Interests: A Postmodern Agenda?

For postmodernist theorists, the relationship between the universal and specific concerns characterising social movements remains problematic. Certainly we can identify a postmodern agenda in Touraine, Melucci and Laclau and Mouffe, which offers a critique of tendencies in political theory to attribute essence and foundation to political action, and cultivates an awareness of the plurality and contingency of human interests. This agenda is seen in the vision each theorist paints of the immanence of social action and identity that emerges among different actors and groups.

For example, Touraine sees post-industrial society as actively responding to circumstances and choosing its own destiny, a society functioning reflexively with the 'increasing ability to act on itself' (1981: 2), of societies able 'to generate their objectives and their normativity' (1981:59). This newly discovered capability stems above all from the new politics of social movements which 'sets up self-managing determination against technocratic management' (1981: 9) – a view sharing Lyotard's preference for 'local determinism' and 'small narratives' expressed in *The Postmodern Condition* (1984).

Consequently, a different view of history that sees social order and change as the outcome of human essence or transcendence, beyond the grasp of human agency, is rejected, because, for Touraine:

> We are moving quite simply to a type of society in which no transcendence – be it of the gods, of man, or of evolution – will any longer force collective action to

take on a meaning by which it is surpassed; we are entering a society which has neither laws nor foundations, which is no more than a complex of actions and social relations. (1981: 2)

An example of this 'transcendent' approach would be the view prevailing in 'industrial society', before the onset of post-industrial society, that progress was judged according to standards that transcended society, such as the power of the technical forces of production and knowledge that stood beyond human influence; or the progress of civilisation marked by human betterment and the increasing satisfaction of human needs. Alternatively, Touraine proposes that 'the history of our industrialisation and the functioning of our industrial society are . . . controlled . . . by actions, by social movements of confrontation' (1981: 32). To which he tersely adds that 'the rest is all metaphysics'.

Melucci, a former student of Touraine, likewise shares this anti-essentialist view in which society is driven by the force of social imagery which has become detached from its material roots and abstracted into systems of symbols and representations, and which now has the power to guide social movements, a development he terms: the 'symbolic challenge' (1985). It is the split between the real and symbolic which, in postmodernist fashion, determines the 'artificial' and 'built' character of social life. Melucci sees that: 'A large amount of our everyday experiences occur (*sic*) in a socially produced environment. Media represent and reflect our actions; individuals incorporate and reproduce these messages in a sort of self-growing spiral' (1985: 804). He asks provocatively, 'Where are "nature" and "reality" outside the cultural representations and images we receive from and produce for our social world?' (ibid.). Yet, despite his unmistakably postmodern account of the power of the symbolic over social reality, Melucci does not forsake his commitment to purposive reflexivity in social action for a vision of the futility of social progress often associated with postmodern writers such as Baudrillard (for example 1983).[1] For what Melucci declares at stake in contemporary movements is:

the production of the human species, at the individual and collective level: the possibility for men, as individuals and as species, to control not only their 'products' but their 'making', culturally and socially . . . What is at stake is the production of human existence and its quality. (1985: 807)

In a way which characterises an essentially Heideggerian moment in recent postmodern thought,[2] Melucci stresses the *contingent* and *indeterminant* nature of social existence:

For the first time societies become radically aware of their contingency, they realise they 'are thrown' in the world, they discover they are not necessary and thus they are irreversibly responsible for their destinies. Catastrophe, suffering, freedom, all belong to the possible future, and they are not fatal events. (1985: 814)

Melucci's 'symbolic challenge' is embraced most fully by Laclau and Mouffe in their account of social movements as engaged in advancing the terms of the democratic discourse begun in the 18th century. This discourse, they argue, has decisively influenced alliances forged between different groups enabling them to form a shared identity out of their differing experiences of oppression. The new politics gains its strength from a discourse which has posed the possibility – the 'democratic imaginary' – that the political universality first raised by the French Revolution could be extended by a 'logic of equivalence' to virtually all groups placed in politically subordinate relations: the non-franchised, women, immigrants, welfare clients, etc. (1985: 129). For Laclau and Mouffe, it is the structure of this discourse, addressing 'the rights of every human being' (1985: 154), which defines positions for individual groups to articulate new identities out of their oppressive relations with powerful others. In the present century this process has been expanded by the formation of the welfare state which 'far from succeeding in integrating different social groups into a cohesive society, in fact laid bare the arbitrary character of a whole set of relations of subordination' (1985: 158). Such a discourse is indeterminate and open to the possibilities of new forms of self-definition and social movement which generate diverse logics of political action: for 'each term of this plurality of identities finds within itself the principle of its own validity without this having to be sought in a transcendent . . . ground' (1985: 167). Laclau and Mouffe oppose the notion, seen in Marxism, that society is a potentially transcendent, complete and 'sutured' totality which predetermines the role of individuals and social classes as *essentially* subordinate, superordinate or equal. Instead the social is defined by the emergence of new social movements which at times coalesce under the identity of an emerging hegemony whilst still retaining their salient identities of difference as gender, ethnicity, age, etc. (Barrett, 1991: 68).

So for Touraine, Melucci and Laclau and Mouffe, the social world is cast in terms of its immanence and contingency, seen in its capacity for self-governance and -guidance; and social movements as conflictual, particularistic, and activist in the pursuit of their social destiny – what Touraine calls 'society's struggle for historicity'.

However, for these writers this postmodern account is offset by moments of grand narrative characteristic of modernist social theory, a turn of thought which is essentialist and universalist, in which the language of solidarity, dialogue and community transcending division and fragmentation comes into play (for example Touraine, 1981: 59–60). I want to suggest that this is not a case of a momentary lapse in their postmodern sensibility into a modern rationalist mode of thought, nor a sign of a transitional stage in developing a more fully postmodern sociology. It is rather the inescapable need to employ universalist concepts in thinking through new problems. Such reconceptualisation, as White has recently stressed, 'should not only address the new problematic, but should be able to show connections with old problematics' (1991: 12). In other words, we should recognise the new problematic which social movement theorists – and many others – have sought to articulate, and the new forms of conceptualisation required, but recognise also that this cannot be understood simply in terms of a shift from foundationalist to anti-foundationalist modes of thought, but rather in terms of a search for new forms of transcendental conceptualisation by which such a shift might be framed. I shall argue later that recent discussion of need when applied to new social movements helps to clarify the terms of this framing.

Both Touraine and Melucci share a sense of a universal process working through the development of contemporary social movements. This is seen most explicitly in Touraine's work: first, in the universal status he accords the cultural field in which antagonists struggle; and, second, in his grand narrative on the emergence of post-industrial society from industrial society, which serves as an essentialist backdrop against which the success of social movements is judged. First, Touraine and Melucci both construct the cultural arena in which social movements struggle against ruling interests as existing independently of the struggle itself. Different social actors are driven by conflicting ideologies and values in seeking the destruction or appropriation of the other. But they belong essentially to the same cultural orientation; for 'Values are always class values, while cultural orientations, although torn apart by class conflicts, have an autonomous existence' (Touraine, 1981: 63). Each cultural orientation is defined by Touraine as a 'field' in which there are 'stakes' valued and desired by two or more opponents. It is this terrain of cultural stakes that extends beyond the different goals and values of opponents and provides them with a universal point of reference: for 'all kinds of social conflicts have in common a reference to "real" . . . actors and to ends which are valued by all competitors or adversaries' (1985: 751). Thus within the broader cultural frame of social movements, shared horizons exist which orient the particular interests of opponents.

Second, the universality of the cultural field is characterised in teleological terms. The cultural orientations which opponents share give way through social movement and conflict to new institutions which come to form the basis for new broadly-embracing cultural fields. In answer to the question he poses about what kind of institutions new social movements will create, Touraine conjectures in a highly suggestive manner – to which we will return. Their role is to serve as 'the embryo of the new institutions, in which dialogue, exchange, and the creation of an autonomous space will enable claims and disputes to gain strength and become politicised' (1981: 23).

It is this articulation of a new sense of autonomy and community that emerges in Touraine's and Melucci's post-industrial/postmodernist philosophy of history by which social movements are to be judged, and which is fleshed out in terms of the new identities and relations the movements actually achieve. Cohen comments on the essentialism implied by this move which inevitably prejudices the radicality of social movements, 'by positing a post-industrial society whose institutions, forms of collective interaction, and consciousness would all be new by definition' (1985: 655, 702–3).

Melucci sees social movements as questioning existing structures and relations beyond their present commitments and reality, and as moving towards a deeper order of understanding: one that discloses the foundations of modern reasoning and in so doing enters the community of modern critical rationality:

> But beyond modernisation, beyond cultural innovation, movements question society on something 'else': who decides on codes, who establishes rules of normality, what is the space for difference, how can one be recognised for not being included but for being accepted as different, not for increasing the amount of exchanges but for affirming another kind of exchange. (1985: 810)

The concepts of 'exchange' and 'dialogue' are key terms in prefiguring a new moral and political universe where difference *and* solidarity are complementary and not opposing ideals. Melucci tentatively outlines a new kind of exchange based on a widening recognition of difference rather than identity alone. Social movement theorists correctly recognise the impossibility of proposing that society is composed entirely according to the principle of identity or of difference alone; of a society, for example, where the identity of equality prevailed, or alternatively, where the principle of social difference of one kind or another ruled. Touraine, for example, argues that 'There is no social relation that is based on equality or on a simple difference, for difference is nothing but the absence of relation' (1981: 33) – and, by the same token, simple equality is the absence of difference (see Walzer, 1983). Yet this insight only compels one to ask how these logically opposing principles are to be combined within a context of widening recognition and understanding.

Melucci likewise does not abandon the principle of identity for difference. For the universal concerns of social movements are seen to penetrate to a deeper understanding of the commonality of human existence, where identity prevails beyond difference as the spheres of address grow wider. The movement from particular to universal is advanced through a process of communication and address. In the struggle to disclose modern forms of rationality and power, social movements develop 'from a particularistic point of view, starting from a specific condition or location (as being young, being a woman, and so on). Nevertheless, they speak to the whole society. The problems they raise affect the global logic of contemporary systems' (1985: 810–11; see Scott, 1990: 67). Melucci tentatively outlines a new kind of exchange based in extending difference within a widening context of mutual recognition.

In these theoretical accounts of social movements we can see the emergence of a logic which is more dialectical than their postmodern agenda, by itself, would allow. Such exercises in hermeneutic understanding between movement and opposition must pass through the social and epistemic relations of modern systems of power in order to transcend them and establish a broader consensus of understanding. The cultural universe depicted by Touraine is itself subject to a deeper – and now increasingly global – logic of history whereby the confrontation between a movement's identity and its opposition parallels the universal confrontation between self and Other.[3] This is none other than Hegel's dialectic of recognition, narrated in his parable of the Master and Slave (see Scott, 1990: 62), in which the self is bent on the appropriation of the Other, and the Other of the self, even to a 'fight to the death for "recognition"' (Kojev, 1970: 7) – a fight which nonetheless eventually leads to a new level of recognition and reconciliation. The source that Touraine has drawn on is fundamental to diverse currents of French intellectual life in the 1960s, passing folk-like through Althusser (1971), Lacan (1977) and Sartre (1976) to Kojev (Hegel's interpolater in 1930s France) to Marx, and back to Hegel.

In contrast to this tradition, Laclau and Mouffe discard the dialectic of recognition by renouncing the idea that the subject is an evolving form of consciousness (1985: 97, 115). Instead discourse articulates positions which political subjects come to fill and articulate for their own political ends. However, this argument is juxtaposed with a different one that rests on the *a priori* status of discourse. On the one hand, the politics of social movements is seen as part of the process of hegemonic formation which is open and indeterminate, a process marked by unlimited meaning (1985: 169). On the other hand, such a discursive formation is endowed with an *a priori* and pre-existing status in determining the essential grounds without which the politics of social movements would not be possible. For example, throughout *Hegemony and Socialist Strategy*, Laclau and Mouffe assert that 'there is no relationship of oppression without the presence of a discursive "exterior" from which the discourse of subordination can be interrupted' (1985: 154). Laclau and Mouffe reject the idea of a universal logic traversing the plurality of radical politics and instead describe the atomised processes of pluralism which are only given shape and identity within the terms of a hegemonic formation. Despite their critique of essentialism, it is the pre-existent characterisation of discourse that provides the limit condition necessary for prosecuting the anti-foundationalist arguments central to postmodernist thought (see Geras, 1987: 65–7; Barrett, 1991: 74) – an anti-foundationalism that in their hands, it should be added, does not seek the complete abandonment of material reality for some 'universal text', but rather endeavours to discern the structuring relations struck between discourse and social reality (see Barrett, 1991: 76–7).

At this juncture we can note that these strands of social-movement theory disclose a universal moment which is out of kilter with the particular moment explored earlier in the section. We can identify three different ways in which recent social-movement theory describes the relationship between particular and universal interests:

1 *contingently*: under a particular set of social circumstances or con-
   tingencies, different interests are articulated with the interests of a
   plurality of differing groups, posing the possibility of hegemonic unity,
   but without there being any logical or pre-ordained linkage (for
   example Laclau and Mouffe, 1985);

2 *dialectically*: different groups with their own interests interact through work, struggle and conflict and come to recognise a wider identity – one which would submerge difference (for example Touraine, 1981);
3 a third relationship is also discernible but less clearly articulated, tending to merge into the first or second, whereby universal recognition permits *identity and difference to coexist* – a position currently explored in feminist political theory (see Bryson, 1992: 168) and in Habermas' theory of communicative action (a position nonetheless distinct from Laclau and Mouffe's contingently cast relations of identity and difference).

The Universal and the Specific: Habermas' Account of Social Movements

It is from Marx and Hegel by way of the different tradition of Critical Theory that Habermas has come to address new social movements in a way that avoids some of the problematic characterisations of other writers. In contrast to Touraine et al., he explicitly thematises the relationship between particularist and universalist concerns in his discussion of social movements. Like other 'identity' theorists (see Cohen, 1985), Habermas characterises social movements by their orientation to specific concerns arising in the cultural field – for example, the needs of marginalised groups for cultural identity – which cannot be allayed by recourse to traditional welfare measures of material compensation and redistribution. Rather, the new social movements seek to overcome the threats to what Habermas terms the lifeworld posed by the extension of the powers of economic and bureaucratic systems under welfare-state capitalism. By the lifeworld Habermas means the everyday presuppositions and beliefs that knit together the relations and communications between members of a social community. By protecting the lifeworld against 'colonising' systems, social movements demonstrate their concern to defend, and in some cases advance, a range of specific cultural objectives about the quality of life. In this way he stresses the particularist concerns of various movements with equality, self-realisation, participation and human rights (1987: 392).

At the same time, Habermas consistently grounds his analysis of difference within what he sees as the universal concern of social movements to recover the communicative foundations of social life. By this he means the assumption that parties to a communication expect that the truth claims one party utters to the other can be redeemed if called upon to do so. This 'communicative ethics' holds, for example, for individuals broadly sharing the same community norms, for scientists engaged in scholarly disputes, and, of importance to the present discussion, for political actors in conflict. For though the latter hold conflicting interests, their dispute cannot be settled unless each party is prepared to listen to the other's viewpoint on the basis that each would expect the other to listen to its own, that is, both parties share an attitude oriented to reaching understanding without which communication would not be possible. Of course, Habermas is fully aware that such reciprocal communication represents an ideal – what he terms an 'ideal speech situation', which may be far from fulfilled in practice (1970). Nevertheless, his claim is that this supposition must hold if communication is to be possible at all. In this way the communicative ethic has a transcendental status in his theory, whatever happens to actual instances of communication that depart from this ideal: ideal speech provides the grounding assumption which Habermas claims must be in place for rational and valid decisions to emerge, and indeed for a just and free society to develop.

It is in this sense that Habermas places social movements within the framework of universalist communicative ethics. He argues that 'A morality is universalist if it accords validity only to norms that all those concerned could approve on the basis of full consideration and without duress' (1989: 41). By critically challenging the policies of ruling groups, social movements are not only exposing those ruling interests which deviate from universal considerations, but, more importantly, restoring these conditions to the public domain for open debate.

Habermas is, however, very circumspect in applying this theory to all movements, preferring to distinguish between, on the one hand, the universalist 'emancipatory' concerns of feminism, which in struggling against patriarchal oppression seek to redeem promises anchored in the universalist foundations of bourgeois and socialist thought; and on the other hand, more 'defensive' movements aiming to stem threats to concrete forms of community life (1987: 393). Yet his account of the principal threats to the lifeworld can be seen to provide an alternative description to that offered by other movements theorists, of the particularist and universalist concerns that provoke social movements into action. Whereas for Touraine, Melucci and Laclau and Mouffe these two kinds of concern remain out of kilter, for Habermas there is an attempt to align them within a single project of universal human emancipation.[4] He gives several examples of this realignment. For example, the threats of excessive complexity foisted by military, nuclear, information technology and other systems on the lifeworld 'go *beyond* the spatial, temporal, and social limits of complexity of even highly differentiated lifeworlds' (1987: 395, emphasis added). Similarly, for the Greens what initiates protest is instances of 'tangible', that is, specific, destruction of the environment. Yet these carry a global significance which affects 'the organic foundations of the lifeworld and [which] makes us drastically aware of standards of livability' (1987: 394). Finally, the cultural impoverishment of the communicative infrastructures of the lifeworld has resulted in the emergence of various movements to protect communities that search for authentic personal and collective identities. These movements involve the 'revaluation of the particular, the natural, the provincial . . . to revitalise possibilities of expression and community that have been buried alive' (ibid.), that is, to rediscover social arrangements guided by a universalistic communicative ethic. Although at no time does Habermas prescribe the universal concerns these movements prefigure, he appears to suggest that even 'defensive' movements concerned with problems of local identity seek to overcome their specific deprivations and immediate needs in order to reach more distant horizons of personal and collective fulfilment. Thus a defence of specific identities and needs provides the grounds for raising more universalistic concerns.

Though they differ in the relationships they portray between the universal and specific, Habermas' characterisation of the universal aspects of social movements is markedly similar in some respects to Touraine's characterisation of the cultural field. Both are couched in terms of a dialectic of recognition which seeks for the ideal but far-from-realised commonality in which the identities of two antagonists merge into a new identity, where each has appropriated the resources of the other, making possible a fuller culture of reciprocity and dialogue. Of course Touraine, as we have seen, and Habermas, both disavow any lapse into historicism and foundationalism (cf Habermas, 1979: 102, 199; 1987: 399–403). However, there is an important difference between their characterisations of the universal concerns of social movements. Touraine describes the cultural field as a normative and autonomous practice; it furnishes a common set of cultural norms towards which opposing parties are oriented. At the point when a movement has reached a new stage of settlement, the resulting cultural field creates new institutions within which opposing identities can participate in dialogue rather than struggle. However, for Habermas the dialogue of ideal speech is not based on normative grounds alone, but on a transcendental presupposition which serves as the basis for guiding the normative conduct of actual instances of speech. His argument thereby operates on two levels: first, the transcendental grounds for reaching understanding which make communication possible, that is, the ideal speech situation; and second the normative ethic which enjoins parties to communicate in an unforced manner in which 'the co-operative search for truth is the only permissible motive' (1978: 363) in reaching understanding, and which thereby serves as a standard for judging actual communications and truth claims.

This suggests that the third way of aligning universal and particular interests, introduced at the end of the previous section, whereby some postmodern theorists seek an accommodation between the principles of identity and difference, is also thematised in Habermas' approach. This is seen especially in his understanding of the normative arrangements required for expressing the different identities formed in the intersubjective process of recognising human need. These arrangements would ensure that each of us has 'the ability to give one's own needs their due in . . . communicative structures' (1979: 78). The possibility that different parties or movements will be able to negotiate recognition of their own separate identities depends on their working collectively to establish arrangements for arriving at consensus. In this way, the recognition each needs of others is inseparable from the mutual recognition they all need in reaching understanding.

For Habermas, the recognition of difference is part of the wider identity of which each is part and by which mutual recognition is achieved. Of course, this formulation and the theoretical conditions underpinning it are highly abstract and almost infinitely generalisable. This problem can only be tackled at the level of application and practice, especially in the everyday world of politics and need, to which the paper now turns.

Social Movements and Social Needs

Having explored the possibility of realigning universal and specific moments in the analysis of social movements, I now want to discuss Doyal and Gough's *A Theory of Human Needs* (1991), which I argue seeks to make explicit these moments and the conceptual connections between them. This framework is applied to the concept of human need, and so provides a way of bringing together an understanding of social movements and their need-orientations. By addressing needs, moreover, we can ground the foregoing theoretical discussion in the practical and material concerns that motivate movements, and see more clearly the ways whereby social-movement goals may come to chime in with more general social concerns.

Doyal and Gough use Habermas' forms of argument to show how culturally specific needs can be articulated in the language of universal needs. Specifically their intention is to demonstrate that we all have the same needs, which are real and objective. Needs are therefore conceptualised independently of a particular social environment (1991: 90). At the summit of what they envisage as a hierarchy of needs stand the needs for physical survival and personal autonomy which represent the minimum basis for individual human existence. In social terms these needs translate into, first, the avoidance of serious harm, and, second, minimally disabled social participation, including critical participation, in one's chosen form of life. These needs are universal in two senses. They define respectively the essentially material nature of humankind, and the basic conditions for rational and self-determining human conduct in the face of technical, moral and political choices.

At the same time, Doyal and Gough acknowledge that such universal needs only make sense in everyday life when spelt out in terms of a lower order of intermediate needs, that is, the basic goods and services that meet specific needs in different cultures, such as adequate nutrition and water, protective housing, non-hazardous work environment, appropriate health care, etc. (1991: Ch. 8). While their discussion conceives needs in universal terms, they recognise that in identifying actual conditions of needing and the satisfiers required, intermediate needs must be interpreted in culturally relative terms, for 'there is no escape from the rules and discourses of one's form of life, there is no neutral reality to which one can turn to assess which approach to need-satisfaction is best' (1991: 43). However, for Doyal and Gough the process of meeting needs is emancipatory and rational, and so cannot be resolved in terms of cultural relativism alone. Rather, progress in meeting needs and procuring their means of satisfaction must be under-taken on a pragmatic basis by discovering what works most effectively in encounters between different cultures. Thereby a 'translation-bridge-head' is established as members of one culture enter another culture and encounter the core activities that are constitutive of the social life of each, and which 'are at the heart of our ability to understand the similarities between alien cultures and our own' (1991: 81). It is, they argue, the ability of individuals to enter into the need-satisfying practices of another culture which enables them to translate the other's culture, language rules and norms into terms that are similar to their own.

In this praxis philosophy, the encounter between two cultures in the discovery of each other's needs bears some similarity to Touraine's account of the struggle between social movements over the stakes in a cultural field. Here both Touraine and Doyal and Gough describe a dialectic between self and Other in the struggle for recognition and understanding, whether over conflicting interests or in understanding culturally different means of need-satisfaction. However, while for Touraine it is the cultural field that the adversaries share and the stakes over which they come into conflict; for Doyal and Gough it is the basic needs that members of different cultures share and the different cultural fields, with their differing ways of expressing and satisfying needs, that they must transcend. Nonetheless, in both cases the structure of interactive-praxis and the development of human understanding (see 1991: 168) accord with the dialectic of recognition.

In the arguments of Doyal and Gough the two higher needs described above – for physical survival and autonomy – represent empirical and transcendental justifications respectively for the universality of core needs. One describes the empirical conditions of human existence; the other the ontological assumption of agency which constitutes the terms of being human. (The consideration here is that to describe all the possible empirical features that necessarily define a human being – for example an indi-vidual's biological and psychological functioning and behaviour – will not be sufficient to exhaust his or her humanity. What has been described still lacks sufficient cause to be called human. This essential quality must lie beyond empirical description at the transcendental level of what constitutes a human being – a point returned to shortly.) It is only a short step to move from empirical and transcendental arguments to a third, normative, argument about need which recognises that if basic needs exist, then modern democratic states are obliged to secure the material means to enable individuals to fulfil their obligations as citizens (1991: 95). Doyal and Gough (1991: 119) develop the transcendental level of their argument by drawing on Habermas' 'ideal speech situation' (1970) and Rawls' 'original position' (1972), which lay down the pre-conditions for rational discourse and distributional justice respectively, to form the normative basis of their theory of need. Thus Doyal and Gough elaborate by these three steps – empirical, normative and transcendental – a theory of need that conforms to the dimensions proposed earlier in relation to Habermas' discussion of social movements. Moreover, as this part of the discussion suggests, we would expect that there is a logic linking the three steps or dimensions with respect to the needs that motivate social movement.

What has been argued here is that it is perfectly consistent to uphold a view which recognises that certain needs have a real, objective and universal status which nonetheless appears in culturally different forms. It would follow that the needs which social movements demand to be satisfied can likewise be cast as real, and yet be present in forms that are socially and politically relative. Doyal and Gough identify such universal needs that different cultural communities or social movements seek to satisfy, whether by productive labour or social struggle. The point is that it is possible to cogently articulate a set of links between the universal and particular dimensions of need.

Drawing on Doyal and Gough's conceptual account of need and on the earlier discussion of social movements, I want to suggest that the universal and specific concerns of social movements can be portrayed in the following three-part schema. *First*, social movements are motivated by single issues represented by concrete objectives which are specific to the more immediate concerns on their agendas: equal pay for equal work; undisputed territory for inhabitants who claim nationhood; removal of pollutants from threatened habitats; freedom from government intrusion into subcultural communities and so forth. Each of these concerns expresses a specific material need which can be understood only in terms relative to the circumstances of a particular movement.

However, the struggle to articulate these concerns must assume, *second*, a normative domain of procedural and substantive guidelines broadly acceptable to movements with cases of need to present, opponents ready to refute these cases, and political actors and parties who mediate and are willing to support cases worthy of policy consideration. This normative domain prescribes procedural rules for how political demands are selected as serious candidates for government policy – whether by democratic agreement, expert decision or elitist dictat – and the substantive criteria by which they are selected (see Taylor-Gooby, 1991: 190). In modern democratic societies this normative dimension is governed by universal considerations which imply that the legitimacy of government requires that the particular interests of different social movements receive a public hearing. The normative dimension of social movement action defines a cultural field in which at least a modicum of norms exists governing political, economic, ethical and interpersonal conduct, determining the value that opposing parties place on the stakes they struggle over, for example the rights of workers to participate with management in managing work, and of welfare claimants to an adequate income. This is the field which Touraine designates as the cultural field and cultural stakes, and which Habermas sees as the one in which truth claims of one sort or another are redeemed. Of course the normative domain is subject to conflict and change, and so is enlarged or reduced as opponents come to acknowledge wider norms of recognition and reciprocity or to retreat into separate worlds of barely negotiable difference. Whatever the case, this domain presents opportunities for knowledge and understanding sought in a struggle for recognition.

But this normative dimension cannot exhaust the universal standards and criteria which guide social movements towards particular concrete ends and valued outcomes. For how can one judge the validity of norms, when frequently parties present their own specific interests in a universal guise, under cover of the ideologies of, for example, national interest, civilised behaviour, the new world order, the imperatives of the market and so on (see Hewitt, 1992)? A test of discernment must appeal to a different order of universality, one involving some form of transcendental argument, that is one that advances a particular concept of human nature concerning its essentially rational (or irrational) and altruistic (or egoistic) propensities. This is an appeal to the ontological grounds of validity when assessing social actions which guide social movements in formulating their human projects and advancing their cases; and which also guide the public in judging which movements, which goals advanced, or which needs met, should be taken seriously in advancing universal needs more generally. This is the *third* transcendental, dimension for analysing social movements – presently most fully developed in Habermas' theory of communicative action. For example, a government's universalist claim to extend the benefits of private ownership of property, shares and pensions to all citizens, so that everyone has a stake in society, would have to be subject to open debate between government and public so that information on the extent of private ownership, and on the extent of deprivation, is published readily and accessibly in a form consistent over time.

The postmodern agenda has led recent theorists to define the demise of old and the birth of new social movements as a rupture, to see the latter as reflecting the spirit of an emerging epoch which has slowly but inexorably become severed from modernity, and which has now come to be characterised by the contingency, particularity and contextuality of social life. Such a view denies that there are universal concerns motivating social movements. Yet, as we have seen, theorists inescapably thematise these concerns in their accounts – if for no other reason than that the logic of explanatory discourse demands the use of universalistic language and concepts in order to couch more particularistic observations. Nonetheless, this is not meant to overlook the substantial changes currently affecting social and political life which are the subject of interest in various areas of study including social policy (cf Chamberlayne, 1991/2; Williams, 1992).

Human Needs and Social Movements

The discussion about universal and culturally relative concepts of human need, and their application to the analysis of social movements, finds a strong affinity in important debates in social policy in the 1980s. A number of debates have recently addressed the issue of universality, as presently discussed, in the more empirical terms of social policy in a postmodern or late-modern era marked by specificity, diversity and fragmentation; for example in relation to citizenship, women, ethnic minorities, and poverty, where in each debate issues about the meaning of universal welfare for socially different groups is posed (for example Williams, 1992).

The final section of the chapter considers the relevance of debates about the concept of poverty and the different relationships between universal and culturally specific needs which can be used to generate insights into the aims of social movements. Townsend's work provides an important empirically based and realist theory of need which I would argue can resolve some of the problems discussed in relation to Touraine and other postmodernists. For Townsend deprivation or need is an objective and real phenomenon which is present only in the cultural forms found in the community or society under review. As his oft-quoted opening sentence in *Poverty in the UK* declares: 'Poverty can be defined objectively and applied consistently only in terms of the concept of relative deprivation' (1979: 31). This claim is elaborated in three propositions about poverty, deprivation and need which it is helpful to rehearse again.

1 Poverty is relative within a given distribution of resources (however defined); for example, poverty is defined relative to average income so that, 'individuals and families can be defined as in poverty when they lack or fall seriously short of the resources commanded by the average members of society' (Townsend, 1967: 43). This represents a normative concept of need.
2 Relative deprivation is defined as an individual's inability to participate in a commonly accepted lifestyle; a further normative concept of deprivation.
3 By operationalising these concepts, the two indicators can be cross-tabulated and two objective propositions established; (a) that there is an inverse relationship between levels of income and deprivation; and (b) that an objective threshold exists for certain families, whereby 'In descending the income scale . . . at a particular point for different types of family, a significantly large number of families reduce more than proportionately their participation in the community's style of living' (1979: 249).

This account provides propositions about need which are similar to those present in the schema about the universal and specific needs of social movements introduced at the end of the previous section. Townsend's concept of poverty delineates two *particularist* norms relative to a specific community or group, which state the terms defining poverty and lack of social participation (that is, 1 and 2 above). He also identifies two universal features. Proposition 3(a) has *normative* relevance in determining levels of acceptable and unacceptable inequality. Proposition 3(b) identifies a realist notion of need, that is, an objective and independently verifiable level of material poverty and deprived lifestyle below which social existence, as defined, is not possible. This constitutes an ontological statement about need and the possibility of human existence, and so refers to the *transcendental* dimension described earlier, which Townsend has cautiously identified empirically as a specific threshold for particular types of household.[5] For the present discussion I have stressed an ontological side to Townsend's concept of poverty; that, for example, human existence is possible only if there are sufficient material resources to enable individuals to fulfil certain social expectations and participate in a given lifestyle. Of course this latter proposition has more immediate policy implications in prescribing a material state in which minimum *levels* of acceptable participation and consumption are identified for specific types of household in a given culture. It therefore prescribes levels of need which governments should aim to secure.

The postmodernist outlook informing recent social movement theory would view a realistic theory of poverty with deep suspicion, as characterised by essentialist arguments that impose an alien notion of reality on individuals and groups who should be free to define their own reality.[6] This outlook would rather endorse the version of a relativist theory of need developed in Mack and Lansley's account of poverty as 'an enforced lack of *socially perceived* necessities' (1985: 39, emphasis added). Here poverty is defined as a lack contingent on the experiences of members of a specific society, community or movement, and is not underwritten by an objective standard lying beyond these collectivities. Townsend has constantly criticised this kind of conventional or subjective view of need for its lack of objectivity and susceptibility to popular prejudice (for example 1979: 46). The difference between conventionalists like Mack and Lansley and a realist like Townsend is that Townsend uses a concept of poverty that is objective in relation to an external and real standard, namely a threshold of deprivation, whilst Mack and Lansley see poverty as an objective condition which exists only within the bounds of a specific cultural group; in this sense its reality and objectivity are culturally relative. The disagreement revolves around the different notions of objectivity the two parties use. Mack and Lansley contend that Townsend has obscured the search for an objective measure of poverty by contrasting 'socially perceived' and 'actual' need. For, 'there is no such thing as an "objective" as opposed to a "socially perceived" measure: items [of need] become objective only when they are *socially* perceived to be so' (1985: 38) – an argument in some respects in tune with the contingent social-activist account of social movements discussed earlier.

Of especial interest to the questions posed in the opening paragraph of this chapter, about the relationship between the needs of social movements and the needs of individuals in society generally, are recent findings of convergence between socially relative and objective definitions of need. Recent studies of deprivation suggest that there is not such a wide difference between definitions of need based on respondents' own judgements of where minimum needs should be drawn (for example, consensus definitions of poverty) and definitions using more objective methods. Similar findings of congruence are found between professional reports and lay self-reports of health assessment (see Whitehead, 1988: 224). Desai's findings after reworking Townsend's data published in 1979 is apposite here. Comparing Townsend's (1979) and Mack and Lansley's measures (1985), he found that the former's objective threshold of poverty and the latter's consensus measure were about 50 per cent and 33 per cent respectively above the Supplementary Benefit level for a two-parent, two-child family (1986: 18). Further, in Townsend's London study (1987), a degree of agreement was also found between subjective and objective measures of poverty generally, prompting Townsend and Gordon to observe that 'People's judgements of the minimum income required to fulfil basic family living standards and meet their minimum social obligations seem to correspond closely with the results obtained by more objective observations of the relationship between income and deprivation' (1989). More speculatively – and controversially given Townsend's earlier doubts about conventionalist approaches – he suggests that 'this demonstrates the intriguing possibility that . . . it may be possible to "objectively" calculate a "poverty line" for most household types that would correspond with the judgements of the majority of the population' (Townsend and Gordon, 1989: 54). Indeed the symmetry between 'conventional'/'relative'/'consensual' measures of poverty and 'objective'/'realist' measures deserves further investigation.

Conclusion

This chapter has argued for the universalisability of some of the needs of social movements. This is possible if one attends closely to the nature of the claims social movements make, particularly to the transcendental grounds underpinning these claims and to the logic linking these grounds to their normative prescriptions. Need claims rest on universalist assumptions about human nature – individual and collective – which when made explicit should provide cogent support for such claims, as Doyal and Gough elaborate. The force of need claims is further tested by reference to the actual practices and policies which purport to rest on such claims, a further step in Doyal and Gough's project.

The postmodern claim that there is no universal human subject – in this case the subject in need – is a powerful claim. However, notwithstanding the diversity and fragmentation of human experience in the late 20th century, the empirical findings of realist social research and the normative force of certain types of need claims suggest the presence of universal needs that underlie cultural and contextual differences (see Brown, 1991).

Recent developments in social policy studies of need provide empirical support for the existence of a universal dimension of need beyond the contextualisations of relative definitions of needs. Moreover, given advances in the methodology of needs research, it is possible to show that, at least in modern democratic welfare states like Britain, a degree of convergence exists between the definitions of need furnished, on the one hand, by realist studies of need and, on the other, by studies of social perceptions of need and need-satisfiers.

Universal needs emerge contingently in the dialogue between social movements representing groups in need, and the wider public and policy makers. Such needs can also be identified by more objective social scientific methods for detecting consensus. Evidence now seems to support the possibility that human dialogue and social science can provide in some instances converging definitions of need. It would be a refreshing thought if this convergence were made possible by the development of a more social-scientifically informed population and a more consensually sensitive scientific community who are both beginning to talk the same language about the core concerns of human life. This would be one of the more significant breakthroughs for social science and social policy in a dawning postmodern or late-modern age.

Notes

1. It is important to stress these political differences among writers otherwise sharing apparently similar postmodern theoretical outlooks (see Ryan, 1988).
2. That is, the essential 'thrownness' of the human condition ('*Geworfenheit*' – see Heidegger, 1962: 174).
3. See Eyerman and Jamison's reading of Touraine (1991: 50, 101).
4. Habermas, however, has become more circumspect about the foundationalist underpinnings of this project (1987: 396–403).
5. This is not to overlook the strong disagreement registered over the existence of such thresholds (see Piachaud, 1981, 1987; Desai, 1986).
6. Touraine and Melucci tend to place the term 'real' and its cognates in inverted commas (e.g. Touraine, 1985: 751; Melucci, 1985: 804).

References

Althusser, L. (1971) *Lenin and Philosophy and Other Essays*. New York: Monthly Review Press.
Barrett, M. (1991) *The Politics of Truth: From Marx to Foucault*. Cambridge: Polity.
Baudrillard, J. (1983) *In the Shadow of the Silent Majorities*. New York: Semiotext(e).
Brown, D.E. (1991) *Human Universal*. London: McGraw-Hill.
Bryson, V. (1992) *Feminist Political Theory: An Introduction*. Basingstoke: Macmillan.
Chamberlayne, P. (1991/2) 'New directions in welfare? France, West Germany, Italy and Britain in the 1980s', *Critical Social Policy*, 33: 5–21.
Cohen, J.L. (1985) 'Strategy or identity: new theoretical paradigms and contemporary social movements', *Social Research*, 52(4): 663–716.

Desai, M. (1986) 'Drawing the line: on defining the poverty threshold', in P. Golding (ed.), *Excluding the Poor*. London: CPAG.

Doyal, L. and Gough, I. (1991) *A Theory of Human Needs*. Basingstoke: Macmillan.

Eyerman, R. and Jamison, A. (1991) *Social Movements: A Cognitive Approach*. Cambridge: Polity.

Geras, N. (1987) 'Post-Marxism?', *New Left Review*, 163: 40–82.

Gibbins, J.R. (1989) 'Contemporary political culture: an introduction', in J.R. Gibbins (ed.), *Contemporary Political Culture: Politics in a Postmodern Age*. London: Sage.

Habermas, J. (1970) 'Towards a theory of communicative competence', *Inquiry*, 13: 360–75.

Habermas, J. (1978) *Knowledge and Human Interest*. London: Heinemann.

Habermas, J. (1979) *Communication and the Evolution of Society*. London: Heinemann.

Habermas, J. (1987) *The Theory of Communicative Action: Volume II: Lifeworld and System*. Cambridge: Polity.

Habermas, J. (1989) *The New Conservatism: Cultural Criticism and the Historians' Debate*. Cambridge: Polity.

Heidegger, M. (1962) *Being and Time*. Oxford: Blackwell.

Hewitt, M. (1992) *Welfare, Ideology and Need: Recent Perspectives on the Welfare State*. Hemel Hempstead: Harvester-Wheatsheaf.

Kojev, A. (1970) *An Introduction to the Reading of Hegel*. London: Cornell University Press.

Lacan, J. (1977) *Ecrits: A Selection*. London: Tavistock.

Laclau, E. and Mouffe, C. (1985) *Hegemony and Socialist Strategy: Towards a Radical Democratic Practice*. London: Verso.

Lukacs, G. (1971) *History and Class Consciousness*. London: Merlin.

Lyotard, J.-F. (1984) *The Postmodern Condition: A Report on Knowledge*. Manchester: Manchester University Press.

Mack, J. and Lansley, S. (1985) *Poor Britain*. London: Allen & Unwin.

Marx, K. (1975) 'Critique of Hegel's dialectic of the state', in L. Colletti (ed.), *Karl Marx: Early Writings*. Harmondsworth: Penguin.

Melucci, A. (1985) 'The symbolic challenge of contemporary movements', *Social Research*, 52(4): 789–815.

Piachaud, D. (1981) 'Peter Townsend and the Holy Grail', *New Society*, Sept: 419–22.

Piachaud, D. (1987) 'Problems in the definition and measurement of poverty', *Journal of Social Policy*, 16(2).

Rawls, J. (1972) *A Theory of Justice*. Oxford: Oxford University Press.

Runciman, W.G. (1966) *Relative Deprivation and Social Justice: A Study of Attitudes to Social Inequality in Twentieth-century England*. London: Routledge & Kegan Paul.

Ryan, M. (1988) 'Postmodern politics', *Theory, Culture & Society*, 5 (2–3).

Sartre, J.-P. (1976) *Critique of Dialectical Reasoning*. London: Verso.

Scott, A. (1990) *Ideology and the New Social Movements*. London: Unwin Hyman.

Taylor-Gooby, P. (1991) *Social Change, Social Welfare and Social Science*. Hemel Hempstead: Harvester-Wheatsheaf.

Touraine, A. (1981) *The Voice and the Eye: An Analysis of Social Movements*. Cambridge: Cambridge University Press.

Touraine, A. (1985) 'An introduction to the study of social movements', *Social Research*, 52(4): 749–88.

Townsend, P. (1967) 'Poverty, socialism and Labour in power', in W. Rogers (ed.), *Socialism and Affluence*. London: Fabian Society.

Townsend, P. (1979) *Poverty in the United Kingdom*. Harmondsworth: Penguin.

Townsend, P. (1984) *Why Are the Many Poor?* London: Fabian Society.

Townsend, P., Corrigan, P. and Kowarzik, U. (1987) *Poverty and Labour in London*. London: Low Pay Unit.

Townsend, P. and Gordon, D. (1989) 'Memorandum' in House of Commons Select Committee on Social Services, *Minimum Income: Memoranda*. London: HMSO.

Townsend, P. (1989) 'Slipping through the net', *Guardian*, Nov.

Veit-Wilson, J. (1987) 'Consensual approaches to poverty lines and social security', *Journal of Social Policy*, 16(2).

Walker, R. (1987) 'Consensual approaches to the definition of poverty: towards an alternative methodology', *Journal of Social Policy*, 16(2).

Walzer, M. (1983) *Spheres of Justice*. Oxford: Blackwell.

White, S.K. (1991) *Political Theory and Postmodernism*. Cambridge: Cambridge University Press.

Whitehead, M. (1988) *The Health Divide*. Harmondsworth: Penguin.

Williams, F. (1992) 'Somewhere over the rainbow: universality and diversity in social policy', in N. Manning and R. Page (eds), *Social Policy Review 4*. Canterbury: Social Policy Association.

12

Understanding Particularism

Paul Spicker

Universalism and Particularism

The kinds of moral beliefs and principles which are usually referred to in
social policy are universal: they apply to everyone, or at least to everyone
who falls within relevant criteria. In social policy, 'universalism' is often
taken in a narrow but 'thick' sense – that is, a highly specific but elaborate
use of the term – referring to a way of distributing benefits and services.
'Universality' is commonly distinguished from 'selectivity': if universal
benefits are available to everyone, selective benefits are available only to
those in need. The distinction of universality and selectivity is mainly about
method; where it touches on principles, it is usually another way of
referring to models of 'institutional' and 'residual' welfare (Spicker, 1988:
162–4). But there is also a 'thinner', broader use of the idea of universality,
found in expressions like 'universal human rights'; that is the sense in which
I shall be using the term here. If universalism means that the same rules are
applied to everyone, residual and institutional models might both be called
'universal' in the 'thin' sense of the word.

Universalist premises of this kind pervade much of the discussion of
welfare: concepts like altruism, freedom or the 'right to welfare' are applied
in general terms, and it is usually taken for granted that they should be – I
have to confess to doing it myself (Spicker, 1988). Fiona Williams' critique
of universalism offers an interesting example, because on the face of it she
is concerned with issues of diversity and difference. She argues as follows:

> The distrust of uniformity and universalism and the recognition of diversity and
> difference has emerged in two ways within social policy. The first has been a 'top
> down' approach to diversity in the form of welfare pluralism. The second has
> been a 'bottom up' development of work around gender in particular, but also
> race, disability, age and sexuality. One consequence of this latter work has been
> to expose the 'false universalism' of the post-war welfare state . . . Whilst welfare
> pluralism stresses the diversity of sources . . . for welfare provision, the second
> places emphasis on the diversity of identity, experience, interest and need in
> welfare provision. (Williams, 1992: 206–7)

First published in *Critical Social Policy*, 39, 1994.

This is not an argument against the universal application of principles; rather, it implies that the traditional interpretation of 'universalism' has not been universal enough.

Critical theory, as outlined by Habermas, has to take a view from outside the society which is being criticised. It depends on a communicative discourse referring to consistent criteria; as such, it is built on universalist premises. Habermas proposes a 'fundamental principle of universalisation', that 'every valid norm must be able to be accepted by all those affected' (cited Kelly, 1990: 147). The universal application of moral norms – applying them to everyone – is based in an argument from consistency: if one accepts a rule in one case, it cannot reasonably be denied in other circumstances which satisfy the same criteria (Habermas, 1990: 68–70). The same principle establishes a presumptive case for equality and social justice: people should be treated equally when other things are equal, and unequally only if they are not (Spicker, 1985). This kind of argument has been taken to be so obvious in the discussion of social policy that the issue of universal application has hardly been discussed. In other areas of academic discourse, however, universalist premises have been seriously challenged. The counter-argument to Habermas is represented, in different ways, by a range of 'communitarian' arguments. Communitarians argue that the values and norms on which a social critique can be founded must be drawn from specific social contexts. An asocial critique has no meaning (see Rasmussen, 1990). Communitarianism can be taken to stand for a highly socialised view of people in which their moral position can be understood only in terms of their social relationships. Communitarian critiques challenge the basis on which judgements about society can be made, and they imply that different standards will be applied in different places.

The debate between universalism and communitarianism cuts across the conventional division of 'left' and 'right' wing; there are left- and right-wing communitarians, as there are left- and right-wing universalists. On the left, communitarian critiques have mainly been directed at the kind of abstract moral theory associated with writers like Rawls or Nozick, and in particular at liberalism (Kymlicka, 1989). Part of the critique of the welfare state with which Williams is concerned has been communitarian rather than universalist: welfare, to be effective, must both recognise the limitations and build on the strengths of existing social relationships. On the right, communitarian premises have been used to challenge some of the general principles, like equality and social justice (see, for example, Charvet, 1983), which have been basic to socialism in the past. The conservative critique has been a powerful one, because it uses the same kind of language and premises as collectivism – a concern with mutual support, diversity, social networks and social context – to argue for social differentiation. It is an argument that communitarian socialists need to come to terms with. This chapter has two main aims. One is to explain the arguments for particularism and communitarianism; the second is to try to reconcile them with the universal values on which socialism depends.

At the simplest level, communitarian ideas imply that there are differences between people, and that these differences must lead to diverse responses. MacIntyre, for example, writes that:

> we all approach our own circumstances as bearers of a particular social identity. I am someone's son or daughter, someone else's cousin or uncle; I am a citizen of this or that city, a member of this or that guild or profession; I belong to this clan, that tribe, this nation. Hence what is good for me has to be the good for one who inhabits these roles. (MacIntyre, 1981: 204–5)

MacIntyre has also argued that norms have to be understood in the context of particular traditions (1988) – and so that they have to be different. Some communitarian thinkers take this much further. Walzer, in *Spheres of Justice*, argues that social principles like justice, equality and need can only be understood and implemented in specific social contexts: his case is:

> that the principles of justice are themselves pluralistic in form; that different social goods ought to be distributed for different reasons, in accordance with different procedures, by different agents; and that all these differences derive from different understandings of the actual goods themselves – the inevitable product of historical and cultural particularism. (Walzer, 1983: 6)

'Particularism', rather than communitarianism, is the true opposite of universalism; it refers to the idea that different standards should be applied to different people (Jones, 1990). The kinds of standards which this argues for are discriminatory. Walzer, for example, is ready to argue for the restriction of immigration, and within that for priority to the relatives of existing citizens. Discrimination is often morally objectionable, and much of it is better explained in terms like 'prejudice' (Allport, 1954) rather than in any moral sense. But discrimination is not necessarily random, irrational or indefensible; it is based on criteria like kinship, friendship, community and nationality. The kinds of responsibilities which people recognise to each other are not universal; they depend on existing ties. The corollary is that people who do not share those ties are left out, and are liable as a result to receive less. The effect of giving priority to family, community or occupational group is to exclude outsiders – people without roots, people from different communities, and those with marginal status – people who are often poor and disadvantaged. So, for example, an appeal for extra resources for Scotland is generally made at the expense of other areas; and where the sons and daughters of council tenants are given priority for rehousing (Kensington and Chelsea has a formal scheme), the people who get left out include incomers, and racial minorities.

It is tempting to dismiss this kind of discrimination as immoral, because much of it is. But it hardly seems reasonable to treat all forms of discrimination in the same way: if there is a moral defect in giving preferential treatment to one's family, arguing for resources for one's home town or region, or special pleading for one disadvantaged group out of many, it hardly seems to fall in the same category as, say, refusing health care to people on racial grounds. That is not to say that there is no connection between this kind of discrimination and disadvantage. If everyone gives preference to their family, then richer families will thrive, and the disadvantage of poor families will be reinforced; if too much is made of community affiliations, ethnic minorities will be excluded; and special treatment for one disadvantaged group is all too often gained at the expense of others. But the position is not simply a moral aberration, which we might choose to tolerate because it is 'understandable'. Particularism represents a set of moral imperatives in its own right.

Universalists have acknowledged the arguments half-heartedly. Titmuss was concerned to establish the importance of social integration, as well as universal social provision (though he couched the arguments for a 'gift relationship' in universalist terms) (Titmuss, 1970). The recognition of duties at the personal level, duties which usually far exceed those required from universal principles like human rights or altruism, is fundamental to much moral conduct. The moral obligations experienced within the family are the archetypal example. Conversely, I suspect we would feel that there was something morally wrong with someone whose commitment for the Third World was so great that he or she subordinated all responsibility to family, friends and community to it. Where there is a tension between the two principles, it is not necessarily the case that universalism should be preferred.

Particularist Beliefs

The universalist ethos has been so much accepted in the academic literature in Britain that it is difficult to find explicit arguments for a particularist approach. Particularism, however, derives from long-standing traditions; it is possible to see, in the growth of communitarianism, references to ancient arguments. Walzer's arguments are influenced both by American pluralism and traditional Judaism. The pluralist tradition in the United States has emphasised community solidarity and diversity. The Jewish tradition is strongly communitarian: according to Jewish law, charity is to be distributed to one's poor relatives before strangers; to Jewish poor before non-Jewish poor (there are also reservations against taking charity from non-Jews); and to the poor of one's own town before the poor of any other town (*Encyclopaedica Judaica*, 1971). The role of 'communitarianism' might be seen as a justification of the kinds of particularist arguments which have long been prevalent in many different societies.

Perhaps the nearest thing to a defence of discriminatory approaches in English writing is found in traditional conservatism. Conservatism has often represented society as a complex, organic structure in which people develop a range of responsibilities of different kinds and at different levels. People are born into families, communities and nations (Clarke, 1975). But there are more fully developed arguments. In European thought, the most important arguments of this kind have been the development, associated respectively with Calvinist and Catholic social thought, of 'sphere sovereignty' and 'solidarity'.

Sphere sovereignty

The idea of sphere sovereignty comes from the Netherlands. It was developed by Groen van Prinsterer, on a prescriptive basis, as a defence of the kinds of social networks which had developed in practice (Dooyeweerd, 1979: 53–4). Kuyper, the leader of the Christian Anti-Revolutionary Party, was to justify the principle in theological terms. He claimed that social diversity reflected the kinds of differences intended by God as part of the creation, and that the duty of the state was to safeguard such boundaries. Kuyper argued that the development of social relationships 'is spontaneous, just as that of the stem and branches of a plant' (Kuyper, 1899: 117). The spheres had developed naturally: 'all together they form the life of creation, in accord with the ordinances of creation, and therefore are organically developed' (1899: 118).

The concept of sphere sovereignty was liberal in its origins. The idea was used to deny state authority in important areas of people's lives, like the family, education and religion. 'In a Calvinistic sense', Kuyper wrote,

> we understand hereby, that the family, the business, science, art and so forth are all social spheres, which do not owe their existence to the state, and which do not derive the law of their life from the superiority of the state, but obey a high authority within their own bosom; an authority which rules, by the grace of God, just as the sovereignty of the State does. (1899: 116)

Each major sphere of society was independent, and authority within that sphere derived from the natural order that existed within it.

One offshoot of Kuyper's arguments was the development of South African apartheid. Kuyper's lectures on Calvinism were published simultaneously in Amsterdam and Pretoria, and the concepts were adopted by those who argued for racial segregation. Skillen and McCarthy argue that this misrepresents Kuyper, who did not 'identify races or nations as social spheres' (1991: 411); but the connection between apartheid and his emphasis on creational differences seems fairly close. Social services under apartheid were segregated very distinctly: there were different medical services, for example, for whites, Asians, coloureds and Blacks.

The moral repugnance which apartheid provokes tends to obscure the force of 'sphere sovereignty' in other respects. In the Netherlands, the main application of the principle has been in the form of pillarisation (Bryant, 1981). The basic structure of society was that people lived in certain cohesive, independent networks. The responsibilities they had, and the responsibilities of others towards them, were determined by the kinds of responsibility which these frameworks established. Dutch social services were developed on the principle of *particulier initiatief*: different social organisations (especially the churches) work in distinct spheres of influence, with their own constituencies, finance and modes of operation (Brenton, 1982). (The word *'particulier'* here has the same effect as that of 'particularism'.) Lijphart distinguishes separate development in the Netherlands from apartheid on two grounds: first, that Dutch particularism is not racist, and second, that apartheid was imposed, whereas separation in the Netherlands was 'self-imposed' (Lijphart, 1975: 186). This is not to deny the common ancestry of the ideas.

'Sphere sovereignty' is vulnerable to the kind of objections which might be made from a universalist perspective. The central texts, by Kuyper and Dooyeweerd, are explicitly conservative in tone; there is an underlying assumption that moral action requires abstinence from intervention; and the concept has a disturbing association with racist ideology. However, the principle has other more attractive features. The idea of community is often valued, especially when it is associated with the recognition of a network of responsibilities (Nisbet, 1953). The strengths of pillarisation in practice include the development of organisations adapted to the characteristics of different communities, the devolution of power from the state, and the fostering and tolerance of diverse arrangements to meet needs. In other words, there is within the idea of sphere sovereignty the kernel of ideas which are now commonly associated with welfare pluralism.

Solidarity

The Catholic model of solidarity defines responsibilities in terms which have to be related to the social circumstances of each person (see Coote, 1989). The concept of solidarity has been of particular importance in France, where the term is widely used to justify provision, and it has been formally enshrined in social welfare law (Dupeyroux, 1989: 290). The idea has become a cliché, used, like 'the welfare state' in the UK, to refer to a broad set of ideals governing the ways in which people support each other. However, where the 'welfare state' emphasises issues like citizenship and the right to welfare (Marshall, 1982), solidarity depends on the place of people within social networks. If a person is part of such networks, there are strong mutual obligations to offer social protection; if not, the emphasis falls on social integration, to ensure that such relationships can be developed.

Solidarity can be understood in two main senses (Spicker, 1991). The first describes a network of mutual support. People come to share, either through affiliation or through reciprocal obligations, both duties to help others and expectations of support. This applies to many different kinds of network, including families, occupational groups and communities. Solidaristic welfare structures are characterised, not so much by common rights and responsibilities as by a complex network of such responsibilities. People have relationships with families, communities and occupational groups; they share rights and responsibilities mutually with others. Much of French social policy has been concerned with the gradual expansion of this kind of mutual network, to incorporate (or 'insert') those left out of society – the 'marginals' (Lejeune, 1988; Alfarandi, 1989).

The second main sense of solidarity is as a form of collective social action – 'fraternity' rather than 'mutualism'. If people act together, it is not just because they have individual interests in common, but because they accept a common social identity as a collective group. There are social preferences, and social forms of welfare – a 'common good' – distinct from the preferences and interests of individuals. Solidaristic measures, by this account, are those which support and reinforce the interests of the group.

Much of the political debate in France has focused on the question of which people should be included within solidaristic networks. The concept of solidarity was taken up by a political movement, 'solidarism'. Solidarism favoured a general extension of the principle to the population as a whole (see Bourgeois, 1897). It tended to assume that solidarities would link together into a widespread, inclusive network. However, not every appeal to 'solidarity' would meet these criteria; there are circumstances in which solidarities are narrowly conceived and defined. The idea, like other forms of particularism, has the potential to be exclusive as well as inclusive.

Solidaristic social networks can be represented in terms similar to the 'spheres' of sphere sovereignty, but the idea also has the potential to be interpreted within a rather more complex framework. Solidaristic arrangements depend on an interaction between individuals and groups, which can overlap and be interrelated. A person might be at the same time a member of a family, a friendly society and a community, and have solidaristic relationships with each. Social responsibility is defined in terms of relationships like these. The primary responsibilities are felt to those with whom one is most intimately connected, and the strength of rights and responsibilities diminishes with social distance. 'One can imagine', Alfarandi suggests, 'a system of concentric circles of solidarity, wider and wider, which goes from the nuclear family to the international community' (1989: 73).

The patterns of particularism associated with these doctrines are complex, and it may be misleading to generalise too strongly between arguments which are themselves rooted in different traditions and ideologies. What the doctrines have in common is a belief that rights and responsibilities are not general, but dependent on specific links between people in different social contexts. They negate universalism.

Assessing Particularism

Particularist doctrines define the boundaries of responsibility. The moral weakness of these beliefs is that they are, in their nature, liable to be exclusive and discriminatory. Particularism has encouraged separatism and racism. However there is a danger, in identifying the particularist approach too closely with these kinds of problems, of losing sight of its moral force.

Particularism can also be held to represent a process which, as long as it is kept within appropriate bounds, is necessary and desirable. There is not just a distinction between in-groups and out-groups. Social relationships form complex networks, and responsibilities have to be defined in a specific context. This is powerful as a description of the way that people live in society. It is also compelling as a moral argument, because the obligations it emphasises are those which we are likely, in practice, to recognise. Values like mutual support, community, personal relationships and loyalty are more usually prized than they are condemned. The principal strength of particularist doctrines is their use of such principles and relationships to reinforce their argument.

The existence of this kind of relationship does help to explain why certain rules are treated as 'moral'. Hume argued that the nature of social morality depends crucially on its utility, and the development over time of moral codes which reflect and support social practices (Hume, 1789: Book III). Burke, similarly, argued that the gradual process of testing such practices led progressively to moral 'prescription', the selection of beneficial (or functional) rules, and the rejection of undesirable ones (Burke, 1790). Morality is not, by this account, universal; rather, it depends on the social context in which it develops. The central defence of the existing structure of rights and responsibilities is that without it, there would be no real 'society' at all. However, although this helps to explain many moral rules, it is not enough to justify them morally: the way things are is not necessarily the way that they should be.

The case for universalism has to be set against these arguments. The argument for consistency seems fairly weak in the face of communitarian objections; it is not that the argument is wrong, but that its scope for application is restricted. There are still some elements of universalism, in particular those associated with human rights, which might be considered important as a precondition of social contact. The provision of welfare is often concerned with 'welfare interests', items which everyone needs, and which are in some sense 'essential' (Feinberg, 1973; Doyal and Gough, 1991). Without food or water, one cannot be a person; without basic material goods, and some (like Townsend, 1979) would argue a great deal else besides, one cannot exist in society with others.

This does not undermine the case for particularism; it only limits it. When particularism is qualified by some universal standards, Jones, refers to it as 'moderate' rather than 'radical' (Jones, 1990: 39). The kind of universalism which this permits is still limited and defined by the context of social relationships in which it is applied. Social duties are still hierarchically ordered, and defined in terms both of existing networks and of social distance. If we pay more attention to a pensioner in Bognor than an orphan in Bogota, it is because we recognise the importance of such networks in shaping the patterns of social responsibility and solidarity which define our actions. We may draw the limits at different stages, but virtually everyone is particularist to some extent. Particularist doctrines suggest that, in the way in which people relate to us, they are not equivalent; we have special responsibilities to some people which we do not have towards others. The effect of the universalist argument might be to impose duties on everybody, but these duties will not be as strong or as demanding as those which are specific to other people.

The Welfare Society

The development and strengthening of this kind of moral relationship have an important potential for improving welfare provision. Arguments for welfare based in reciprocity are often stronger (as Titmuss realised) than others based in a non-specific altruism. The French system has developed on the basis of 'solidarity' or mutual aid (Dupeyroux, 1989). The kinds of networks developed in France have deficiencies, but for those who are covered they are often notably superior to the kinds of provisions offered under the universalist welfare state in Britain.

However, a system of solidaristic networks does not look very much like a universal welfare state. Universal principles, like 'social justice' or the 'right to welfare', offer basic standards; they can also be used, in the application of rules like 'territorial justice' within the NHS, to justify an attempt to equalise provision and resources. By contrast, solidaristic arrangements, insofar as they are based in relatively small, overlapping groups, are diverse; the kinds and levels of protection which they offer depend greatly on the context of both the person who is being helped and the group to which the need is referred. The main aim of mutualism is social protection: people should not have to suffer destructive changes in their lives because of needs like sickness, unemployment or old age. This often implies unequal treatment – because a person in a better position has further to fall than a poor person.

The 'institutional model' of welfare has similar concerns – the development of systems to protect people against socially defined needs. If this is what the 'welfare state' is like, it does not have to be seen as monolithic (Titmuss, 1974) or even egalitarian (Spicker, 1988: 159–61). However, the model associated with this argument is not so much the traditional 'welfare state' as what Titmuss and Robson called a 'welfare society' (Titmuss, 1968: 11; Robson, 1976). For many, this is now associated with a concept of welfare pluralism. An important element within the discussion, though, has been a critique of the universalist pretensions of the welfare state; the welfare state cannot do everything. The welfare society is one in which people recognise responsibilities towards each other, through a system of 'gift-reciprocity' which binds together the various actors in society.

The development of the concept of a welfare society has depended on a picture of a diverse, multifaceted set of social relationships – including the kinds of relationships considered in sphere sovereignty. The arguments for independent provision include the belief that diversity complements existing provision, fosters innovation, increases flexibility and choice, and offers alternative perspectives from state welfare. For those (on both right and left) who think that state welfare can be restrictive and repressive, the devolution and decentralisation of welfare can be seen as a means of empowering people.

This argument is not necessarily particularist, but it is very likely to be. The emphasis on diversity is difficult to reconcile with the norms usually associated with universal principles of distribution, like minimum guarantees or optimal provision. It can be argued that there are different routes to achieving basic standards; and if there are different routes, one has to ask on what basis they can be judged. There are some answers which might be compatible with universalism: that the standard to be achieved must depend on the choices of the people being served; or that the best location for decisions is at the level where they will apply (a principle also, incidentally, compatible with sphere sovereignty). But there are also answers that are particularist: that the standards cannot be seen in the abstract, but have to be translated into a form which is compatible with the social context in which they are applied; that although basic standards are desirable, it is for every moral community to decide how, and whether, to pursue them; and, of course, that different standards should apply to different people.

The Limits of Particularism

Particularism and communitarianism present an important challenge for socialists. The arguments are framed in terms very similar to those which socialists themselves use, referring to social networks, mutual aid and collective action. These are ideas which socialists are likely to approve of. At the same time, some aspects of particularism are repellent; the idea can be used to justify racism, inequality, patronage and injustice. My own position is ambivalent, as might by now be clear; I am both attracted and appalled by the concepts. The problem is to find some way of taking on board what is valuable in the particularist approach without conceding its disagreeable points.

Jones takes the view that it is at least possible to reconcile particularism with some universal values:

> strictly, there is no reason why moderate particularism should not also accommodate an idea of universal rights of citizenship – if by that we mean only that there are certain rights which every political community must accord to its members. (Jones, 1990: 40)

This is probably right, though there are some reservations to make about it. Universal rights have to be interpreted and realised within a social context, which means that they are subject to particular applications. Particularism is necessary, and perhaps even desirable, to the extent that it provides the means through which people are able to exercise rights and duties, and by which they participate in society. It ceases to be defensible in cases where it contradicts other kinds of moral principle, like the right to welfare. This is an important limitation, but it still implies a significant qualification to universalism – that some degree of particularism, and so of discrimination between groups, is desirable. The main issue is to decide where the boundaries lie.

The weakness of moderate particularism is that it assumes the status quo to be desirable unless some argument can be made to the contrary. This is the basis for many of the arguments which are actually made. For example, people commonly use the rules of inheritance and succession to offer property, some protection and, where possible, some advantages to others. This is largely defensible in terms of the social framework which I have been describing. The main reservation to make is that the result of such rules may not be socially just; the position after succession has to be reviewed and if necessary altered to prevent unacceptable inequalities from arising. However, there are also cases in which the assumption seems unwarranted. Particularism is an argument for discrimination, and there are wholly unacceptable grounds for discrimination. In cases where a landlord will not accept a tenant on the grounds of race, or where politicians appoint unqualified members of their families to public office, it is not generally the practice to say that 'this would be reasonable were it not for some other values which it contradicts'. On the contrary, they are unreasonable, and there is something wrong with a principle which states otherwise.

It is not enough, then, to try to reconcile contradictory values. What needs to be done is to find a different way of appealing to values like 'community' and 'solidarity' which does not leave room for exclusion and injustice. There have been a number of attempts to do so. The idea of community is ambiguous; it can refer, amongst many other definitions, to a network of social relationships, a geographical area, or a group of people with common interests. To make the emphasis on community as inclusive as possible, the idea has to be taken in a fairly comprehensive sense. It might, for example, be taken to mean a geographical area – so that everyone within that area makes up part of the 'community' – or to a widely spread group of people, defined in terms of their common rights or citizenship. David Miller argues that the idea of community can effectively be identified with the nation state (1990: Ch. 9); others, like Ruth Lister, try to define 'citizenship' as widely as possible (1990). The solidaristic approach equally depends on establishing the broadest possible terms for the inclusion of people at the margins. The issue is implicit within Titmuss' understanding of 'gift-reciprocity' (1970); a more fully elaborated example is Bill Jordan's 'socialist model' of welfare (1987: 42). It is possible to represent all these arguments in terms of 'moderate particularism', which would suggest that there is some inconsistency in the positions they hold. I think, though, that the case which communitarian socialists wish to make can be argued without any theoretical inconsistency.

People's lives develop within a particular social context, and they are structured in terms of that context. This is the central case for the development of 'particular' rights and responsibilities. Social relationships, and social networks, are the means through which people are able to make a reality of their hopes or aspirations. The view which this represents is a form of freedom in a 'positive' sense – the freedom to do things. More importantly, it is freedom in a collective sense. People can only be said to be 'free' or 'unfree', not when they act in isolation from others, but when their actions are seen in relation to others (Spicker, 1985). In order to be free, people must be able to choose; they must have the power to choose; and they must not be prevented from choosing. In principle, freedom can be increased without diminishing the freedom of others; people collaborating, for example, can all increase their range of actions. In a social context, however, people's freedom tends to be limited by the structure of power: in these circumstances, the power to act can be increased only through a relative increase in their power, and a reduction in the power of others.

Another way of saying this is that there must be a redistribution of power. The idea of 'empowerment' means that people who are relatively powerless are able to gain more power. The term has only recently come into widespread use, and it tends to reflect its origins in social work practice. Solomon, in the earliest use I have been able to identify, defines empowerment as:

> a process whereby the social worker or other helping professional engages in a set of activities with the client aimed at reducing the powerlessness stemming from the experience of discrimination because the client belongs to a stigmatized collective. (Solomon, 1976: 29)

This has subsequently been extended to refer to:

> the mechanism by which people, organisations and communities gain mastery over their lives. (Rappaport, 1984, cited in Holdsworth, 1991: 3)

A protest against the closure of a local school or hospital is almost invariably made in competition with the allocation of resources elsewhere. Positive action for racial groups, such as 'Black' housing associations, always runs the risk that in compensating for the disadvantages for one group it may work to the detriment of others. Empowerment has to be taken, then, as a relative concept. The test which has to be applied is a relative one: what is the balance of power, and to what extent does it produce disadvantage?

Increasing people's freedom, and reducing their disadvantage, are general principles, even if they can only be understood in a social context; they apply to everyone. If principles like 'community' and 'solidarity' are advocated as a means of empowerment and the removal of disadvantage, there does not have to be any inconsistency. But this means that they must be treated as secondary rather than primary values; universal claims like freedom and equality have priority. It is only when socialists advocate 'community' and 'solidarity' as values in their own right that they come close to a particularism which can undermine universal claims for equality and social justice. There are dangers, but the theoretical problems can be resolved.

There are still important practical problems. Communitarian values have to be applied within a particular social framework. It is often assumed that if people who are most vulnerable and most often excluded are given power, they will ensure that others like them who have been excluded will be given greater opportunities. The reverse may well be the case. Tenants in poor estates do their utmost to keep out 'problem families'; parents of children in schools where many children do not speak English (notably in the Dewsbury case) have tried to take their children out. This may be distasteful, but there is nothing surprising in it. Empowerment means that people are gaining power in a competition for scarce resources. It means that they will have the opportunity, as others have, to protect their own situation, and that of those they care about. They are being given the opportunity to participate – to take part in social relationships and networks. People are being empowered to do the kinds of things which other people do; and the kinds of things which other people do are often discriminatory. The real dilemma for communitarian socialism rests not, then, in the need to reconcile universalism with particularism in theory, but in the problem of respecting universal values in practice.

Acknowledgements

Thanks are due to Tony Black and Richard Freeman for comments, and to Will Storr and Graham Room for help with 'sphere sovereignty'.

References

Alfarandi, E. (1989) *Action et aide sociales*, 4e edn. Paris: Dalloz.
Allport, G. (1954) *The Nature of Prejudice*. Cambridge, MA: Addison-Wesley.
Bourgeois, L. (1897) *Solidarité*, 2nd edn. Paris: Armand Colin.
Brenton, M. (1982) 'Changing relationships in Dutch Social Services', *Journal of Social Policy*, 11(1): 59–80.
Bryant, C. (1981) 'Depillarisation in the Netherlands', *British Journal of Sociology*, 32(1): 56–74.
Burke, E. (1790) *Reflections on the Revolution in France*. New York: Holt, Rinehart & Winston (1959).
Charvet, J. (1983) 'The idea of equality as a substantive principle of society', in W. Letwin (ed.), *Against Equality*. London: Macmillan.
Clarke, D. (1975) 'The Conservative faith in a modern age', in P. Buck (ed.), *How Conservatives Think*. Harmondsworth: Penguin.
Coote, N. (1989) 'Catholic social teaching', *Social Policy and Administration*, 23(2): 150–60.
Dooyeweerd, H. (1979) *Roots of Western Culture*. Toronto: Wedge.
Doyal, L. and Gough, I. (1991) *A Theory of Human Needs*. London: Macmillan.
Dupeyroux, J.-J. (1989) *Droit de la Securité Sociale*, 11th edn. Paris: Dalloz.
Encyclopaedica Judaica (1971) 'Charity', 338–53 of Vol. 5. Jerusalem: Kether.

Feinberg, J. (1973) *Social Philosophy*. Englewood Cliffs, NJ: Prentice Hall.

Habermas, J. (1990) 'Discourse ethics: notes on a program of philosophical justification', in S. Benhabib and F. Dallmayr (eds), *The Communicative Ethics Controversy*. Cambridge, MA: MIT Press.

Holdsworth, S. (1991) *Empowerment Social Work with Physically Disabled People*. Norwich: University of East Anglia Social Work Monographs.

Hume, D. (1789) *A Treatise of Human Nature*, edited by L. Selby-Bigge. Oxford: Clarendon Press, 1888.

Jones, P. (1990) 'Universal principles and particular claims', in R. Goodin and A. Ware (eds), *Needs and Welfare*. London: Sage.

Jordan, B. (1987) *Rethinking Welfare*. Oxford: Blackwell.

Kelly, M. (1990) 'The Gadamer/Habermas debate revisited', in D. Rasmussen (ed.), *Universalism versus Communitarianism*. Cambridge, MA: MIT Press.

Kuyper, A. (1899) *Calvinism: Six Stone Lectures*. Amsterdam: Höveker and Wormser.

Kymlicka, W. (1989) *Liberalism, Community and Culture*. Oxford: Clarendon Press.

Lejeune, R. (1988) *Réussir l'insertion*. Paris: Syros-Alternatives.

Lijphart, A. (1975) *The Politics of Accommodation*. Berkeley: University of California Press.

Lister, R. (1990) *The Exclusive Society*. London: Child Poverty Action Group.

MacIntyre, A. (1981) *After Virtue: A Study in Moral Theory*. London: Duckworth.

MacIntyre, A. (1988) *Whose Justice? Whose Rationality?* London: Duckworth.

Marshall, T.H. (1982) *The Right to Welfare*. London: Heinemann.

Marx, K. and Engels, F. (1848) *The Communist Manifesto*, edited by A.J.P. Taylor. Harmondsworth: Penguin.

Miller, D. (1990) *Market, State and Community*. Oxford: Oxford University Press.

Nisbet, R. (1953) *The Quest for Community*. Oxford: Oxford University Press.

Rasmussen, D. (1990) *Universalism versus Communitarianism*. Cambridge, MA: MIT Press.

Robson, W.A. (1976) *Welfare State and Welfare Society*. London: Allen & Unwin.

Skillen, J. and McCarthy, R. (1991) *Political Order and the Plural Structure of Society*. Atlanta, GA: Scholars Press.

Solomon, B. (1976) *Black Empowerment*. New York: Columbia University Press.

Spicker, P. (1985) 'Why freedom implies equality', *Journal of Applied Philosophy*, 2(2): 205–16.

Spicker, P. (1988) *Principles of Social Welfare*. London: Routledge.

Spicker, P. (1991) 'Solidarity', in G. Room (ed.), *Towards a European Welfare State?* Bristol: SAUS.

Titmuss, R.M. (1968) *Commitment to Welfare*. London: Allen & Unwin.

Titmuss, R.M. (1970) *The Gift Relationship*. Harmondsworth: Penguin.

Titmuss, R. (1974) *Social Policy: An Introduction*. London: Allen & Unwin.

Townsend, P. (1979) *Poverty in the United Kingdom*. Harmondsworth: Penguin.

Walzer, M. (1983) *Spheres of Justice*. Oxford: Blackwell

Williams, F. (1992) 'Somewhere over the rainbow: universality and diversity in social policy', in N. Manning and R. Page (eds), *Social Policy Review* 4. Canterbury: Social Policy Association.

Index

abuse: of elderly 128; of disabled 90
access: for disabled 101, 105; to participation 193
actuarial tables, sex-based 137
Age Discrimination in Employment Amendment 136
ageism 10–11, 144; conflictual 127; women and 132–3
Alexander, Lionel 31
Aliens Act, 1905 27, 34–5, 64
Aliens Defence League 32
Aliens Order, 1920 44
Aliens Order, 1953 44
Aliens Restriction Act, 1914 41
Aliens Restriction Amendment Act, 1919 41
altruism 52, 53, 220
American Association of Retired Persons (AARP) 135–6, 144
Americans for Generational Equity (AGE) 127
Andrews, G. 179
anti-collectivism, relation between race and welfare 6, 50–1
anti-discrimination legislation 95, 105–8
anti-semitism 27, 28–35, 64
apartheid 224
Arnstein, S. 188
Association for Retired Persons (ARP) 137–8, 144
autonomy, need for 210, 211

Bayley, Michael 79
Begum, Nasa 46, 89, 90
Ben-Tovim, G. 49, 53, 62
Benton, Sarah 160–1
Bevan, Aneurin 44, 45
Beveridge, William 54
Beveridge Report 43–4
Bhavnani, K. 60
Black people 7; access to housing 69; exclusion from welfare rights 45–6, 50–1, 52–3, 55–7, 63; immigration of 44–5; and social reproduction 66–8; *see also* Black women
Black feminism 58–61

Black Health Workers and Patients Group 68, 69
Black women 67, 72; as NHS workers 59, 65, 66–7; sexuality of 118
Board of Deputies 38–9; and naturalisation 42; protest at social legislation 39, 40, 41
Boer War 33
Bondfield, Margaret 32, 40
Bourne, J. 57, 60
Brah, Avtah 49, 66, 71
Brien, Frank 32
Brisenden, Simon 90, 92
British Brothers League 29, 32
British citizenship, acquisition of 42–3, 162–3
British Council of Organisations of Disabled People (BCODP) 96, 102, 106–7
British Nationality Act, 1982 42, 162
British Pensioners and Trade Unions Action Association (BPTUAA) 139, 140
British Pensioners' Charter 139
Bryan, B. 69
Burke, E. 227

capitalism 62, 78
Carby, Hazel 59, 68
caring 8, 89–90; *see also* community care; women, as carers
change, and involvement 184
charities 102
Charlton, Val 15
chauvinism: of labour movement 29, 30–1, 32; and welfare legislation 38, 43–4, 47
child allowances 43
Child Benefit Act, 1977 67
child support 25
Christianity, and morality 114–15
Chronically Sick and Disabled Persons Act, 1970 104
citizens' charters 179
citizenship 149, 150–1; and participation 179–80, 190; requirement for pensions 36, 37, 39; rights of 157, 161, 163–5, 166, 179; and social power 156–66; women and 168, 169–73; *see also* British citizenship